Quality Assurance in Higher Education

The quality of teaching and learning is one of the major issues in higher education. This book provides an analytical account of the changes to the quality assurance of UK universities and colleges from 1992 to the present day. It documents the increased involvement of the state and the associated debate about the regulation of professional activities. All the key developments and issues are covered, including the background to the ongoing debate, the evolution of the post-1992 quality regime, the role of the Higher Education Quality Council (HEQC), changes to teaching quality assessment, the creation of a single system, and the formation and evolution of the Quality Assurance Agency (QAA).

As former Chief Executive of the HEQC, Roger Brown writes with authority derived from his experiences in the thick of quality assurance. He argues that the external quality assurance regimes in the UK since 1992 have not provided good value for money, and draws from the lessons learned over the last decade to establish the conditions required for the effective regulation of teaching and learning.

Quality Assurance in Higher Education
The UK Experience Since 1992

Roger Brown

RoutledgeFalmer
Taylor & Francis Group

LONDON AND NEW YORK

First published 2004 by RoutledgeFalmer
2 Park Square, Milton Park, Abingdon, Oxon OX14 4RN

Simultaneously published in the USA and Canada
by RoutledgeFalmer
711 Third Avenue, New York, NY 10017

RoutledgeFalmer is an imprint of the Taylor & Francis Group, an informa business

First issued in paperback 2011

© 2004 Roger Brown

Typeset in 11/12pt Garamond 3 by
Graphicraft Limited, Hong Kong

British Library Cataloguing in Publication Data
A catalogue record for this book is available
from the British Library

Library of Congress Cataloging in Publication Data
A catalog record for this book has been requested

ISBN 13: 978-0-415-33492-1 (hbk)
ISBN 13: 978-0-415-51134-6 (pbk)

Contents

Foreword by John Stoddart   x
Preface   xiii
List of acronyms   xv

Introduction   1

Argument of the book 3
A note on methodology 4
Plan of the book 5

1   **Background and context**   9

Introduction 9
UK higher education at 6 May 1991 9
Government policy towards higher education 10
The economic ideology of education 11
The evaluative state 12
The regulatory state 14
The audit society 15
The regulation of the professions 19
The regulation of higher education 23
Efficiency from above: the politics of performance assessment 25
Collaborative self-regulation 26
Quality enhancement 28
The regulation of teaching and learning 30
The quality of regulation 32

2   **Establishing the framework**   35

Introduction 35
The pre-1992 arrangements 35

Higher education: a new framework 37
The new quality assurance arrangements 38
Quality assessment 39
The 1991 white paper: analysis 39
The 1991 white paper: reactions 41
Constitution, organization and resourcing of HEQC 43
CDP and CVCP views of quality assurance 45
The establishment of assessment 46
Relationship between HEQC and the HEFCE
  Assessment Unit 46

3   **The HEQC 1992–97**   49

Introduction 49
Overview 49
Audit 50
Enhancement 62
Other functions 69
International links 70
Envoi 71

4   **Assessment**   73

Introduction 73
The assessment method 74
Assessment: for and against 79
The demands on institutions 84
Violation of academic autonomy and the creation of a
  compliance culture 85
Hard managerialism 88
Damage to Britain's international reputation for quality 90
The quality of the process 91
Institutional bias 94
Value for money 97
Assessment in Scotland and Wales 98

5   **The creation of the single system**   101

Introduction 101
September 1993 to December 1994 102
December 1994 to September 1995 104
HEQC's position 107

September 1995 to October 1997 110
The Dearing Committee 116
The new agency's inheritance 118

6   The Quality Assurance Agency 1997–2002   121

Introduction 121
Overview 121
The new chief executive 123
The new quality process, March 1998 to December 2000 124
The new quality process, January 2001 to August 2002 131
Scotland and Wales 135
The Better Regulation Task Force 136
Information 137
Enhancement again 137
External examining again 138
The new process: envoi 139
The quality infrastructure 140
Professional training 143
Degree awarding powers and university title 144
Subject review and institutional audit 145
The Thames Valley affair 146
QAA 1997 to 2001 146

7   UK quality assurance: past, present, future   151

Introduction 151
The past 151
The future 158
Accountability and enhancement 160
Key requirements for an effective quality assurance regime 162
The purpose of quality assurance 162
Focusing on what matters for quality improvement 163
Strengthening self-regulation 163
Making quality assurance more meaningful to those involved 164
Diversity and innovation 164
Quality control 165
Accountability 166
Coordination 166
A Higher Education Audit Commission 167
Envoi 169

Appendix 1   Definitions used in the book   173

Appendix 2   Chronology of attempts to achieve
              an external quality assurance regime   175

Appendix 3   Information requirements   178

Appendix 4   Benchmark statements   181

References   183
Index   196

This book is dedicated to my HEQC colleagues

Foreword

Evaluation, assessment and assurance of academic quality is intrinsic to higher education. As with any profession that sets its own standards and is subject to constrained resources, questioning and evaluating quality takes place at a variety of levels – the individual (the reflective practitioner), peer networks of scholars, the department or discipline, the institution, and at system-wide level. And as with other professions that consume significant amounts of public funding, the emphasis has changed in recent decades from a focus on the individual – in this case teacher, scholar, researcher – and reliance on traditional forms of peer review, to the systematic application of external judgements that aim to satisfy the need for accountability. Universities, in particular, have perceived this external dimension at best as an added burden, but more commonly as intrusive or unnecessary. As higher education institutions have grown more complex and managerially more sophisticated, the criteria for evaluation have moved from informal, tacit and essentially internal academic values to wider and more explicit criteria which take into account broader socio-economic considerations. This both reflects and has contributed to the ongoing debate about the purposes of higher education, the role of the teacher in higher education and the relationship between research and teaching. It has also highlighted the distinction between the accepted approaches to evaluating quality and standards in higher education, compared with other levels of the education system where inspection is accepted as the norm.

The issue at the heart of the quality debate, therefore, is not whether higher education should be subject to evaluation and assessment but who should do it, how it should be done, what criteria should be used and what sanctions might be deployed if what is assessed is found wanting. The latter point has exercised higher education institutions particularly in the context of a perceived threat to create a direct link between teaching quality and funding – and both the Teacher Training Agency/Office for Standards in Education (OFSTED) experience and the recent further education approach certainly offer lessons here – but to date the link in general remains relatively loose, and the league tables which were so hotly contested less than a decade ago appear to be providing a foundation for a freer higher education market, where quality is expressed in terms of a range of factors rather than academic criteria alone.

Indeed, there is a growing number of examples of higher education institutions that are examining and addressing quality through holistic approaches grounded in organizational development and institutional performance rather than conventional academic quality assurance processes alone. That the Higher Education Funding Council for England (HEFCE) is investing in a number of projects designed to explore the relationship, for example, between the current Quality Assurance Agency (QAA) processes and the European Foundation for Quality Management (EFQM) model, is testimony to official interest in a broader conception of quality in higher education.

The changes to the higher education system introduced by the 1988 and 1992 Acts marked a significant shift of emphasis in the relationship between government, funding bodies and institutions. These landmark pieces of legislation heralded a subtle dilution of institutional autonomy and a move towards a more centrally planned system, with the funding bodies losing their purported buffer role and acting more or less directly as agents of government. Funding was increasingly earmarked to achieve policy aims through a series of special initiatives, a regional substructure was established, and the emphasis on public accountability and transparency became ever more explicit.

A redefinition of the issues surrounding quality assurance was an important part of this redefinition of the balance of power between the government and the sector. Unfortunately, the debate was often confused and defensive – on all sides – it was often based on assertion rather than being firmly rooted in reality, evidence or experience. The experience of quality evaluation at system level in the 1990s is one of competing agencies, of a defensive sector engaging with a new agenda under considerable political and resource pressures. This was a period of great change and undoubtedly considerable progress, but it was at a high opportunity cost to both the autonomy of the university sector and its traditional collegiality. Ultimately the only guarantor of high quality and standards of teaching, learning and research is the professionalism of the academic community itself. While, of course, trust and respect for professional judgement must be earned and justified, an effective assurance and validation system must support, not undermine that professionalism. Accountability to students, employers and government on the one hand and institutional self-improvement, enhancement and innovation on the other must be in balance. A rigorously self-critical profession, learning from experience and regulating itself, is sustainable in a way that a system of imposed external controls will never be.

Dr Roger Brown's personal account of quality assurance in the last decade provides an interesting case study in the regulation of the profession, with important lessons for other service sectors such as health. He is uniquely qualified to comment on this particular period in the evolution of academic quality assurance processes in the UK. His career has encompassed senior roles in the civil service and a higher education funding council, and a period as chief executive of a major representative body during which he was involved in high-level negotiations with government. He was Chief Executive of the Higher Education Quality Council (HEQC) in the period up to its being replaced by the Quality Assurance Agency for Higher Education – a change which marked a watershed in relations between higher education and its external scrutineers. He is now principal of a major college of higher education, and is able to reflect on the events of the 1990s from several angles.

John Stoddart

John Stoddart was Chairman of HEQC between 1992 and 1997. He was Principal and Vice Chancellor of Sheffield Hallam University (previously Sheffield City Polytechnic) between 1983 and 1998. He was awarded the CBE for services to higher education in the 1995 Queen's Birthday Honours List. He has also been awarded honorary degrees by the Universities of Coventry, Middlesex and Humberside and by the Council for National Academic Awards.

Preface

Like it or not, quality assurance has become a major preoccupation for many concerned with higher education in the last 15 years or so. While this is a phenomenon by no means confined to the UK, the UK has arguably had more than its fair share of difficulty in establishing stable quality arrangements. However while these changes have been numerous and important, they have so far lacked any systematic account or analysis.[1] This book seeks to remedy this gap. It draws on the author's involvement at key stages, chiefly during his time as Chief Executive of HEQC between 1993 and 1997.

While this is primarily an historical account, it also speculates on a number of issues, such as the reasons for the increasing interest in quality assurance, the balance between accountability and enhancement, and how to create the conditions for quality improvement. Most critically, studying the relevant literature, as well as recalling and describing the events that took place, has only strengthened the author's conviction that self-regulation within a selective external regime concerned primarily with quality improvement is the only effective mode of regulation for higher education if appropriate levels of quality are to be sustained.

The book is dedicated to my HEQC colleagues who achieved such a lot in such a short time. A number helped me with the book, including Vaneeta D'Andrea, Carolyn Campbell, David Parry, Norman Sharp and Peter Wright. Peter Williams and Robin Middlehurst both read and commented on the chapter dealing with HEQC. I would also like to acknowledge cooperation and encouragement from a wide group of other people including Geoffrey Alderman, John Brennan, Roger Cook, Gillian Evans, Martin Johnson, Roger King, Mike Laugharne, Jethro Newton, John Stoddart, Simeon Underwood, Sue Wright and David Young. Sincere thanks go also to Ronald Barnett. I should also like to thank Universities UK and the Standing Conference of Principals for granting access to their papers. QAA kindly granted access to the HEQC records. Lynne Banin, Elaine Creeser, Brenda Fisher, Hazel Flynn and Barbie Panvel all provided valuable assistance. David Parkins kindly gave us his permission to use his artwork.

However my greatest thanks go to my indefatigable and always cheerful research assistant Lilian Winkvist. Given the other pressures on my time as the head of a major higher education institution, it would not have been possible even to contemplate this project without the quality of assistance that Lilian has provided. I am especially grateful to her.

Note

1 A notable exception is the unpublished thesis by Dr Juan-Francisco Perellon (2001), to which reference will be made.

Acronyms

AAU	Academic Audit Unit
AUCF	Average Unit of Council Funding
AUQA	Australian Universities Quality Agency
BTEC	Business Technology Education Council
CDP	Committee of Directors of Polytechnics
CHES	Centre for Higher Education Studies, Institute of Education, University of London
CNAA	Council for National Academic Awards
COSHEP	Committee of Scottish Higher Education Principals
C-SAP	Centre for Learning and Teaching – Sociology Anthropology Politics (University of Birmingham)
CVCP	Committee of Vice Chancellors and Principals
DENI	Department of Education for Northern Ireland
DEL	Department for Employment and Learning
DES	Department of Education and Science
DfES	Department for Education and Skills
DOH	Department of Health
ECTS	European Credit Transfer System
EFA	Efficiency From Above
EFQM	European Foundation for Quality Management
ESRC	Economic and Social Research Council
FDS	First Destination Survey
FE	further education
FHEQ	Framework for Higher Education Qualifications
GCSE	General Certificate of Secondary Education
GSP	Graduate Standards Programme
HE	higher education
HEFCE	Higher Education Funding Council for England
HEFCW	Higher Education Funding Council for Wales
HEI	higher education institution
HESA	Higher Education Statistics Agency
HESDA	Higher Education Staff Development Agency
HEQC	Higher Education Quality Council

HMI	Her Majesty's Inspectorate
HMSO	Her Majesty's Stationary Office
HQ	*higher quality*
ILT	Institute for Learning and Teaching
ILTHE	Institute for Learning and Teaching in Higher Education
JPG	Joint Planning Group
LSE	London School of Economics
LTSN	Learning and Teaching Support Network
NCIHE	National Committee of Inquiry into Higher Education
NHS	National Health Service
NPM	New Public Management
NUS	National Union of Students
OD	Operational Description
OFSTED	Office for Standards in Education
PCFC	Polytechnics and Colleges Funding Council
QAA	Quality Assurance Agency
QCA	Qualifications and Curriculum Authority
QEG	Quality Enhancement Group
QSC	Quality Support Centre, Open University
RAE	Research Assessment Exercise
REEs	Registered External Examiners
RHA	regional health authority
SCOP	Standing Conference of Principals
SEDA	Staff and Educational Development Association
SHEFC	Scottish Higher Education Funding Council
SCOTCATS	Scottish Credit Accumulation and Transfer System
SRHE	Society for Research into Higher Education
SWOT	Strengths, Weaknesses, Opportunities and Threats
THES	*Times Higher Education Supplement*
TQA	Teaching Quality Assessment
TQEC	Teaching Quality Enhancement Committee
TQM	Total Quality Management
TVU	Thames Valley University
UCAS	University and Colleges Admissions Services
UFC	Universities Funding Council
UUK	Universities UK

Introduction

Higher education does not lack accountability, rather it lacks enough of the proper kind and is burdened with too much of an unproductive kind.
(Albjerg Graham, Lyman and Trow, 1995: iv)

On 16 May 1991 the Government published a White Paper, *Higher Education: A new framework* (DES, 1991), announcing its intention to abolish the 'binary line' between the existing universities and polytechnics, and enabling the latter to acquire a university title. The White Paper included proposals for a new quality assurance regime which would for the first time bring the regulation of all institutions' teaching and learning activities within an over-all statutory framework. The proposed dual quality assurance regime would consist of, first, an assessment by the higher education funding councils (the non-governmental organizations allocating public funds for teaching and research to the higher education institutions in England, Scotland and Wales respectively, each answerable to the Secretary of State) of the quality of teaching and learning at subject level in institutions; and second, audit by the Higher Education Quality Council (HEQC) (an agency owned by the institutions through their representative bodies, the Committee of Vice-Chancellors and Principals (CVCP) (now Universities UK), the Committee of Directors of Polytechnics (CDP) and the Standing Conference of Principals (SCOP)) of institutions' quality control mechanisms.[1]

The legislation to create this dual system of quality assurance was enacted the following year. The first assessments took place in 1993. HEQC was incorporated in May 1992 and commenced operations in September 1992.

Not much more than a year later, in September 1993, the principal rep-resentative body for higher education – the CVCP – agreed at its residential conference to press for a single quality assurance regime: a single quality process operated by a single quality agency. Fifteen months later, in December 1994, the Secretary of State for Education and Employment asked the Higher Education Funding Council for England (HEFCE) Chief Executive, Professor (now Sir) Graeme Davies, to review the arrangements introduced the previous year, in consultation with the sector. However, although supported by the

CVCP Chair, Professor Davies' proposals for a single system, with assessment as the core process, were rejected by the vice-chancellors in June 1995. There then followed negotiations between CVCP, HEFCE and the Department, leading to agreement in September 1995 on the principles of a new quality framework.

Between December 1995 and December 1996 a Joint Planning Group (JPG) established by CVCP and HEFCE with as Chair the former Vice-Chancellor of the University of Glasgow, Sir William Kerr Fraser, worked to produce detailed proposals. In December 1996 the JPG recommended that a new framework bringing together assessment and audit should be administered by a new agency. This would carry out the assessment functions of the funding councils and the audit and other functions of HEQC. The Quality Assurance Agency for Higher Education (QAA) came into existence in March 1997 and took over HEQC's staff and functions in August 1997. The staff of the English and Welsh Funding Councils' Assessment Units were transferred later in the year. In the meantime, in July 1997, the National Committee of Inquiry into Higher Education under Lord Dearing made wide-ranging proposals on quality including a new quality 'infrastructure' of precepts and guidance covering both quality and standards.

The QAA began work in the autumn of 1997 on a new quality process, eventually known as Academic Review, which incorporated the notion of 'variations in intensity' of external scrutiny. This was finally agreed in January 2000. The new methodology was introduced in Scotland in October 2000 and was due to be introduced in England in October 2001. But it was abandoned in March of that year following intensive lobbying of the Government by a small group of universities. In August 2001 the Agency's Chief Executive John Randall resigned. Discussions about a new audit-based method continued, and this was eventually approved by the Government in March 2002. The detailed methodology was published in August 2002. The first audits were undertaken in the early months of 2003. At the time of writing (May 2003) it remains to be seen whether this regime will prove to be more durable than those it has replaced.

In May 2002, the Funding Council announced the setting up of a further committee under Professor (now Sir) Ron Cooke, Vice-Chancellor of the University of York, to review the work of the various agencies concerned with quality enhancement. The Teaching Quality Enhancement Committee, of which the author was a member, produced an interim report in August 2002 and a final report in December 2002. The Committee recommended the creation of a single agency for quality enhancement, and this was endorsed in the White Paper *The Future of Higher Education* in January 2003 (DfES, 2003a).[2]

There have therefore been no fewer than three major changes of external quality regime in a decade, as well as a number of smaller ones (David Parry (2002) suggests that over the 10-year period there were actually 10 different external regimes or major modifications to existing regimes.) A lot of energy has gone into the discussion, and there has been prolonged and sometimes bitter wrangling and infighting. This book looks at the reasons for this lack of stability and at some of the lessons that can be learnt.

Argument of the book

Like all publicly provided services, UK higher education faces increasing pressure for accountability (as a minimum, the rendering to second and third-party stakeholders of an account of what one is doing and why). These pressures reflect the greatly increased scale and cost of higher education, increasing consumer awareness and the ideological revolution that has led the Government increasingly to treat higher education as if it were a private good. These pressures are by no means confined to the UK, although the UK system's response to them has led to a uniquely painful series of adjustments.[3]

As with many other professions, the traditional form of regulation in higher education has been self-regulation, by individual institutions and by the academic community collectively. We now have a mixture of self-regulation and external regulation, although self-regulation is still the principal mode. There has nevertheless been a continuing disagreement about the purposes, coverage, form and ownership of quality assurance. It is this that explains the lack of stability in the various quality regimes since 1992. The latest framework conciliates rather than resolves these differences.

The argument has sometimes been couched in terms of self-regulation versus statutory regulation. This is much too simple, dangerously so. Few people now believe in pure self-regulation: that universities and colleges should be free to run their courses and qualifications without any external scrutiny or supervision. Equally, few argue that universities should have their teaching closely monitored and controlled in the way that, for example, the school curriculum and examinations are currently supervised and controlled by the Qualifications and Curriculum Authority (QCA), the three exam boards and the Office for Standards in Education (OFSTED).[4] The argument therefore is about where the line should be drawn, and who should draw it.

An ancient philosopher – probably not Plato – said that the beginning of wisdom was the grasp of the obvious. It seems obvious to this writer at least that the main form of regulation applicable to higher education has to be self-regulation, by individual universities and colleges and by the wider academic community that those institutions constitute. The reasons are both philosophical and practical.

Philosophically, only practising teachers can determine the academic value of a proposed programme of study, a student's dissertation or project, or an award. Only those who design and deliver programmes and assess and accredit students are in a position to assure (that is, ensure) the quality of those programmes and qualifications. No one else can do so. Practically, the scale, complexity and quickly changing nature of the modern higher education curriculum mean that there is no real alternative to self-regulation.

The issue is not self-regulation or external regulation, but what are the conditions, and in particular what is the kind of external quality regime, which will promote rigorous (that is, honest and tough) self-regulation as opposed to clever games playing. More generally, how can academic staff be encouraged to take quality seriously by looking critically at what they offer their students, and be both willing and able to improve it, taking advantage of relevant theory and practice where this is helpful? How, in short, can they be encouraged to bring to their teaching, assessment and quality control activities the same habits of scholarship that they bring to their other scholarly activities (Brown, 2001e, 2001f)?

Towards the end of the book (Chapter 7) the author puts forward his own thoughts about how to create an environment in which quality improvement becomes the norm. It is argued there that the crucial test of any external quality regime is not whether it delivers sufficient reassurances to external stakeholders, still less what it costs the institutions, but whether it promotes or sets back effective self-regulation. This is because ultimately it is the quality of academic self-regulation which determines the value of the assurances and information which can be given to students and other third parties, and not, at least in normal circumstances, the external regime.

In his excellent lecture *A Sovietological View of Modern Britain*, to which extensive reference is made in Chapter 1, Ron Amann describes how a Soviet system of government did not disappear with the Berlin Wall but moved west to modern Britain's public sector. He remarks on how, as in Stalin's Russia, able individuals have come forward to manage public institutions under the new arrangements while 'Those who keep faith with the traditional values are often treated with pity and contempt – as relics of the old world who have not quite "got their act together"' (Amann, 1995: 6).

This book will show how the sector has indeed failed to 'get its act together'; how the leadership of the sector has failed to believe in, demonstrate the advantages of, and really fight for effective self-regulation; and how as a result we have had, and still to a large measure have, an external quality regime for teaching that is seriously sub-optimal. It will also show what needs to be done if self-regulation is once again to be made effective and quality properly assured.

A note on methodology

Before we get too far it may be worth saying something about the author and the methodology adopted. This is in large measure an insider's view of what happened and why. As, successively, the first (and as it proved last) Chief Executive of the CDP (May 1991 to December 1992), Head of Research and Strategy at the CVCP (January to June 1993), and Chief Executive of HEQC (July 1993 to August 1997), the author was centrally involved in the discussions about both the establishment and the revision of the 1991–2 arrangements. He continued to inform himself about the further changes from 1997, and had access to most of the key documents and personnel. This more or less direct involvement has been supplemented by close study of the relevant documentary sources prior to 1991 and by interviews, conducted by Lilian Winkvist, with the some of the principal actors.

Inevitably an account by an insider will incur charges – almost certainly well founded – of bias. To these charges the author can only plead guilty, but with the following pleas in mitigation. It is not necessarily the case that being closely involved in events in itself prevents one from taking a wider view. In setting up the post-1991 arrangements, and in the revisions in 1995–6, both the Chair of the CDP and HEQC (John Stoddart) and I were keenly aware of the wider ramifications (more aware, it can be argued, than many others of those involved).

Second, this account of what happened is placed within a wider conceptual and analytical framework, drawing in particular on the literature on public regulation. Finally, the author has gone to some lengths to report not only the facts but his own understanding and interpretation of these, indicating where this is particularly limited, or partial.

At the same time, there is much to be said for an insider's account, provided it is controlled in this way. Just because the author was involved in these events they can be described with a precision, and a flavour, that it may be difficult for outsiders to understand or convey. Without such an account, in fact, it may be difficult for students of the subject to comprehend some of the quite remarkable things that happened. The second 'justification' is that given the closed and even secretive nature of policy making in this particular policy area, it is often quite hard for those not directly involved to find out what is going on, let alone make sense of it. Even now there are some aspects of what happened that remain poorly understood, on the author's part at least. We may in other words have little alternative but to rely on insider views, at least until policy making in higher education is properly opened up, and issues of the kind discussed in the book attract the attention of serious academic researchers.[5] The final argument is that the author's unusual – possibly unique – experience as, successively, senior civil servant, Funding Council Secretary, CEO of a major representative body, CEO of an agency, and Principal of a large institution, gives him a good understanding of how public policies are made both generally and in higher education in particular.

The remainder of this Introduction describes the overall plan of the book.

Plan of the book

Chapter 1 outlines the historical context in which the developments covered in the book took place, and reviews the relevant literature on the regulation of teaching and learning in higher education. It offers a model for analysing the regulation of teaching and learning in higher education.

Chapter 2 describes the 1991 White Paper proposals and the thinking behind them. Reference is made to the existing quality regimes in the two separate sectors of higher education, and to developments therein from the mid-1980s onwards. The main part of the chapter deals with the representative bodies' response to the White Paper: broadening the role of the sector's own agency and narrowing and limiting the remit and resourcing of the Funding Council's units. The chapter then describes the establishment of the HEQC and the assessment units. It ends by discussing HEQC's relationships with the CVCP and the HEFCE Assessment Unit.

Chapter 3 is about HEQC's role and achievements. It looks in some detail at the Council's audit and enhancement work. Other areas are covered more cursorily.

Chapter 4 describes the establishment and evolution of assessment in England: the initial methodology; the 1994 evaluation; the changes that followed from 1995; and the further changes up to 2001. Briefer sections then describe the evolution of assessment in Scotland and Wales.

Chapter 5 gives a detailed account of the single-system discussions between September 1993 and August 1997. It describes the 1993 CVCP Residential Conference and its outcome; the work of the CVCP working party under Sir Frederick Crawford, Vice-Chancellor of Aston University; the review by Professor Davies; the creation, work and report of the Joint Planning Group; the report of the Dearing Committee; and the establishment of the new agency.

Chapter 6 deals with the work of the QAA from the point at which it took over its new functions to the final approval of the latest quality process. The chapter therefore covers the Registered External Examiner episode; the formulation of Academic Review; the development of the quality infrastructure (the qualifications framework, subject benchmark statements, programme specifications, code of practice); the introduction of Academic Review in Scotland and its abandonment in England; and the discussions about the new process. It also describes the work of the Cooke Committees on information and enhancement.

Chapter 7 begins by summarizing the reasons for the changes since 1992. It offers an assessment of the new quality assurance process and the chances of at least a degree of semi-permanence. Are the 'quality wars' over or have they merely gone underground? Will the new process survive until it achieves 'steady state' in 2005, or will a further round of complaints from the sector, or indeed from students paying 'top-up' fees, undermine it? Will the QAA be able to recover its credibility, or will there be moves to incorporate it into a wider and more streamlined regulatory regime? Chapter 7 also looks at the relationship between accountability and enhancement. It sets out the requirements for an effective quality regime, and outlines ways in which these requirements can be met. It concludes with a plea that we try to learn from the wasted effort of the past 10 years and establish arrangements with at least some degree of permanence.

Notes

1 The definitions used in the book are given in Appendix 1; the acronyms are listed on pages vii to viii.
2 A detailed chronology of developments between May 1991 and May 2003 is given in Appendix 2.

3   Four features have been distinctive in the British approach. First, the focus of the external reviews. Some countries (a majority) focus mainly on subjects or programmes. Others focus on institutions. But only the UK chose to introduce reviews at both levels simultaneously, initially implemented by separate organisations. Second, only in the UK has external review resulted in public gradings of quality. Third, only in the UK did review, initially at least, focus particularly on direct observation of teaching. Fourth, although members of the academic community have provided the vital foot soldiers in UK quality procedures, their status has been rather that of the 'hired help' of the agency rather than the leaders and definers of the process. In a number of countries, national subject committees – not seen in UK higher education quality assurance since the demise of the Council for National Academic Awards – have played lead roles in the implementation of quality assurance procedures, acting on behalf of the quality agency. Taken together, these features of the British approach have made the implementation of quality assurance particularly intrusive and divisive and lacking in legitimacy within the academic community.

(Brennan, 2002)

For a recent review of quality assurance internationally, see Brennan, 2001. (See also Brennan *et al*, 1991; Brennan and Shah, 1997; El-Khawas and Shah, 1998; Brennan and Shah, 2000a, 2000b, 2002c; Gaither, 1998.)
4 A predictable exception is the former Chief Inspector of Schools (Woodhead, 2000). But even in relation to the schools there is no clear evidence that the benefits of such control outweigh the detriments (Aitkenhead, 1998; Barnard, 1998; Brighouse, 1998; Budge, 1998; Doe, 1998; Hunter, 1998; Mansell, 2001; Pyke, 1998; Wragg, 2000).
5 As John Brennan says, 'academics have rarely, alas, been operating in researcher mode when they have addressed quality issues' (Brennan, 2001: 22).

1 Background and context

The implications of New Public Management ideas in public administration have been contested. Introducing these new ideas in a public university system should make an apt case for the exploration of the potential and limitations of New Public Management as a universal approach to management reform. In higher education where institutional autonomy and academic freedom are fundamental values, the compatibility between the rationale of the reform policies and the substantive field in which they are supposed to operate is posed more acutely than in most other policy fields.

(Bleiklie, 1998)

Introduction

It seems to be generally agreed that, in common with other publicly funded activities, the external regulation of universities has increased in both scope and specificity, particularly since the early 1980s. There have been various attempts to account for this and to assess the benefits and detriments. This chapter outlines the historical context in which the developments covered in the book took place and reviews some of the relevant literature. It concludes by proposing a model for analysing the regulation of universities' teaching and learning.

UK higher education at 6 May 1991

In May 1991 there were 1.176 million students in UK higher education, 748,000 full-time and 428,000 part-time (Government Statistical Service, 1993: 7). Numbers had risen rapidly since the mid-1980s due chiefly to the success of the new General Certificate of Secondary Education (GCSE) in improving retention rates in post-compulsory education and also to the Government's intention – announced in the Secretary of State Kenneth Baker's speech at Lancaster University in January 1989 (Baker, 1989) – to expand the system so as to bring UK participation rates into line with those of our major industrial competitors.

These students were to be found at two main categories of institution: the existing universities (including for this purpose the Open University) and the polytechnics and colleges, which formed the so-called public sector of higher education. The latter had absorbed the bulk of the expansion in demand at the cost of a substantial reduction in the unit of funding. As a result, their total student numbers now exceeded those of the established universities: 652,000 students against 524,000 at the existing universities. (Government Statistical Service, 1993: 7).

A major facilitator of this public sector expansion was the incorporation of the polytechnics and colleges through the Education Reform Act 1988, and the subsequent leadership and development of the new sector under Sir Ron (now Lord) Dearing and Dr (now Sir) William Stubbs at the Polytechnics and Colleges Funding Council (PCFC), the government agency allocating public funds to these institutions. By contrast, and in spite of having their own new funding council (the Universities Funding Council or UFC), the old universities showed not only slow growth but also a distinct reluctance to lower their costs, a factor which was to contribute in no small measure to the Government decision to abolish the distinction between the two groups of institutions.

Both the universities and the polytechnics and colleges were – and in their post-1992 form are – legally autonomous, privately owned organizations. The pre-1992 universities generally have charters, the post-1992 institutions are mostly higher education corporations, a specific category of company created by the 1988 Act. This legal autonomy is particularly important for quality since by law universities are answerable only to themselves for the standards of their awards. This legal autonomy of the institutions can be distinguished from the wider notion of academic autonomy, as the freedom within the law to question received wisdom and put forward new or unpopular opinions, enshrined in section 202 of the 1988 Act (HM Government, 1988).

Government policy towards higher education

The basic theory underlining the creation, terms of reference, composition and modus operandi of the new funding councils was that universities and other higher education institutions had to become both more efficient in their use of resources and more responsive to the needs of the economy. The classic statement of this case came in the 1985 Green Paper on higher education: 'the Government believes that it is vital for our higher education to contribute more effectively to the improvement of the performance of the economy' (DES, 1985).

To give effect to this, the 1987 White Paper *Higher Education: Meeting the Challenge* (DES, 1987) announced that two new funding bodies would be created which would be directly answerable to the Secretary of State and have powers to 'contract' with the institutions: that is, to allocate funding in return for the achievement of certain broad goals. The necessary legislation was enacted in 1988 as the Education Reform Act. By May 1991 the

Polytechnics and Colleges Funding Council (PCFC) had begun to give effect to this policy, the Universities Funding Council (UFC) was still finding its way.

Two other manifestations of the Government's wish to see universities becoming more efficient and economically responsive were the report of the Jarratt Committee on university management in 1985 (CVCP, 1985) and the first Research Assessment Exercise (RAE) in 1986. The former sought to remodel internal university governance and management along private sector corporation lines, with vice-chancellors becoming chief executives rather than academic leaders. The latter introduced the systematic external evaluation and ranking of all publicly funded university research, an exercise which was repeated in 1989, 1992, 1996 and 2001 and which is itself under scrutiny at the time of writing (HEFCE/SHEFC/HEFCW/DEL, 2003).

As well as the Department and the funding councils (and the research councils for some research), the other principal actors in determining policy were the bodies representing the heads of institutions, of which there were then three: CVCP, CDP and SCOP (representing the HE colleges). Of these, CVCP was by far the oldest, going back to 1918. CDP had been formed in 1970 as the last polytechnics were being designated under the 1968 Education Act. SCOP dated from 1978. These organizations were – and are – in effect trade associations, making representations and lobbying government about policies, disseminating advice and guidance to members, and delivering certain functions on their behalf, chiefly negotiating staff salaries under national bargaining arrangements with the relevant trade unions.

We now turn to a brief review of some of the relevant literature on the regulation of higher education.

The economic ideology of education

In an important series of writings, Tapper and Salter argue that since the war institutional autonomy has gradually reduced because of the view that successive governments have taken about the overriding importance of an efficient and dynamic economy. Moreover, this reduction was both inevitable and right, given higher education's unique social role as the creator and legitimator of knowledge and status (and hence its accretion of socio-political power). The result has been ever more extensive and intrusive attempts to influence the behaviour of universities in the service of the Government's goals for the economy (cf Watson and Bowden, 1999; Kogan and Hanney, 1999).

According to this thesis – which in general terms the author accepts – it was also inevitable that these attempts to control the universities should embrace the quality and standards of student learning, and that this should eventually involve – in the QAA – 'a pliable instrument of ministerial will' (Salter and Tapper, 2000: 84). By the same token, HEQC ('chosen champion of the HEIs'), which attempted to represent the academic community and to protect self-regulation, was doomed: 'as a political strategy to deal with an aggressive state it was unsustainable' (ibid: 77). This is also the view of the only other study known to the author of the events described in this book (Perellon, 2001).

For reasons that will be explained in detail later, the author does not accept this judgement. While government interest in universities' performance is unavoidable, it is not inevitable that the regulation of quality and standards should have developed as it has, nor will the present arrangements necessarily persist. The author's long experience of policy making, in various public contexts, suggests that nothing is inevitable until it happens, and that there are almost always alternatives to be considered, and choices to be made, as in this case. Moreover the sector need not be supine but can influence the policies that are applied to it, if it has effective leadership (something which was, as we shall see, largely lacking in this case).

The evaluative state

An enormous literature has grown up around the notion of 'the evaluative state' (Neave, 1988; Henkel, 1991; Pollitt, 1993; Kettl, 1997; Neave, 1998). In a useful review Dill (1998) refers to the 'essential principles' of this approach as being:

- The separation of the government's interests as the 'owner' or financial supporter of an agency from its interests as the purchaser of the services of that agency.
- Operational specification, in output terms, of the performance objectives of government agencies, i.e. performance measurement.
- Aligning accountability with control by delegating to agencies increased authority over inputs and decisions about resource use.
- Encouraging accountability for performance through reliance on explicit contracts, competition amongst service providers, and privaisation within government agencies.

(Dill, 1998: 361)

In the earlier article Neave argues that evaluation (of the performance of universities) has always been an intrinsic part of public policy making on higher education, and a legitimate one. However, the expansion of such evaluation, in particular through the establishment of powerful intermediary bodies such as the French Comité National d'Evaluation, HEQC, the Swedish Högskolverket, the Flemish Vlaamse Interuniversitaire Raad and for that matter the Dutch Vereeniging der Samenwerkende Nederlandse Universiteiten, represents a step change:

> In essence . . . the Evaluative State reflects an attempt to go beyond historic modes of evaluation, to enforce more precise and more rapid responses from institutions of higher education by devising a highly

elaborate and more widely ranging instrumentality of judgement than existed earlier. This instrumentality, if regularly applied, is dynamic and grounded upon a principle of contractualisation fundamentally different from the implicit ideas of contractualisation which bound State and university together in Europe for the best part of the 19th and 20th Centuries.

(Neave, 1998: 282)

In the later article, Neave draws attention to the way in which the state can change these agencies if they are not seen to be doing their job in helping with the overall steerage function. He gives the abolition of HEQC and the establishment of QAA as an example. As we shall see, the author considers this too simple an explanation for what actually happened in this particular case.

In an important article, Bleiklie (1998) challenges the views of both Tapper and Salter and Neave. While institutional autonomy is certainly a feature of some traditional views of the 'normative space' of university policy, it is not of all, and particularly not of the 'rationalist' perspective which emphasizes the role of universities in helping societies to meet their social and economic needs (and hence the need for societal control over them).

Just as there are different perspectives on the role and functions of universities which coexist, so there are different sets of expectations, which 'are processes of gradual sedimentation rather than sequential stages' (Bleiklie, 1998: 304). The main ones are:

- the university as part of the national civil service and as implementer of public policy;
- the university as an autonomous cultural institution;
- the university as a corporate enterprise, as a producer of educational and research services.

It is to the last of these that the emphasis has now shifted. So it is inevitable that the most important issue facing universities (and the state in its view of universities) is efficiency: 'related to the rapidity and cost at which it produces useful services, research and candidates for the benefit of users, be they the university's own faculty, administrators, employers of university graduates, or buyers of research' (Bleiklie, 1998: 307). This requires both a strengthening in the administrative aspect of university governance and a shift in the position of the state:

From a traditional ex ante regulation in the shape of established rules, practices and budget decisions, the State has moved to emphasise ex post facto control. The focus lies on performance in relation to deliberately formulated policy goals. The central idea is that if state agencies are provided with clearly formulated goals and a set of incentives and sanctions invoked in response to actual behaviour, efficiency will thereby increase. When emphasis shifts from rule production and rule adherence to goal formulation and performance control, evaluation becomes a core activity and thus changes the way the State goes about its business of governance.

(Bleiklie, 1998: 307)

The regulatory state

A parallel literature has grown up around the 'regulatory state'. Cope and Goodship (1999: 4) identify three sets of pressures that have contributed to this. At the 'macro' level, 'states are restructuring themselves and the societies they govern so as to remain competitive in the global market place. This shift from a welfare state to a competition state constitutes a significant pressure upon governments to increasingly regulate public service provision so that spending is both directed towards achieving centrally set policy goals and contained within centrally set budgets'.

At the 'meso' level, New Public Management (NPM) aims to remove differences between the public and private sectors, and shift ways of doing business in public organizations away from complying with procedural rules towards getting results (Cope and Goodship, 1999: 5). This involves both centralizing and decentralizing: 'NPM separates steering from rowing, leaving the centre to steer while other agencies row' (Osborne and Gaebler, 1992, quoted in Cope and Goodship, 1999: 5).

At the 'micro' level, increasing regulation serves the interests of both politicians and bureaucrats, enabling them to increase their control and their ability to ensure that regulatory agencies serve their interests, and not necessarily those that the agencies ostensibly serve.

In a recent review article Moran notes that the modern regulatory state was effectively invented in the United States, where business was controlled by law-backed specialized agencies rather than through public ownership. Since the 1960s such regulation has been weakened by a 'crisis of command' as regulation was extended to areas such as social policy which were much less easy to control in this way, and where the law could not be wholly relied upon. Instead of trying to find ways of restoring command, however, the academic literature has asked 'what kind of spirit should animate this regulation?' (Moran, 2002: 397).

Three sets of answers can be found. One is that in the end the only effective regulation is self-regulation. Another, associated with Braithwaite (Ayres and Braithwaite, 1992), is that successful regulation is eventually about persuasion and dialogue in the regulatory process, what is called 'responsive regulation' (Moran, 2002: 398) Yet another view, articulated by McBarnet and Whelan (1991) is that non-formal modes of regulation are just as afflicted as formal ones where there is no community of interest. Instead, 'Attempts to induce co-operation in the spirit of regulation only produce creative compliance – ingenious obedience that ignores the spirit of regulation if it happens to get in the way of the pursuit of comparative advantage' (Moran, 2002: 400). We shall see some of this when we look at assessment.

Where does Britain stand in this discussion? Moran finds two distinct but linked sets of literatures, both highly relevant to this book. The first concerns the historic British preference for self-regulation, much of which 'turned on appropriating public authority while evading mechanisms of accountability for the exercise of that authority' (Moran, 2002: 405). The second, which owes much to Foucault, emphasizes regulation as a project that involves the reconstruction of social understanding 'such that effective systems of control are those that involve the internalisation of control norms' (Moran, 2002: 405). This view is given its classic statement in Michael Power's critique of accounting (1994, 1997).

The audit society

Power's argument is that there has been a 'veritable explosion' of audits in many different fields as government has sought to devolve many of its functions while retaining a regulatory oversight. Audits are not simply a response to problems of accountability, but also shape the contexts in which they are demanded. Audits are justified in terms of organizational transparency and improvement of organizational performance, but they are often very specialized and opaque to the general public. Yet their record in improving performance is highly questionable: as the Professor of Accounting at the University of Essex said in an article in the *Guardian* on 20 February 2002, 'No scandal has ever come to light because of audit firms or the professional accountancy bodies' (Sikka, 2002).[1]

In fact, audit is more likely to reduce trust further than to restore it. What is needed is a 'broad shift' in control philosophy: 'from long distance, low trust, quantitative, disciplinary and ex-post forms of verification by private experts to local, high trust, qualitative, enabling, real-time forms of dialogue with peers. In this way, we may eventually be in a position to devote more resources to creating quality rather than just policing it' (Power, 1994: 49). This last sentence is particularly relevant to this book.

One particularly striking statement in Power is that audit is not simply a technical practice but an idea:

> [It] has become central to ways of talking about administrative control. The extension of auditing into different settings, such as hospitals, schools, or to companies, laboratories, and industrial processes, is more than a natural and self-evidently technical response to problems of governance and accountability. It has much to do with articulating values, with rationalising and reinforcing public images of control.
>
> (Power, 1994: 5)

This argument has been taken forward in relation to higher education by Shore and Wright. Analysing both research and teaching assessment, the authors suggest that rather than improving quality and empowering those involved, 'these processes beckon a new form of coercive authoritarian governmentality' (Shore and Wright, 1999: 1). Echoing Power, the authors explore how modern audit systems and techniques function as 'political technologies' for introducing neo-liberal systems of power where professionals have been 'reinvented as units of resource whose performance and productivity must constantly be audited so that it can be enhanced' (ibid: 3). Moreover, the professionals 'internalize' the new 'expert' knowledge in order to reform themselves (ibid: 4).

In the 1980s it was assumed by government that market forces provided the best model of accountability, and that without such a market the best way of instilling private-sector values and practices was through the technology of accountancy. In higher education, the introduction of audit:

> was designed to create an efficient, accountable system that could be standardised, disciplined and continuously improved. The means for realising these objectives were new disciplinary norms, institutional procedures and bureaucratic agents which together precipitated a radical change in academics' own sense of themselves as professionals. As a result, the progressive advance of this neo-liberal form of governance has systematically reconfigured the university sector as a docile auditable body.
>
> (Shore and Wright, 1999: 7)

RAE, TQA and particularly the QAA's post-Dearing quality framework (see Chapter 6) all illustrate how audit culture functions as a political technology:

> First, they focus on policing an organisation's own systems of control – the control of control. Second, they create new intermediaries, seemingly independent of government, who, in turn, present people with new expert knowledge through which they can reform themselves. Third, they rely on techniques of the self that render political subjects governable by requiring that they behave as responsible, self-activating free agents who have internalized the new normative framework. Fourth, they require disciplines to re-organise themselves so as to be more centralised, accountable, and therefore, auditable.
>
> (Shore and Wright, 1999: 10)

Ironically, such an approach actually threatens quality. Instead, 'What we are witnessing here is the imposition of a new disciplinary grid which, by inculcating new norms, "empowers" us to observe and improve ourselves according to new neo-liberal notions of the performing professional' (Shore and Selwyn, 1998, quoted in Shore and Wright, 1999: 14).

Similar criticisms of the Audit Society are voiced in eloquent form in the 2002 BBC Reith Lectures (BBC Radio 4, 2002). Lady O'Neill quotes Dr Johnson: 'It is happier to be sometimes cheated than not to trust' (O'Neill, 2002a). She shows how, paradoxically, the emphasis upon accountability and transparency, while ostensibly about restoring trust, particularly in professional judgements, has in fact undermined trust by constraining and weakening professional practice. As a result 'We are heading towards defensive medicine, defensive teaching and defensive policing' (O'Neill, 2002b). Moreover, while the ostensible aim is accountability to the public, 'the real requirements are for accountability to regulators, to departments of government, to funders, to legal standards. The new forms of accountability impose forms of central control – quite often indeed a range of different and mutually inconsistent forms of central control' (O'Neill, 2002b: 4).

Another trenchant critic of the audit society is Professor Ron Amann. In a 1995 lecture (Amann, 1995), Professor Amann, then Chief Executive of the Economic and Social Research Council, more recently Director General of the Centre for Management and Policy Studies at the Cabinet Office, drew attention to the parallels between central planning in the former Soviet Union and the reforms of the British public sector in the 1980s and 1990s.

Amann's central thesis is that, like the Soviet state, British government – at least under Mrs Thatcher and Mr Major, and now, almost certainly, Mr Blair – was engaged in social engineering, 'imposing a general "social interest"' through command and control methods which, while they were perfectly rational at the micro level, were profoundly irrational at the macro level. As in the Soviet Union, those operating the system found all sorts of ways of coping with the requirements laid on them while collectively subverting the underlying intentions.

Amann's critique is so good that, as well as deserving to be much better known, it should be read in its entirety. One or two comments have a particular pertinence to this book. In particular:

As public institutions, such as universities for example, began to construct 'bids' to the central funding bodies for resources (in Bristol, in this instance, rather than Moscow), it was of course appreciated in a vague sort of way that some kind of quality control would be required, otherwise the more unscrupulous institutions would 'play games'. Doubtless it was hoped initially that this would be a lightly managed process. However, the official fiction of the minimalist response, which is still maintained by many purchasing organizations, stands in dramatic contrast to the actual volume of the documentation which they demand and receive and the time taken to produce it. The fact that space in aircraft hangars was required to house the aggregate university response to the last HEFCE Research Assessment Exercise makes the point in graphic terms. . . . Like the horizon, the objective of assured institutional accountability receded as one paddled clumsily towards it.

(Amann, 1995: 4–5)

We shall find precisely this in the QAA's version of 'lightness of touch'!

Amann echoes Power in asking why the new administrative arrangements 'have not, for the most part, been theorized or contested in systemic terms':

> The answer to that question is both interesting and complex. It is, of course, tempting when viewing the British professions under siege today to see parallels with the unfortunate Soviet 'bourgeois specialists' of the 1920s: a group of engineers and managers far too sensible, pragmatic and conscious of their own worth to recognize a fundamental political challenge – until it was too late and they were wheeled out of their factories in barrows. But that would be a harsh judgement. In any event, groups which are subject to a concerted political and ideological attack of this kind have to make a psychological adjustment which they are usually too proud to admit. It is a classic dilemma of the persecuted minority, torn between the decision to fight (or, in this case, to challenge the new orthodoxy) or to acquiesce gracefully, grab what advantage they can, and keep their powder dry. Many are the Vice-Chancellors and public sector Chief Executives, facing the new bodies which encroach upon their traditional autonomy, who might echo Cyril Washbrook's definitive view of fast bowlers: 'Nobody likes 'em but it's not everybody as'll let on'.

(Amann, 1995: 5–6)

Finally, Amann deals very crisply with the claims made by the Government that the new approach has improved efficiency:

> To get a better grip, purchasing and regulatory bodies stipulate more and more performance indicators, amounting in the case of the NHS Trusts to an intrusive form of micro-management, accompanied by official rhetoric about vibrant managerial autonomy. (You always know that something is up when official protestations of this sort occur – this is pure *vran'yo*, almost on a par with Agitprop statements about Soviet 'democracy of a new type' which allegedly stimulated turnouts of around 99% by an enthusiastic and grateful electorate).

(Amann, 1995: 7)

Precisely this can be found in Government and Funding Council statements about the efficacy of assessment.

In another important article, Graham and Barnett (1996) review the successive notions of quality held by those responsible for the regulation of teacher education (unfortunately considerations of space prevent the author from doing justice to this and other professional areas of the curriculum in the context of the book's main story). They echo the points made by Power and others about definitions of quality not being 'neutral' but actually constituting a crucial matter in the ideological formation of those being regulated. They suggest a two-dimensional framework for understanding these various approaches.

The first axis is that of power, and whether it lies with the state or with the providers of the service. Following Lukes (1974), they distinguish between the 'coercive', 'agenda setting' and 'ideological dimensions' of power. They comment that:

> In Britain and elsewhere, management by the state of the discourse of quality is a crucial element in the agenda-setting process and associated belief system . . . By setting the political agendas, proposing legislation for debate, producing national reports (Apple, 1986), initiating White Papers, and establishing governmental agencies with remits couched in the terminology of accountability and of quality, arguably the State has caused (quality) itself and its associated terminology to become common sense and everyday categories in education.
>
> (Graham and Barnett, 1996: 172)

The second axis is communication, and whether the assurance process is, one, closed and bureaucratic or open and dialogical in character, and two, purely judgemental or aimed at assisting providers and improving their own teaching practices. Graham and Barnett (1996) then plot various assurance processes (see Figure 1.1 on p 20). They comment that the dialogic half 'is being rapidly vacated, as bureaucratic systems take over, making summative judgements, often expressing State agendas' (ibid: 175). In their view, HEQC was not immune from this even though it started on the right side of the line!

Finally, Graham and Barnett comment on the potential impact on institutions' internal systems:

> in working out their own internal quality arrangements, institutions are becoming more managerial and less collegial themselves. The external patterns of quality evaluation are being institutionalised within institutions and the embryonic professionalism of self-critique is faltering. The more strategic systems of quality assurance are likely to colonise the dialogical and self-reflective. These can only be speculations for future empirical enquiry.
>
> (Graham and Barnett, 1996: 175)[2]

The regulation of the professions

The Teacher Training Agency is merely the latest vehicle through which the Government has sought to regulate the performance of the teaching profession

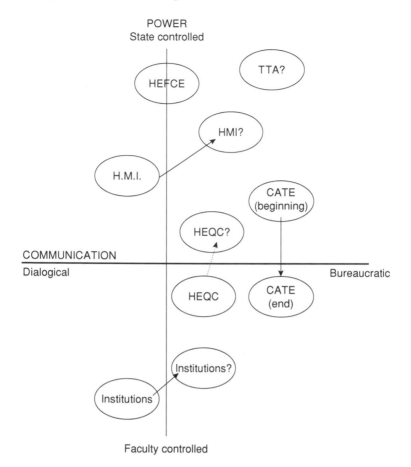

Figure 1.1 The relationship of the bodies that monitor quality in teacher education.

(for another and very similar critique to Graham and Barnett see Foreman-Peck, 2001). Of course, teaching is not the only profession to have been subject to increasingly close external regulation. An instructive and highly relevant case is that of medicine.

Historically, there was little direct regulation of doctors. The General Medical Council enforced minimum standards but had no overall interest in accountability. The Royal Colleges and other professional bodies inspected and accredited medical schools. However, the NHS Act 1990 introduced the concept of medical audit, which involved all medical staff in the critical examination of the quality of care and practice (HM Government, 2001).

Hunter argues that clinical governance is 'possibly the most significant feature of the Government's NHS modernising agenda', and means achieving a 'fundamental shift in the power balance' between doctors and managers:

'professionalism as a style of managing is no longer in vogue following a series of scandals' (such as at Bristol) (Hunter, 2002: 11).

The reference to Bristol is a reference to the report of the Bristol Royal Infirmary inquiry (HM Government, 2001). Hunter worries that the new approach:

> could result in the de-professionalisation of clinical work through a process of creeping bureaucratic monitoring and performance evaluation. In the 'wrong' hands, clinical governance could grant permission to Ministers to intervene at will to 'sort out' difficult, non-compliant doctors. Indeed the new Health Act contains reserve powers giving Ministers the powers of precisely this type.
>
> (Hunter, 2002: 12)

Hunter emphasizes the importance of retaining the best features of professionalism by not constraining them through 'narrow managerialism'.

Salter (2000) claims that over the previous two years trust between patient and doctor was 'politicised'. In the face of 'what is widely, if wrongly, perceived as a crisis of trust in the medical profession' the government response was frenetic, verging on what might be best described as 'policy panic':

> In an impressive display of energy, the policy making machinery has gone into overdrive in the production of regulatory policies designed to deal with the concerns of the public and, it is hoped, defuse the issue. These policies include: revalidation, re-certification, continuing professional development, continuing medical education, clinical audit, medical audit, critical incident reporting, adverse event reporting, risk management, rapid response teams, annual appraisal, quality assurance and, of course, clinical governance. To implement these policies new organisations have mushroomed in the fertile soil of the NHS. They include: the Modernizing Agency, the National Institute for Clinical Excellence, the Commission for Health Improvement, the National Clinical Assessment Authority, and the Assessment and Support Centres.
>
> What is unclear, and perhaps intended to remain unclear, is how these well-intentioned but diverse policies will relate one to the other, how accountability lines will be drawn, how a doctor will be required to move seamlessly through the expanding web of surveillance without becoming hopelessly entangled in its procedures, and what effect greater regulation will have, if any, on public trust. Part of the problem for the analyst, and presumably also for the professionals and managers, is the tendency of the government to create numerous and overlapping forms of accountability with obscure, if not opaque, relationships one to the other.
>
> (Salter, 2000: 1–2)

However, this increase in external accountability is not simply the result of government attempts to increase its power. In another article, Salter describes the 'rise of the active citizen'. He suggests that, for example, 'the rise of complementary medicine is a clear indication of the erosion of the profession's cultural authority and legitimacy':

> As citizens come to see themselves as active consumers of healthcare, rather than passive recipients of authoritative clinical decisions, so they are in effect redefining their welfare citizenship, their healthcare rights, their expectations and their political demands. [They] . . . are increasingly taking the view that since medical regulation is for them, they should be actively involved in determining what it is trying to achieve, rather than being dependent upon a professional definition of appropriate outcomes.
>
> (Salter, 2002: 62)

In a recent report, Calman, Hunter and May (2002) reviewed the implementation of the present Government's health policy two years into the NHS plan of 2000. Their criticisms are familiar:

> Without trust there can be no sensible way of running a complex system like the NHS. But modern trust does not entail a retreat into outmoded models of professional paternalism. Rather, it is underpinned by the values of open debate, scepticism, inquisitiveness, and the pursuit of continuous learning and improvement. All of these are in short supply when the policy context is dominated by a centralising government intent on controlling the agenda.
>
> (Calman, Hunter and May, 2002: 4)

Moreover:

> Across the service, senior management time is overwhelmingly taken up with demands from the Government and the regulatory agencies, and the consequences of the current reorganisation Shifting the Balance of Power. This can result in senior management neglecting the most important challenge – improving front-line services.

At the same time:

> The introduction of 'franchising' and attempts to import private sector expertise into the NHS give the false impression that improvement will automatically result from placing new management on top of NHS Trusts. However, only front-line management can undertake detailed redesign of services and improve the use of information. Most change

occurs from the inside out, at the front-line of service delivery – where the NHS often fails patients.

(Calman, Hunter and May, 2002: 7)

The regulation of higher education

In the article already referred to, Dill shows how some of the problems with external regulation generally also apply in higher education through evaluation exercises like the RAE and TQA. One of these problems is that the regulatory agency will substitute its own values for those of the external stakeholders on whose behalf it is purporting to act, a danger which is increased by the difficulties of measuring the quality of academic outputs (de Vries, 1996). A related problem is the familiar one of regulatory 'capture', where the community being evaluated substitutes its own values for those of the regulator. Another difficulty is that performance measurement in higher education is quite costly:

> These [costs] include not only the direct costs of assessment, but also the indirect costs associated with mis-measurement, as, for example, when a focus on teaching presentations retards more effective and efficient innovations in teaching and learning, or when a reliance on discipline-based peer review discourages research developments in applied and multi-disciplinary areas. The process of external assessment can also entail special costs. These include the emotional costs amongst those observed in the case of UK assessments and the substantial opportunity costs in faculty time if occasional external assessments encourage the creation of Potemkin Villages of quality assurance. External assessments are also often only loosely co-ordinated with internal processes of planning and resource allocation, thus limiting their potential impact. To evaluate the alternative of the Evaluative State effectively we need more systematic research on the full costs and benefits of such evaluative processes.
>
> (Dill, 1998: 364)

Amen.

Dill then compares the alternatives of competitive markets and control by the 'academic guild'. Governments have attempted to move the regulation of higher education in the competitive market direction by improving the quantity and quality of information for students. This passage is so good that it deserves to be quoted in full for all those (such as the present Government) who would see an expanded quasi-regulatory role for external information:

> It is presumed that even if a 'price' were created for academic programmes through the adoption of tuition fees, students lack sufficient

information about the quality of academic institutions or programmes to make choices that will be efficient for the overall society. It is further assumed that if such information were to be provided publicly by academic institutions under government mandate, or by independent quality assurance agencies carrying out government policy, subsequent student choices would provide incentives for institutions to improve their academic quality. This simple logic lies behind the development and publication of academic quality assurance information in many countries. However this logic rests upon a long and complex causal chain, which assumes first that reliable and valid measures of academic quality can be created; second, that, if provided, students will use such information in their decisions to enrol in higher education; and third, that institutions as a consequence will respond to declining student numbers and act to improve the quality of their academic programmes.

(Dill, 1998: 365–66)

Dill is far from being dewy-eyed about the academic guild and particularly the increased specialization of knowledge, which has undermined genuine collegiality, and the abiding preference of many academic staff for research over teaching. However, he sees some possibilities for renewal through the global pressures for specifying both academic and individual professional standards, and through changes at the level of individual institutions designed to restore collegial accountability.

The latter agenda – which could include such things as faculty-led, subject-level assessment systems, mirroring government-mandated external assessments, including required self-assessments and external peer reviews, and articulated with institutional resource allocation processes – represents a 'middle way' between the extremes of external regulation through markets or agencies on the one hand, and self-regulation on the other. Dill concludes: 'The policy choice, I would suggest, is not between an imperfect evaluative state and a perfectly competitive market or a perfectly influential academic guild, but between three imperfect institutions. Which of these forms of co-ordination, and in what circumstances, may produce the greatest overall benefit for society is still unclear' (Dill, 1998: 370–71).

Cave, Dodsworth and Thompson (1995) have similar doubts about pure self-regulation, but are less enthusiastic about competitive markets and more positive about external regulation. Like Dill, they refer to the work of James and Neuberger (1981), and the risk that, left to themselves, academic staff will pursue their own interests at the expense of their students and other stakeholders. (cf Adam Smith's remark that universities were inefficient because 'they were run for and by the same people') However, market mechanisms are unlikely to resolve satisfactorily the information failures inherent in the nature – or notion – of higher education as a product. A further, and in their view conclusive, argument for some form of external regulation is the strain that increased competitive and commercial pressures are placing on quality levels.

Efficiency from above: the politics of performance assessment

In an early, and prophetic, article, Pollitt (1987) reviewed the different kinds of performance assessment that had by then been developed across the UK public sector, and the potential implications for higher education. Pollitt distinguished two approaches: those that had 'efficiency' as their main driver and which were usually sponsored or imposed from above (what he christened 'Efficiency from above' or 'EFA' schemes), and those that were more concerned with quality and effectiveness and which grew up in a particular institutional setting (Pollitt, 1987: 88–89). Pollitt described these as 'ideologies' because the underlying approach 'infects almost every detail of the actual mechanism used' (Pollitt, 1987: 95). We shall have cause to recall these words when we come to the development of assessment and the single system debate.

As ideologies the two approaches were fundamentally incompatible:

> The 'EFA' model sees individuals as needing to be formally 'incentivised', and sanctioned, to ensure sufficiently rapid change. Thus it is management's task to create such a framework, and to excite otherwise subdued or dormant aspirations for improved performance. Hierarchy, competitiveness and the 'right to manage' are implicit throughout this approach. The professional development model, on the other hand, is more egalitarian, less individualistic, more communitarian. Professionals co-operate to improve each other's performances, and monetary rewards (or negative sanctions for persistent under-performance) are not necessary to sustain the process.
>
> (Pollitt, 1987: 94) (cf Elton, 1986)

Indeed, rewards or sanctions may well destroy the aim of development because this requires openness and frankness about strengths and weaknesses, something that can be counterproductive in an EFA regime.

There is one other comment of Pollitt's that is particularly relevant to the single system discussion. He remarks that:

> Variations in schemes to suit local circumstances are likely to be more acceptable within the professional-development approach (because of its emphasis on the control of the process by those immediately involved – a kind of 'local democracy'). The 'EFA' approach, by contrast, usually requires standardised measures so as to provide the centre with the data on which to base decisions to shift resources from the less to the more efficient 'providers'.
>
> (Pollitt, 1987: 95)

This was precisely the factor that made it so difficult to develop a selective or 'lightness of touch' approach to assessment.

Pollitt suggested that if higher education was to escape the worst rigours of EFA (which it was already beginning to experience with the RAE, which was run for the first time the year before his article was published) it should consciously attempt to involve students and other 'consumers' much more fully in the assessment process. There is no evidence that anyone in higher education heeded either these warnings or this advice.

Collaborative self-regulation

In separate books and articles, Kells and Jackson (a former HEQC colleague) have identified a range of possible regimes for regulating teaching and learning and the conditions that are necessary if such regulation is to succeed (Kells, 1992; Jackson, 1997a, 1997b, 1997c, 1998). The main thesis is that while in theory either pure self-regulation or external regulation (that is, regulation by an agency separate from and independent of those being regulated) is possible, in practice most regulatory systems are 'collaborative', involving not only institutions and agencies but other groups such as professional and statutory bodies, subject associations, credit consortia and so on. Perhaps the most valuable and relevant part of Kells' work as far as this book is concerned is the statement of the conditions necessary for an effective 'collaborative' self-regulatory system. These are:

- Government oversight is important: without the threat of intervention in the event of serious malfunction or lack of effort in the self-regulation system, some drift away from serious and responsible effort can occur. Some external regulation is essential.
- However, higher education institutions, through their leaders, should design, fund and control the regulatory system. This is necessary to establish 'ownership' of the system's purposes and procedures.
- The activities of self-regulation should be managed through a collaborative, inter-university, 'buffer-type' organization.
- Processes of interaction, particularly self-assessment processes, should be the heart of the system. The advantage of professional judgement, particularly self-assessment, is that it provides a firm basis for sustained change as a result of the regulatory act. Comparative or externally referenced indicators and other information can only provide a signal or starting point.
- External validation is needed in the self-regulation system. Without such validation, through peer review, self-regulation is less credible.
- Agreed upon frameworks for evaluation are necessary.
- Purposes and meanings must be functionally aligned. A system seeking to reassure the public must have a procedure such as peer review to provide second-party validation. A system seeking to stimulate improvements

should not publish the failures of the institutions and programmes, or publish rankings of indicators about them, before any improvement can be enacted (cf Pollitt). As we shall see, most of the official statements of the objectives of quality assurance since 1992 have sought to combine assurance and enhancement.

- Sufficient time and resources must be provided to develop the system. The maturation of standards and training systems, and the building of mutual trust and confidence between institutions and government, is a slow and demanding process requiring considerable attention on the part of the leaders. Those with interests in the development of these systems must be realistic and patient. Moreover there are no inexpensive regulation schemes: they are, like democracy, just less expensive than the alternatives!
- High priority for the regulatory system and an environment of trust must be established by institutions and government leaders. In particular the climate for self-regulation must be carefully nurtured and continuously attended to by leaders.
- Incentives and sanctions must be applied according to the purposes of the system and the circumstances in the country.
- Information must be adequate to inform the judgements to be made in the system.
- The consequences of self-regulation must be integrated with the budget and planning functions of institutions and the other systems thereof.
- Self-regulation should be a cyclical process gaining effectiveness over time (Kells, 1992: 58–64).

Kells' book was published in 1992 but had been prefigured in a number of publications from 1972 onwards. Had those determining the various quality regimes we have had since 1992 paid it any attention at all, many of the subsequent mistakes might have been avoided.

Jackson reinforces the importance for self-regulation of having a clear framework of standards or criteria so as to provide a credible basis for consistent external judgements, as well as for effective self-evaluation. Such a framework needs to be at system, institutional, sub-institutional (that is, departmental) and individual levels. As we shall see, this was the purpose of HEQC's Graduate Standards Programme.

As already noted, Kells, like Pollitt, stresses the need for the purposes and means of any regulatory system to be functionally aligned and compatible. Both Kells and Jackson draw attention especially to the difficulties (though not the impossibility) of combining in a single quality regime the different purposes of accountability and improvement (cf Pollitt, 1987; Middlehurst and Woodhouse, 1995; Vroeijenstijn, 1995).

Kells in particular emphasizes the benefits of a developmentally focused regulatory system, and this has been taken up by a number of other writers (eg Harvey and Knight, 1996; Biggs, 2001; Gosling and D'Andrea, 2001; Elton, 2002). At the same time he is scathing about comparative ratings:

> One matter that must be addressed with regard to self-assessment pro-
> cesses is the almost universal, and understandable, reluctance of faculties
> to expose any of their weaknesses or problems in such a process which
> involves external visitors and where government officials and journalists
> may be able to get access to the report of the visitors. The answer lies in
> the fundamental balance between public assurance and internal control
> that must be carefully maintained if these processes are to result in
> improvement and, therefore, a higher level of quality over time being
> reported to the public. It also points to the basic difference between
> inspectorial, ratings-oriented processes that seek to measure and report
> comparative quality, and the self-based processes that seek improvement
> and a betterment of the system.
>
> (Kells, 1992: 91–92)

This leads us naturally to the subject of quality enhancement.

Quality enhancement

In another piece that should be required reading for all interested in quality assurance, another former HEQC colleague distinguishes several stages in developing approaches to quality: quality control, quality assurance, quality enhancement and quality transformation.

> An initial stage will involve specifying what one is trying to achieve in
> relation to a set of purposes and goals. In order to measure levels of
> attainment, standards will also need to be part of this specification.
> Typically, the next stage of development will involve quality control, ie
> procedures to check whether objectives have been achieved at the desired
> performance level. Beyond this level lies quality assurance, which involves
> establishing that there are systems and procedures in place to ensure that
> objectives are met consistently and reliably, and that they are periodically
> reviewed. Quality enhancement can be conceived as a subsequent (and
> consequent) stage of each of these dimensions. For example, quality
> enhancement should follow from quality control by correcting errors or
> plugging gaps in the achievement of objectives. . . . At levels beyond this,
> quality enhancement becomes quality transformation.
>
> (Middlehurst, 1997a: 48–49)

Both quality assurance (that is, accountability) and quality enhancement depend on an appreciation of the context and meaning of quality for an individual, group or unit, and should be built upon a specification of educational purposes, aims and objectives as well as standards to guide judgements. But the two are hardly similar: 'Quality assurance is concerned with establishing that objectives are being achieved consistently and reliably, whilst quality enhancement is concerned with improving on or changing the original objectives, aims or purposes' (Middlehurst, 1997a: 48). While quality control and quality assurance may be necessary or unavoidable to provide reassurance to third-party stakeholders, quality is most likely to be promoted if it becomes a way of life in the organization. This reflects the approach of total quality management.[3]

It is sometimes argued that quality assurance will in itself lead to quality enhancement. Middlehurst demolishes this argument with characteristic elegance:

1. The first flaw is that there is a necessary relationship between accountability and improvement; this is not the case, since they may each serve a range of different purposes and interests, some of which are likely to be in conflict with each other. . . .

2. A second flaw is that the motivations which drive individuals and institutions to be 'accountable' in response to the interests of external stakeholders are the same motivations as those which drive improvements in practice. [But] The motivations involved are not the same. Accountability as currently practised relies largely on extrinsic motivation [while] effective and sustained improvement tends to rely on intrinsic motivation, often linked to notions of professionalism . . . improvement relies on individuals and groups engaging with the desired objectives and a commitment to their achievement. Unless the improvement is driven by a large measure of intrinsic motivation, the best that can be hoped for is compliance with external requirements. . . .

3. A third issue involves the concept of quality enhancement that is linked with accountability. In many cases, quality enhancement is only associated with the outcomes of quality control, assurance or external evaluation. This may mean that there is a greater concentration on incremental and largely reactive improvements in practice rather than on more radical reassessment and redirecting of practice. At a time when higher education needs to be looking outwards in order to act on the basis of external intelligence, and when scarce resources, technological developments and market pressures require urgent and often radical reactions from institutions and academic units, incrementalism is an insufficient and possibly dangerous response.

4. [In short] over-concentration on 'rendering an account' to external audiences can take time and resources away from delivering high-quality educational research, or finding out the real needs of students and sponsors and developing new approaches to satisfying their requirements in cost-effective ways.

(Middlehurst, 1997a: 51–54)

In another important article, with George Gordon, Middlehurst (1995) draws on the general literature on quality improvement, as well as well tested models such as Investors in People and the European Quality Award, to focus more closely on the role and importance of effective leadership and professional development in establishing the conditions for general quality improvement.

> Leadership is important in relation to quality because it offers a vision and idea of what is possible, a strategy for moving in this direction and a means of achieving individual and collective commitment to the goals of continuous improvement which underpin quality . . . leadership is needed to interpret, to help share, to motivate and to enlist the support of individuals and groups in relation to the changes required. It is also needed to define and preserve those aspects of higher education tradition which are essential.
>
> (Gordon and Middlehurst, 1995: 276;
> cf Middlehurst, 1997b and Gordon, 2002)[4]

The regulation of teaching and learning

This brief review of the literature suggests four 'dimensions' for analysing the nature of any regulatory regime for teaching and learning:

- the balance between internal and external regulation;
- the mode(s) of regulation;
- the purpose of the regulation;
- the nature and extent of the activities being regulated.

The balance between internal and external regulation

The issue here is how far institutions are free to regulate themselves, and how far they are subject to external regulation, that is, regulation by an agency external to and independent of the institution. A secondary issue is how 'free' the institution being regulated is to ignore the regulatory outcomes (Hughes, Mears and Winch, 1997). The polytechnics and other 'public sector' HE providers were initially subject to quite close regulation by the Council for National Academic Awards. Although over time this regulation became more general – moving away from the close scrutiny of courses to the periodic review of institutions – CNAA continued to exercise ultimate control over the institutions' academic provision. (HMI also continued to inspect them.) Nevertheless those institutions that had attained accredited status were in very large measure self-regulating, while those which were Associates also had a quite significant measure of autonomy. However, other than in certain professional areas (including Initial Teacher

Training), the teaching and learning activities of the pre-1992 universities were effectively free of any external regulation until the establishment of the Academic Audit Unit in 1990 and the 1992 Further and Higher Education Act (see Chapter 2).

The mode(s) of regulation

The issue here is whether external regulation is carried out by the academic community collectively, by the government or an agency under its control, or by both together (Jackson's 'collaborative regulation') (Jackson, 1997a).

The purpose of the external regulation

The issue here is whether the external regulation is aimed primarily at improving institutional effectiveness in teaching and learning, or at improving the efficiency of the resources used for teaching and learning. A key indicator here is the presence or absence of graded outcomes from the regulatory intervention; a secondary one is whether the regulators' reports are published. In its original form audit was purely developmental, with not even a threshold judgement, and the reports themselves were not published. Assessment always involved graded judgements, either overall or in relation to individual aspects of provision, and the results were always published (though initially there was also a longer and more detailed report that was confidential to the institution).

Nature and extent of the activities being regulated

The issue here is whether the regulatory process focuses on:

- academic standards: the level and quality of the student achievement denoted by the award; and/or
- academic quality: the quality of the teaching, the process by which students are brought to a particular level of achievement; and/or
- academic quality assurance: the means by which standards and quality are monitored and protected; and/or
- academic information: information about the standards, quality and quality assurance of the provision concerned.

Like the CNAA in its latter days, audit focused on institutions' quality assurance arrangements. Assessment looked at the quality of teaching and learning and the 'student experience'. From the mid-1990s there were moves to see that an integrated process of quality assurance also addressed institutions' academic standards.

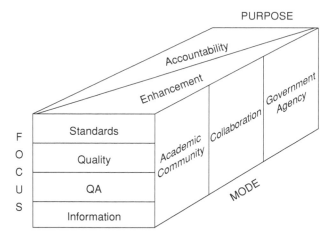

Figure 1.2 Overall model of regulation.

Overall model

From these various dimensions can be derived various regulatory regimes (see Figure 1.2).

The quality of regulation

Finally, whilst there is a considerable literature on regulation in general and a smaller one on the regulation of higher education, there is not nearly as big a literature on the quality of regulation, although Kells and others have talked about the need for 'meta-evaluation', an overall evaluation to establish whether the regulatory regime is achieving its purposes and whether, if it is not, corrective action is called for. The question here is how to ensure that the regime produces valid, reliable, consistent and transparent outcomes (judgements and reports) as economically as possible. This is by no means straightforward. To quote the present author:

> Issues here include the comprehensiveness, clarity and consistency of the guidelines and codes on which judgements and decisions are to be based; the selection, recruitment, training and development of those making the judgements and decisions; the management of the various evaluation processes and the calibration and moderation of outcomes; the provision of appeals and corrective actions where necessary; and the quantity and quality of the management time and attention devoted to them.
>
> (Brown, 2000c: 340; cf Brown, 1999c)

These questions are important because, as we shall see, inadequate quality control played an important part in undermining assessment. It is time to begin our story.

Notes

1 It is a pity therefore that the rumoured explanation for the running aground in July 2002 of the British destroyer HMS Nottingham off the Australian coast – that at the time the captain was in his cabin filling out his risk register – turns out to be apocryphal.
2 In a more recent study, Henkel (2000a) looks at the notion of academic identity. She argues that the higher education reforms and consequent changes in the academic community have created an impetus towards a more structured environment, encouraging new, 'professional' academic identities. She also asks whether the reforms have not made the institution more important than the disciplines.
3 It is not one of the purposes of this book to espouse any particular theory of quality. For a good recent review of the application of various quality theories to the public services see Gaster and Squire, 2003. Birnbaum's 2000 article 'The life cycle of academic management fads' is also worth a read.
4 The importance of leadership in the public sector has recently been emphasized in a research study by the Performance and Innovation Unit of the Cabinet Office (Cabinet Office, 2000).

2 Establishing the framework

> The prime responsibility for maintaining and enhancing the quality of teaching and learning rests with each individual institution. At the same time, there is a need for proper accountability for the substantial public funds invested in higher education. As part of this, students and employers need improved information about quality if the full benefit of increased competition is to be obtained.
>
> (White Paper, *Higher Education: A new framework*) (DES, 1991: 24)

Introduction

This chapter describes the quality assurance arrangements to which UK higher education institutions were subject prior to 1992; the Government's proposals for changing these (in the 1991 White Paper) and how these were modified through interaction with the representative bodies; the differences of view about quality assurance between the representative bodies; and the relationships between the HEQC, CVCP and the funding councils' assessment units.

The pre-1992 arrangements

Although there were some common elements before 1992, the two sectors of higher education were subject to very different quality regimes. (For a more detailed account of the immediate historical background to the 1992 changes see Perellon, 2001.)

The universities

With the important exception of certain professional areas (see below), the existing universities were not before 1992 subject to any external quality regime. The absence of such regulation of the universities' core activity was indeed remarked upon regularly by successive Ministers and Secretaries of State. It was in response to these concerns that CVCP in 1983 established an Academic Standards Group under Professor Philip Reynolds, Vice-Chancellor of Lancaster University.

The Committee's report, which appeared in 1986, covered a wide range of topics and included three formal codes of practice (on external examiners, postgraduate training and research, and research degree examination appeals), as well as two papers on the maintenance and monitoring of standards, which offered universities 'points of reference' for self-comparison (CVCP, 1986).

The Committee completed its work in 1986. In 1988 CVCP inquired into the extent to which universities had implemented the recommendations in the earlier report. Although most universities had adopted most of the recommendations, doubts remained. In particular, the Department continued to be sceptical. As a result the group was re-established in the autumn of 1988 with as Chair Professor Stewart (now Lord) Sutherland, Principal of King's College London (later Vice-Chancellor of the University of London and of the University of Edinburgh). This produced a further report in 1989 on the implementation of the codes of practice. In the same year, and after some internal debate, CVCP decided, on the group's recommendation, to go a step further and establish an Academic Audit Unit to scrutinize institutions' quality control systems. The unit commenced operations the following year.

The public sector

By contrast to this somewhat laissez-faire regime, the polytechnics and colleges were subject from their inception to dual external oversight by, first, the Council for National Academic Awards (CNAA) (and for their vocational awards the Business and Technical Education Council – BTEC, now EdExcel), and second, inspection by HMI.

CNAA has been described as 'a national network for quality assurance' (Silver, 1990). It was established in 1964 as a guardian of academic standards in the non-university sector. Its basic purposes were to award degrees and to safeguard the quality of degree courses in polytechnics and colleges. While over time it moved away from the close scrutiny of individual courses to the periodic review of institutions, delegating responsibility for course validation and approval to those judged to have the requisite degree of maturity as 'accredited' institutions (Harris, 1990), as an awarding body it retained ultimate control over the institutions' academic provision. However CNAA was not just a regulatory body. The Council also saw the academic development of the sector as a key part of its remit. It explored and in effect legitimized a series of developments which together transformed higher education: new subjects like business studies, new means of delivering programmes such as modularization, and new ways of recognising learning such as credit accumulation and transfer. In addition the Council's network of subject committees and boards provided an invaluable means of staff and professional development and communication.

HMI carried out in relation to the polytechnics and colleges broadly the same functions as it discharged in relation to the schools: a combination of formal inspection at institution or subject level, and informal consultation and advice. While resources were stretched by the huge expansion and differentiation of the system, HMI continued to make important interventions in individual institutions. From 1989, and following discussions between Dr Stubbs and Dr Terry Melia, Senior Chief Inspector, HMI judgements became the basis for certain funding decisions by the PCFC, in particular helping to determine how many additional funded places were allocated to individual institutions. It was this dual system of accreditation and inspection that was now in effect to be extended to the universities.

Professional training

All institutions, whatever their status, that want their programmes to be recognized by a professional or statutory body, as conferring exceptions or advanced standing in relation to their qualifications, must have those programmes accredited by that body or by someone acting on its behalf. This has always presented considerable challenges to institutions because fitness for professional practice may not mean the same as fitness for academic award. Indeed CNAA did a considerable amount of work in this area to try to align its regulations and practices with those of the professional bodies. Finally, all institutions offering courses of Initial Teacher Training, whether at undergraduate (BEd) or post-graduate (PGCE) level, had to have these formally inspected, and approved, by HMI (although in the existing universities the convention was that HMI was invited in by the institution concerned). This continued in an intensified form under OFSTED from 1996.

Higher education: a new framework

The White Paper published on 6 May 1991 began by reviewing the progress that had been made by the higher education system in becoming larger, more efficient and more responsive to the needs of business and commerce without any reduction in quality. This expansion should continue so that, by 2000, 'approaching one in three of all 18–19 year olds will enter higher education' (DES, 1991: 10). The 'real key' to achieving such expansion in a 'cost-effective' way lay in greater competition for funds and students, and this could best be achieved by 'breaking down the increasingly artificial and unhelpful barriers between the universities, and the polytechnics and colleges' (DES, 1991: 12).

This meant creating a single funding structure for all institutions of higher education; establishing new higher education funding councils in England, Scotland and Wales (and eventually Northern Ireland) to distribute those funds; extending degree awarding powers to major institutions

and winding up the CNAA; offering the title of university to those polytechnics that wished to adopt it, and subject to the development of suitable
criteria, other major institutions; and creating a common quality assurance
regime for teaching.

The new quality assurance arrangements

The White Paper defined the various aspects of quality assurance in higher
education as follows:

- Quality control: mechanisms within institutions for maintaining
  and enhancing the quality of their provision.
- Quality audit: external scrutiny aimed at providing guarantees that
  institutions have suitable quality control mechanisms in place.
- Validation: approval of courses by a validating body for the award of
  its degrees and other qualifications.
- Accreditation: in the specific context of the CNAA, delegation
  to institutions, subject to certain conditions, of responsibility for
  validating their own courses leading to CNAA degrees.
- Quality assessment: external review of, and judgements about, the
  quality of teaching and learning in institutions.

(DES, 1991: 24)

The White Paper stated:

> There is a common view throughout higher education on the need for
> externally provided reassurance that the quality control mechanisms
> within institutions are adequate. Quality audit is a means of checking
> that relevant systems and structures within an institution support its
> key teaching mission. This audit role is currently played by the CNAA
> in relation to most polytechnics and colleges, and is currently being
> developed in the university sector by the recently established Academic
> Audit Unit.
>
> The Government accepts the views put to it by some representatives
> of universities and polytechnics that, in a unitary system, this quality
> audit role should become the task of a single unit in which the insti-
> tutions have the major stake. It believes that any doubts about the
> effectiveness of self-regulation are more than offset by the self-interest
> which institutions will have in demonstrating that internal quality
> controls continue to be rigorous. The unit's remit would desirably cover
> arrangements in all higher education institutions throughout the United
> Kingdom.
>
> The Government intends to include reserve powers in the legislation
> to ensure the satisfactory establishment of the unit.

(DES, 1991: 26–27)

Quality assessment

To complement quality audit, however, 'arrangements are needed to assess the quality of what is actually provided *and these assessments should continue to inform the funding decisions of the Funding Councils*' (DES, 1991: 28–29) (author's emphasis). There were two ways in which such assessments could be developed: through quantifiable outcomes (performance indicators and calculations of added value) and through external judgements on the basis of direct observation of what was provided, including the quality of teaching and learning, management and organization, and accommodation and equipment. While quantitative measures were valuable, they could not in themselves provide a comprehensive view. A Quality Assessment Unit would therefore be established within each funding council with full-time professional staff recruited from HMI and elsewhere. Its precise role would be for the funding councils to determine, in consultation with institutions and subject to guidance from the Secretary of State. The units would be required to establish 'steering committees' comprised mainly of institutional representatives, to advise them on operations (DES, 1991: 29).

As well as maintaining 'constructive relationships' with the institutions, the units would be expected to 'consider how best to make available to potential students and employers information about the actual relative quality of institutions and of the courses they provide' (ibid: 30). Finally, the units would be expected to monitor and encourage developments in higher education, for example the development of performance indicators, access policies and responses to changing student profiles, links with industry and commerce, and the industrial and commercial relevance of provision (ibid: 30).

The 1991 white paper: analysis

Bearing in mind the literature review in the last chapter, there are a number of comments that can be offered.

First, the starting point for the new arrangements – establishing a uniform quality regime for the whole sector for the first time – was not concern about quality. The issue was more about how quality was to be protected as the expansion continued, competition intensified, and institutions came under increasing pressure to use their resources more efficiently. At the same time comparative information about quality would help that competition by directing students towards the 'best' universities (as the RAE had directed funds to the best research departments). There was also the point that, having been given the job of funding the institutions, the Funding Council had to have some way of judging value for money. It was this that provided the basic rationale for assessment.[1]

Second, the basic premise of the new arrangements – to improve efficiency by enhancing competition – was itself highly questionable. Was an adequately funded expansion so unthinkable? How, on the other hand, could quality be protected if the unit of funding were to fall, as fall it must since otherwise the phrase 'efficiency gains' had no meaning. (In the event the unit of resource will have fallen by about a third in real terms over the period 1989 to 2004.) Even accepting the need to reduce funding per student, was greater institutional competition, compared for example with a greater degree of planning, the best means of securing efficiency gains and protecting quality? Last, even if greater competition was desirable, bearing in mind David Dill's wise words (see Chapter 1), was comparative information about institutions and courses necessary, helpful, sensible or even meaningful?

Third, the quality arrangements pointed in different directions, reflecting quite different views as to what quality assurance should be about. To quote the present author:

> Underlying audit is the view that the fundamental purpose of external quality assurance is to reassure the institution and those associated with it that its quality assurance policies and procedures are working as intended. Audit works on the assumption that quality improvement is most likely to be achieved through the 'internal' professional motivation to do better rather than by 'extrinsic' motivators such as money or prestige. Hence the information in audit reports is aimed mainly at those in the institution concerned.
>
> Underlying assessment, however, is the view that the fundamental purpose of external quality assurance is to reassure external stakeholders – primarily but not only the Funding Councils – about value for money. This is done by providing information about the effectiveness with which 'subject providers' within institutions are achieving their object-ives. Assessment works on the assumption that quality improvement is most likely to be achieved through the motivation to compete to win additional students or resources.
>
> Both processes are conducted by peer review and lead to published reports. But while audit reports contain what is at most a threshold judgement, and have no financial consequences for the institution con-cerned, assessment reports contain a ranking or grading, or a series of gradings, and do have financial consequences for the institution. TQA is thus an example of what Chris Pollitt has christened 'Efficiency from Above' (Pollitt, 1987).
>
> (Brown, 1997a: 5–6)

These conflicting perspectives were the main source of the continuing prob-lems with the subsequent arrangements.

Finally, as well as being remarkably imprecise as regards the benefits, the White Paper set an unwelcome precedent by nowhere stating the costs or the resourcing implications of the new regime, either for the Government or for the institutions. As we shall see, this was not the least of the problems that arose with the new arrangements.

The 1991 white paper: reactions

Overall the CDP was naturally delighted with the general thrust of the White Paper, the main concern being the absence of a timescale for implementation. (In the event the legislation was included in the Queen's Speech at the start of the 1991/2 Parliamentary session, and enacted just before Parliament was dissolved following the announcement of the 1992 General Election.) However CDP had mixed feelings about the proposed quality arrangements. Eventually it was decided that every effort should be made to restrict the scope of assessment while the role of the institutionally owned audit unit was expanded; CVCP and SCOP agreed.

As regards assessment, the author recalls very vividly a debate in CDP between Professor (now Sir) David Watson, recently appointed Director of Brighton Polytechnic (now the University of Brighton) and shortly to become Chair of HEFCE Teaching Quality Assessment Committee, and his erstwhile boss Dr (now Sir) Clive Booth, then Director of Oxford Polytechnic (later Oxford Brookes University). David sought to persuade the committee that the polytechnics should seize the opportunities provided by the new methodology to demonstrate their superiority at teaching, just as the RAE would inevitably confirm, at least for a long while to come, the existing universities' superiority at research. Clive argued that, in spite of the rhetoric, the established institutions' superior resourcing, and the favourable penumbra associated with research, would always win out. We shall see in Chapter 4 how that particular argument came out.

At any rate, CDP tried to water assessment down. But it was hampered by two things. First, it proved difficult to get CVCP energized, possibly because the Committee was more concerned with the provisions in the draft legislation that might have enabled the Secretary of State to intervene in the affairs of an individual institution, provisions which were successfully modified through CVCP efforts. Second, CDP's overriding concern was to get the legislation agreed, since an election was clearly imminent and a successor government, even one formed by the same party, might have very different Parliamentary priorities. CDP did however succeed in getting one amendment accepted, to ensure that the HEFCE's Quality Assessment Committee had a majority of institutional members.

As regards audit, CDP's view, led by John Stoddart, was that if it could not take over CNAA, the sector should grasp the opportunity to set up an institutionally owned body which would protect standards across the newly unified sector. However, institutional audit was insufficient: there needed also to be a research/dissemination of best practice function along the lines discharged by the CNAA's Quality Support Group, whose role had recently been evaluated and confirmed by the Committee for Information and Development Services (of which John was Chair).

As a result of further discussions with CNAA officers, CDP also came to accept that it would be valuable to continue the Council's work in promoting credit accumulation and transfer and, in conjunction with CVCP, in accrediting recognized providers of Access Courses. These ideas were discussed not only with CNAA but also with the Department. A working party was established of institutional heads from both sectors, to hammer out proposals. The resulting document, sent to the Department in October 1991 by the chairs of the three bodies, could be said to be the sector's 'quality manifesto'.

The letter stated firmly that the institutions collectively had a responsibility to ensure adequate systems of quality assurance across the entire sector. Quality assurance embraced both the monitoring of institutional quality systems and, 'equally important', quality support and enhancement (for which reason a broader title for the organization than 'audit unit' was preferred). Moreover the growing need in higher education for accessibility and flexibility of provision meant that the new organization should also embrace the central running and further development of credit accumulation and transfer schemes and the recognition and development of Access Courses. Above all, 'A strong QA organisation will provide both necessary public assurance of institutional quality and act as an additional input to a pluralistic assessment of quality in higher education.' (CVCP/CDP/SCOP, 1991, para 5.vi)

The letter flagged up very clearly the risk of duplication between the new organization and the funding councils' assessment units. While recognizing that the funding councils needed access to sources of quality assessment (sic), the institutions had 'major reservations' about the functions of assessment and funding being in the same hands: advice on quality should be given independently of the funding operation. How that might be achieved should be discussed. The Assessment Unit could for example be advised on the discharge of its assessment functions by a steering committee, of which institutional representatives nominated by CDP/CVCP/SCOP should form the majority. One function of such a committee would be to comment on and approve the annual work programme. The units could be staffed primarily by secondments or by temporary appointment of subject experts, rather than through a permanent staff.

It followed that the functions of the unit should be to:

  — advise the Funding Council on available sources of information relevant to quality within particular subject areas;
  — *provide responses to specifically focussed questions in particular subject fields by the Funding Councils*; [present author's emphasis]
  — visit institutions to observe practice;

- present its advice in such a way as to leave the Funding Councils to make any judgement which might affect institutional funding;
- avoid replicating the activity, including collection and publication of data another relevant information, of other agencies including the QA organization;
- publish an annual report.

(CVCP/CDP/SCOP, 1991, para 6)

The Department accepted, and indeed welcomed, the representative bodies' initiative in establishing HEQC, and soon the giving of advice to the Department about applications for degree-awarding powers was added to its functions.

While these decisions were being made, the Further and Higher Education Bill was being taken through Parliament (HM Government, 1992). In general the relevant provisions were those prefigured in the White Paper. Section 70 provides that each funding council shall:

(a) secure that provision is made for assessing the quality of education provided in institutions for whose activities they provide, or are considering providing, financial support . . . and

(b) establish a committee, to be known as the 'Quality Assessment Committee', with the function of giving them advice on the discharge of their duty under paragraph (a) above and such other functions as may be conferred on the committee by the council.

In addition section 82 provided that:

(2) Any two or more councils shall, if directed to do so by the Secretary of State, jointly make provision for the assessment by a person appointed by them of matters relating to the arrangements made by each institution in Great Britain which is within the higher education sector for maintaining academic standards in the institution.

In his letter of 13 March 1992 confirming the Government's acceptance of the representative bodies' proposals for the new QA organization, the Minister for Higher Education, Alan Howarth MP, confirmed that the Government did not intend to take up the reserve powers. This was to be the high water mark of self-regulation. Little was it realized that it would be so short or that it would be undermined from within the sector.[2]

Constitution, organization and resourcing of HEQC

As the result of the discussions between the representative bodies and the Department it was agreed that HEQC should be constituted as a company limited by guarantee, the owners being the representative bodies. The Board of Directors should comprise equal numbers of university and polytechnic heads plus two college representatives. There were also to be two – later increased to four – independent (that is, employer) members. The new Council would initially have three arms, concerned respectively with audit, enhancement, and credits and access, together with a small secretariat. The Council would be funded by institutional subscriptions, but the monies for this would be earmarked in the institutions' initial funding allocation by the new Funding Council. Resource cover for these in turn would be found by reserving a proportion of the funds allocated each year for CNAA in the monies received by higher education from the Department. Initially this figure was £2.5 million but was soon increased to £3.2 million. Also as part of these discussions, and to underline the Council's semi-statutory nature, it was agreed that it would be a condition of receiving public funding, reflected in the Funding Council's Financial Memorandum with the institutions, that universities and colleges should subscribe to HEQC. HEQC was incorporated on 12 May 1992.

A good deal of discussion took place about the position of chair. Eventually agreement was reached by the representative bodies that since the enhanced organization was CDP's idea it was appropriate for it to be chaired by John Stoddart. This arrangement was never subsequently questioned, although 'old' vice-chancellor attendance at the Board was generally less good than 'new' vice-chancellor attendance. For quite a long time after 1992, HEQC was the only sector agency, the Board of which was chaired by a post-1992 Vice-Chancellor.

Discussions also took place between the representative bodies about finding a chief executive. Agreement proved difficult. Eventually John Stoddart, concerned about possible loss of momentum, suggested to CVCP that the new Council should appoint the CNAA Chief Executive, Dr Malcolm Frazer, and this was agreed on the basis that he would do the job alongside his CNAA role, until his planned retirement. In the author's view Dr Frazer did the sector a very considerable favour by agreeing to this arrangement, although it was a great pity that the CNAA records did not come to the HEQC.

Dr Frazer in turn appointed the heads of the three functions: Peter Williams (previously Head of the Academic Audit Unit and now Chief Executive of QAA), Professor Mantz Yorke (Liverpool John Moores University) and Harry Mitchell (formerly the CNAA Officer for Scotland). The Company Secretary, Graham Middleton, was already Secretary of CNAA.[3]

In January 1993 Dr Frazer announced his intention to retire later in the year, and the post was advertised. The present author was appointed following a public selection process, and took up his post in July. Just over two months later the CVCP Residential Conference decided to enter into discussions with other parties to reduce the external quality burden by creating a single quality system which would combine the functions of audit and assessment. Almost from the start, HEQC was living on borrowed time.

CDP and CVCP views of quality assurance

Before leaving this initial phase it may just be worth commenting on the differences of perspective between CDP and CVCP about the character and role of the HEQC.

As already mentioned, John Stoddart's initial view was that rather than abolish CNAA, the institutions should take it over. The sector should thus take collective responsibility for its own quality and standards in a very clear and public way. By contrast, CVCP had taken some while to create a sector-wide agency – the Academic Audit Unit – and even this was contested.[4]

Lying behind this were quite different views of what was meant by the 'sector' and what was meant by 'quality assurance'. The polytechnic directors, although ambitious for their institutions and highly individualistic, nevertheless accepted that there were certain purposes for which they needed to act collectively. CNAA, HMI, PCFC and CDP itself had played key roles in the development of their institutions, and this was appreciated, if not always celebrated. By contrast, the older universities were (and still are) much less ready to act in a corporate fashion or to respond positively to the need for collective agencies, particularly if it meant some curtailment in their own freedom of institutional action.

There were also differences of view about quality assurance. For the existing universities quality was inherent in the qualifications of the students enrolled, the qualifications of the staff recruited and trained through the PhD, and in the central role of research; there was little need for formal procedures. For the polytechnics, by contrast, formal structures were needed precisely because the students and staff were not as well qualified (and this provided protection for the students and for the degree), as well as to respond to external regulation. Even when they came to accept external regulation (through the AAU and HEQC), the vice-chancellors were also, for a long time, reluctant to accept that anything other than the audit of institutional arrangements was needed if standards were to be maintained. They certainly did not see the need for an enhancement function. For quite a long while after HEQC's establishment, there were arguments each year as to whether the subscription should not cover just the audit function, with the Council's other work being supported only by those institutions that wanted it.[5]

Finally, there was a basic ambivalence about CVCP's attitude to the HEQC. At times CVCP was happy for HEQC to act as its quality assurance 'arm'. At other times, and particularly as the debate about a single system hotted up, there was not a basis of confidence between the two bodies. Quite late in HEQC's existence, for example, there remained concerns about CVCP's ability to 'control' HEQC and the other agencies such as the Universities and Colleges Admission Service (UCAS) (also run by an ex-public sector CEO), concerns which are also reported in Dr Perellon's study (2001). In view of their later problems with QAA (see Chapter 6), this can only be seen as ironic.

While there was certainly more that HEQC should have done to engage with vice-chancellors, the author believes that CVCP collectively never really understood the purpose or functions of HEQC. It is not even certain that many vice-chancellors understood, or believed in, collective self-regulation, a point to which we will return (see Chapter 7). It perhaps did not help that the Chair and Chief Executive of the HEQC were the former Chair and Chief Executive of CDP, whereas the chairs of the CVCP and chief executives of HEFCE tended to come from the old universities.[6]

The establishment of assessment

Discussions also took place between the Department and the funding councils about the establishment of the assessment units. The Department had initially planned to move some 30 to 50 HMI into the assessment units, to constitute the assessment staff. This was opposed most vigorously by the Chair-designate of the new single Funding Council (Sir Ron, now Lord, Dearing) and the Chief Executive (Professor, now Sir, Graeme Davies), who both feared an adverse reaction from the universities. In the event only a handful of HMI were transferred, though the HMI influence remained in the subject-based assessment model adopted.

One of the first acts of the new Funding Council was to establish its Assessment Committee under the chair of Professor Watson. The committee's first meeting was on 24 September 1992. For a while official leadership was offered by Professor Alan Hibbert (formerly Deputy Chief Executive of CNAA and Director of Programmes at PCFC, later a colleague at Southampton Institute) and Alun Thomas (now Assistant Principal at Bath Spa University College). When they left the Council, Dr Paul Clark (Dean of Science at the Open University) was appointed Director of Assessment, a post he filled until 1996.

Relationship between HEQC and the HEFCE Assessment Unit

The Council's manifesto document had, as already noted, warned the Government of the risk of duplication between the two processes. Partly to anticipate this, it was agreed that an HEQC representative should attend meetings of the funding councils' assessment committees and that a Funding Council representative should attend HEQC's Audit Advisory Committee. In addition the author chaired regular liaison meetings with the three funding councils which also involved senior colleagues from the HEQC. Robin Middlehurst explored with Dr Paul Clark the scope for assessment outcomes feeding into HEQC's enhancement work. John Stoddart and I had regular informal meetings with Professor Watson and Dr Clark. All of this was reflected in a publication by the two councils in January 1994 (HEFCE/ HEQC, 1994).

The *Joint Statement* summarized the main features of audit and assessment, described these reciprocal arrangements, and outlined the collaboration which was taking place in a number of areas, notably our agreement that simultaneous visits would be avoided wherever possible, and that audit visits would not normally trail in a subject area currently or recently assessed.

Very little came of this joint effort, for two main reasons. First, because for much of this time, particularly in England, those responsible were struggling to make assessment work. As we shall see in Chapter 4, the initial method – involving judgements of 'excellence', 'satisfactory' or 'unsatisfactory' on the basis of institutional quality claims – was soon changed, after independent evaluation and much criticism, to a universal visit method with numerical grades (from 1996). These changes preoccupied an already hard pressed staff so that they had little time or energy for cooperation either with HEQC, or with others with cognate responsibilities, such as the professional and statutory bodies or the NHS (where, as we shall see, HEQC took the lead in developing cooperation protocols which were subsequently ratified by HEFCE).

An illustration of the pressures which HEFCE was under came when HEQC and HEFCE exchanged information in early 1997, and the question arose as to whether staff in either organization actually read each other's reports. When one of my colleagues mentioned that he read every published

Figure 2.1 Watchdogs at war: with vice-chancellors pressing the Education Secretary to decide on a single agency to monitor quality, the quality council bared its teeth while the funding council softened its act.
Source: *Times Higher Education Supplement*, 23 September 1994
Cartoonist: David Parkins. Used with permission.

quality assessment report, and indeed circulated details for colleagues preparing audits, his opposite number was amazed, saying that they had no time to read their own reports, never mind anyone else's!

Perhaps once these transitional issues had been resolved, as they largely were in England by 1997, and in Scotland and Wales somewhat earlier, cooperation might have developed, particularly as relations at the personal level remained generally good. But by this time the second factor intervened: the single system genie was loose, and neither party could afford to get too close to the other, or give any public credence to the other's method. The position was well summed up by a cartoon published on the front page of the *Times Higher Education Supplement* soon after the Department's willingness to see the system reviewed was announced.

The cartoon (Fig. 2.1 on p 47) showed the Secretary of State, Mrs Shephard, with a rosette in her hand. HEQC was depicted as a poodle baring its teeth to look fierce, HEFCE was shown as a bulldog attempting to smile.

HEQC nevertheless got down to work. Chapter 3 describes this in greater detail.

Notes

1 There was also an argument that the continuation of RAE meant that some assessment regime for teaching was necessary if teaching and learning were to receive the attention they deserved within institutions.
2 In effect, the establishment of the QAA amounted to the invocation of the reserve power.
3 Mantz Yorke was succeeded by Robin Middlehurst in April 1994. Harry Mitchell left the council in December 1993 and was not replaced.
4 According to Lord Sutherland, there were three views. While the majority favoured the establishment of the Audit Unit, some favoured the equivalent of HMI for the universities, and others argued for the imposition on the then university sector of the equivalent of CNAA procedures. The last fell on the fact that the universities had already had their own degree-awarding powers. The lobby for HMI was used to support the case for the unit (personal communication to the author, May 2003).
5 The irony of course is that this means collective arrangements, via the Funding Council, over which the institutional heads have far less control. The White Paper *The Future of Higher Education* (DfES, 2003a) described in Chapter 7 lays no fewer than 56 implementation tasks on HEFCE, leaving virtually none to the representative bodies.
6 The HEFCE chief executive has always been an old university vice-chancellor. The current President of Universities UK, Professor Roderick Floud (London Guildhall University, now London Metropolitan University), is the first CVCP/ Universities UK chair or president from a new university.

3   HEQC 1992–97

> The work done in the 1990s by the Higher Education Quality Council
> (HEQC) which had both quality audit and quality enhancement as distinct
> functions and which was in some senses ahead of its time in its approach.
> (HEFCE/UUK/SCOP, 2003: 4)

Introduction

This chapter describes the work of HEQC. An overview summarizes how the
organization and its agenda evolved in the light of emerging priorities as
they appeared to the Council and its chief stakeholders. The main part of the
chapter then deals in some detail with the work of the Council's two main
arms: audit and enhancement. A final section deals much more briefly with
the Council's other work: the handling of applications for degree-awarding
powers and university title, Access Course recognition, credit-based learning, the Council's international work, and its role in Scotland and Wales

Overview

My first objective on taking up the post of Chief Executive in July 1993
was to raise the Council's public profile. Having as CDP Chief Executive
been instrumental, with John Stoddart, in creating a more widely ranging and potentially powerful organization, I was concerned about the
momentum that had been lost even before I learnt on the grapevine of the
new CVCP Chair's ideas about a single system. I therefore looked around for
issues with which the Council could identify itself. These were not long in
appearing.

   In January 1994 the Secretary of State, John Patten MP, visited Singapore
and Malaysia. He was assailed on all sides with complaints about the lengths
to which British universities – some though by no means all 'new' – were
going to attract students. These complaints raised questions in his mind
about the abolition of the binary line. Were academic standards now being
compromised? Almost as soon as he was back, one of his senior officials

telephoned me to see whether, if the Secretary of State were to ventilate his concerns about standards, HEQC would be able to respond in any way on behalf of the sector.

We had already been put on notice about the external examiner system (see below). We had also – following a hint from John Stoddart – begun to have some discussions internally about how to give greater attention to how academic standards were defined and protected. I therefore confirmed that it would. At a major speech at the HEFCE annual conference at Keele University in April, Mr Patten therefore stressed the importance the Government placed upon 'broad comparability' of standards between institutions, and asked HEQC to give greater emphasis to this in its work.

This meant that the Council would give greater attention within audit to how institutions established and monitored the standards of their programmes and the associated awards. In addition, the Council's quality enhancement work would be reoriented so as to include a range of projects to explore how institutions actually went about formulating their academic standards. This was the beginning of what became known as the Graduate Standards Programme (GSP), the single most important and influential achievement in UK quality assurance in the entire period since 1992.

Audit

The origins and setting up of the Academic Audit Unit (AAU) were described in Chapter 2. In what follows the author has relied heavily on a paper by its former head, Peter Williams, now CEO of the QAA (CVCP, 1992). The audit process went through a number of stages between October 1990 (when the AAU came into being) and August 1997. The main ones were:

1. The initial AAU audits of 27 universities between February 1991 and June 1992, working to a methodology broadly laid down by the unit's Management Board.
2. The review and evaluation by HEQC which led to a number of mostly incremental changes.
3. The extension of the process to institutions' collaborative provision.
4. The extension of the process to institutions' overseas provision.
5. The refocusing on standards following Mr Patten's April 1994 speech.
6. The revision of the process ('continuation audit') after the completion of the first cycle in the summer of 1997.

The AAU phase

As described by Peter Williams, the bare bones of the initial AAU audit method were 'enquiries by groups of three unaccompanied peer auditors; the use of primary documentation; visits of three days; a focus on four main areas of scrutiny; and reports which would remain the property of each university' (Williams, 1996: 2). The other key point was that quality arrangements could only be seen in terms of institutions' own aims and objectives: there could be no absolute 'gold standard'. As we shall see, there has over the decade been a shift away from this towards a fitness of purpose approach.

The AAU itself operated under the following terms of reference:

1. To consider and review the universities' mechanisms for monitoring and promoting the academic standards which are necessary for achieving their stated aims and objectives;
2. To comment on the extent to which procedures in place in individual universities reflect best practice in maintaining quality and are applied in practice;
3. To identify and commend to universities good practice in regard to the maintenance of academic standards at national level;
4. To keep under review nationally the role of the external examiner system;
5. To report to the CVCP via the Management Board.

(CVCP, 1992: 5)

The underlying approach was to ask:

*   What are you doing?
*   Why are you doing it?
*   How are you doing it?
*   Why are you doing it that way?
*   Why is that the best way of doing it?
*   How do you know it works?
*   How do you improve it?

The Management Board proposed that auditors should make these enquiries in respect of four main areas of scrutiny:

*   the provision and design of courses and degree programmes;
*   teaching and communication methods;
*   academic staff, and
*   means of taking account of external examiners' reports, students' views on courses, and views of external bodies.

(CVCP, 1992: 8)

The AAU reports adopted a format of 'points for commendation' and 'points for further consideration'. As a matter of policy, no overall judgement was offered. The aim was to provide a non-adversarial commentary on what the auditors saw as the strengths and weaknesses of each institution's arrangements, as they were revealed in the four areas of scrutiny. It was consistent with this approach not only that the report became the property of the institution, but that the AAU did not assume a right of entry, although any failure to invite the unit could potentially have difficult public consequences for the institution concerned.

In January 1992 Peter Williams produced an annual report based on experience to date. The report is valuable both as an account of the unit's early work, which laid the foundations for audit's subsequent development under HEQC, and as an early indicator of a number of issues that were to recur throughout the period, and indeed do so today.

After a description of how the auditors had approached their task, Peter commented on the state of quality assurance. Overall, it appeared, the institutions audited were beginning to come to terms with the requirements of a more systematic approach. However, 'the intensity with which this is being done . . . cannot but be a reflection of the comparatively minor place which some of these questions have hitherto occupied on institutional agendas' (CVCP, 1992: 21). Inevitably universities differed greatly in how far down this particular road they had gone. While some had just begun to come to terms with the concepts and demands of quality management, others were in the course of refining already effective procedures, although even here these tended to be the least costly.

Turning to current practices, the report noted that while few universities did not have in place, or had not proposed for early implementation, detailed criteria for designing and approving new programmes of study and a regular rolling programme of course or departmental reviews, the art of identifying qualitative indicators was still in its infancy. Moreover, there was still too little innovation in teaching and learning:

> Where innovation has taken place, it is often at the initiative of individual members of staff; and it is with some disappointment that we report that too few members of the academic staff encountered by the audit teams seem to be devoting much time to curriculum development or innovative teaching methods or practices. There continues to be an overwhelming reliance on the chalk and talk approach, with technology as an adjunct. . . . More generally, the consequences of the expected expansion of students for the aims, objectives and structure of programmes of study have yet to be seriously addressed, even though the lead time for development and testing of the new methods and models is fast disappearing.
>
> (CVCP, 1992: 23)

We shall return to innovation in Chapter 7. Academic staff development and training also left a good deal to be desired:

> The common attitude encountered by the Unit in its discussions with academic staff has been that the training of lecturers to be effective

teachers is a matter essentially for the beginning of their careers, and that it has little relevance to longer-serving or part-time colleagues. . . . The increasing use, even reliance, on non-traditional sources of teaching, such as temporary lecturers, post-graduate students, technicians and ad hoc assistants also gives the Unit some cause for concern. . . . The comparatively modest impact of staff development and training so far is unlikely to be improved until there is a pervasive acknowledgement that the professionalism of university teaching staff involves an actively professional commitment to teaching as well as to research.

(CVCP, 1992: 24)

So also did the assessment of teaching:

It is abundantly clear . . . that the quality of teaching has not been generally or systematically assessed, that its status as a contributory factor in promotions is widely perceived to be subsidiary to that of research (not withstanding its formal equality of esteem in most promotions procedures), and that, in consequence, many academic staff do not feel much encouraged to pursue a career path which they believe can satisfy only a limited ambition.

(CVCP, 1992: 25)

External examiners apart, universities also had some way to go in evolving effective and economical systems of feedback. Whilst some progress had been made with student feedback, 'the use made of graduate and employer feedback seems to be altogether more rudimentary and is typically left to the initiative of departments or individuals' (CVCP, 1992: 26).

Finally, while the auditors had found that external examiners were for the most part discharging their responsibilities in a fully professional way and that departments and institutions were in most cases following up their comments and recommendations with due diligence:

The demands being made upon external examiners are increasing, the rewards they receive are small, and their ability to act effectively as the guardians of quality and standards for the university system as a whole is beginning to come under strain. . . . With the increased concern for quality and standards, the time may be approaching when a general inquiry into the working of the external examiner system will be desirable.

(CVCP, 1992: 26–27)

Almost as revealing and interesting as the Director's report is an appendix in which 'an auditor' offers a SWOT analysis of university quality assurance. As strengths, the auditor mentions the commitment and sense of professional pride that university teachers had in (in particular) their honours courses, and their routine acceptance of external examiners. The major weakness was that:

> it is relatively rare to find a UK university teacher who really sees the systematic incorporation of evaluation and structured feedback as an essential part of effective teaching. Such evaluation is not yet seen as a necessary routine part of teaching practice. Performance of students in traditional exams is often taken to be sufficient and indeed, the only valid evidence of the effectiveness of teaching. Training designed to improve teaching performance is seen as, at best, an optional extra – at worst as an insult.
>
> (CVCP, 1992: 30)

The main reason for this in the author's view was the dominance of specialist honours courses in single disciplines, and the institutional structures of the universities which reflected and entrenched this. Meanwhile one or two government initiatives, notably Enterprise in Higher Education[1] were helpful to teaching innovation:

> As yet, I do not think that the attempts of the UFC to install competitiveness into the education market has had any noticeable effect on quality assurance. There is not clear evidence that potential students, when they come to select their campuses, are in any real sense influenced by knowledge of teaching standards, and certainly not by knowledge of the effectiveness of quality control mechanisms. There is thus no very great incentive to teaching staff to devote prime time and effort to innovations of this kind: competition, inasmuch as it has a visible effect, leads to innovation in the content of courses on offer. All the bureaucracy involved in quality control is thus, by and large, seen as a waste of valuable time and hence deeply resented.
>
> (CVCP, 1992: 30–31)

Perhaps of most interest of all, to anyone concerned with raising the quality of university teaching or at least making it more uniform, is what the auditor saw as the principal problem:

> The greatest threat is undoubtedly the prospect of another UFC research selectivity exercise. The overriding urgency with which university departments seek to maximize their research outputs (and inputs) is currently the main obstacle to innovation in quality assurance and, indeed, to the systematic improvement of teaching. Not only is time short, but resources in general are painfully inadequate to support innovations in teaching. (Whether this is internal or external I refuse to say)!
>
> (CVCP, 1992: 31; cf Hannan and Silver, 2000
> and Southampton Institute, 2000)

The evaluation of audit

At its first meeting in July 1992, the HEQC Board decided that the council should publish audit reports. Otherwise audit should continue essentially unchanged pending a review after a year. The areas of scrutiny were however revised so as to be:

- programmes of study;
- teaching, learning and communication;
- academic staff;
- assessment and classification procedures;
- verification, feedback and enhancement;
- promotional material (this was at the request of the Department which had received a number of complaints about misleading prospectuses and other promotional material).

In July 1993 the Council commissioned Coopers and Lybrand to undertake a review. The overall aim was to see whether and how the audit method should be adapted to meet the needs of a larger and more diverse sector, educating students for a wider range of purposes. The consultants' conclusion, which was echoed in the consultation responses (the report together with the Council's initial response was circulated to all institutions for comment), was that audit had achieved a great deal, had had an important impact on individual institutions, had helped to raise the profile of quality assurance, and had begun to disseminate good practice. It was also, in general, being done well. But it had considerable further potential to fulfil its objectives, particularly in relation to public accountability, good practice, and serving audiences wider than higher education institutions.

A number of essentially incremental changes were made as a result of the evaluation. These covered such matters as the rationalization of documentation requirements, the form of reports, new arrangements for a follow-up after one year, quality control within what was now the Quality Assurance Group, and publicity for audit reports. However, the most important change to the audit method under HEQC was introduced not as a direct result of the evaluation but through some of the consultation responses from institutions. These were to the effect that the 'points for further consideration' listed at the end of reports should be given an order of priority. Accordingly it was decided (by Peter Williams in consultation with the Audit Steering Council) that in future (that is, in audits conducted from the latter part of 1994 onwards) such points should be grouped into three categories:

- those deemed by the Council to be 'necessary' for the maintenance of academic quality and standards;

- those considered to be 'advisable' for the better ordering of the institution's arrangements;
- those that were thought to be simply 'desirable' for the institution to consider.

Although this initially caused some problems of interpretation, through careful management this potentially radical change to create, in effect, a quality 'threshold' was introduced without controversy either among the auditors or among the institutions.

Learning from audit

Another of my concerns as HEQC Chief Executive was that neither the Council nor the institutions was getting the full benefit of the wealth of material – facts, comments and judgements – contained in the audit reports. Accordingly I asked the Council's Quality Enhancement Group to make an analysis of the reports written on the 69 universities audited between April 1991 and April 1994. The analysis covered not only the reports themselves but also the material on which they were based. This was a landmark publication, and demonstrated that HEQC was serious about providing material to support institutions' efforts at quality enhancement. The report, which came out in September 1994, was also an example of teamworking within HEQC: although the project was led by Claire Matterson from the Enhancement Group, those working with her included two colleagues from the Quality Assurance Group.

Overall the report charted the progress of many institutions since the late 1980s in establishing formal, institution-wide quality arrangements. Nevertheless some of the messages – about the internal evaluation of teaching and learning, the use of feedback, and staff deployment and development – were the same as in the AAU report.

The strongest criticisms concerned student assessment:

> Students often require more information on the assessment methods and criteria used to judge their performance. Students (both within and across universities) may not be receiving fair and equal treatment in terms of the marking scales used to assess performance, the criteria used, or the methods used to record achievement eg degree classification. The methods used to monitor the effectiveness of assessment practices are, mostly, rudimentary.
>
> (HEQC, 1994d: xxii)

These included very variable use of external examiners.

Finally, the report contained a summary of the findings of the Council's first 'validation audits'.

The validation audits

HEQC had had the benefit of a 'valedictory despatch' from the CNAA. This paper, which was considered at a Board meeting in the autumn of 1993, drew the Council's attention to a number of areas of potential concern. Prominent among these was the spread of various forms of off-campus provision: particularly, but not only, franchising (the process by which the awarding institution approves an external institution or body to offer all or part of a programme normally designed and already offered by the franchising institution). HMI had also raised the issue (*Higher Education in Further Education Colleges*, 228/91/NS). The Council therefore decided to undertake separate audits of universities offering their awards for programmes run in collaboration with partners.

The method to be used was very similar to that in use in the 'on campus' audits, the starting point being an exploration of the awarding institution's validation and other procedures. Auditors were expected to address:

- the awarding institution's arrangements for securing and testing (and subsequently for maintaining the currency of) information about the external institution, its financial and other resources, the qualifications and experience of its teaching staff, its processes for deciding and implementing academic policy, and the effectiveness and appropriateness of its quality control procedures;
- how academic standards and quality were controlled, maintained and where appropriate enhanced by the awarding institution; and
- how the quality of the students' experience in the external partner institution was defined, controlled, monitored and maintained.

In carrying out their enquiries the auditors might decide to meet staff and students from the partner institution or institutions, including on their own premises, not with the aim of probing their systems per se but to see how the links with the awarding institution were understood and operated. To assist them the auditors had the benefit of *Notes of Guidance for the Audit of Collaborative Provision* (HEQC, 1995e). There was also a separate document entitled *Some Questions and Answers for Participants in HEQC Collaborative Audit Visits* (HEQC, 1995f).

Learning from Collaborative Audit: An interim report, published in April 1995, set out the findings of the first 14 collaborative audits. The overall conclusion was that:

whilst there are examples of good practice, some universities have yet fully to come to terms with the quality assurance demands of their collaborative activity. This is seen most clearly in the whole area of monitoring and review but it also applies, to a lesser extent, at other stages as well. Unless institutions are able to bring at least the same degree of consistency and rigour to the quality assurance of their collaborative provision as they apply to the internal provision for which they are wholly responsible, there must be a risk that collaboration in all its forms will come to be seen as second best. Since collaboration is a means of responding more suitably and flexibly to external demands on the system, this would be a considerable setback not only for the students and employers concerned, but also for higher education as a whole.

(HEQC, 1995d: 2)

The overseas audits

HEQC first became aware of concerns about institutions' overseas collaborative arrangements from the initial audits of collaborative provision in 1993/4 and from the representations made to the Secretary of State on his visit to Malaysia and Singapore.

Conscious of its responsibilities to the sector, HEQC sent out its own fact-finding teams to a number of major overseas 'markets' in 1995. Their conclusion was that there was prima facie evidence that the quality of some UK higher education being delivered abroad was not being fully assured. This appeared to be the result of innocent negligence, naivety and possibly malpractice. Problems seemed to be most evident in collaborative links with private education providers, particularly where state provision was inadequate; there were less obvious difficulties where there was a strongly regulated and respected state system able to meet most local demand. There needed to be a code of practice specifically aimed at overseas collaboration (this was published in October 1995: HEQC, 1995b), and there should be a pilot programme of audits which should involve visits not only to UK universities and colleges, but also to their partner institutions abroad. At this point the Council ran into resistance from the CVCP, whose Chair, Professor (now Sir) Gareth Roberts, Vice-Chancellor of the University of Sheffield, was reluctant to see auditors going overseas.

I proposed that before reaching a final view the Council should consult the relevant government departments. Accordingly, I wrote to the Foreign and Commonwealth Office, the Overseas Development Administration and the Department for Trade and Industry, as well as the British Council and the Department for Education and Science, setting out the issues. I also talked to the officials concerned, some of whom I knew from my Whitehall days, and explained the issue. All these departments confirmed our preference to visit although the DES, true to form, sat on the fence even though it was their Minister who had started the ball rolling! I was therefore able to inform the CVCP of the overall Whitehall view, and this enabled them to change their attitude.

As a result, between April and June 1996 audit teams visited 20 overseas partners in Greece, Hong Kong, Malaysia, Singapore and Spain. The outcomes were published in December 1996. Overall these offered a reasonably reassuring picture. Partnerships had mostly been initiated and developed cautiously. Programme delivery appeared to have been generally undertaken with serious regard for quality and standards. But there was little room for complacency. The audits showed a range of systems and procedures in operation, and some evidence of variations in both coverage and effectiveness. There were five main areas of weakness:

- the establishment and formalization of partnerships, including implementation;
- validation and approval procedures;
- communication, monitoring and feedback processes;
- academic standards;
- recognition, publicity and promotional issues.

Some of these overlapped with the findings from the domestic collaborative audits. It was clear that even many institutions with sound internal quality systems struggled with the quality of their collaborative provision. The following year HEQC auditors visited partner institutions in 10 countries (Bahrain, Bulgaria, Germany, Greece, Hungary, India, the Netherlands, Oman, Poland and the United Arab Emirates). In each case the UK institution had not been audited in this way in the previous year.

Many of the problem areas identified in the pilot overseas audits recurred in the 1997 ones. In an article in the *Journal of International Education* in 1997 I highlighted four underlying issues:

1. The confusion or conflict in universities' objectives in establishing partnerships;
2. The continuing and serious tendency to underestimate the challenges of delivering British higher education programmes and experiences in a different culture;
3. The excessive reliance, in developing and managing partnerships, on committed individuals;
4. The evidence that universities, as corporate entities, were not sufficiently informed about, and were not exercising proper oversight of, what was being delivered in their name.

(Brown, 1997c: 15–21)

It was clear that institutions were paying greater attention to HEQC's code, a revised and expanded version of which was published in 1996, but many weaknesses remained. What was needed was a better balance between the undoubted benefits and the potential costs and detriments.

The decision to extend audit to institutions' overseas collaborative partnerships, to send auditors overseas, and to publish the resultant reports required considerable courage on HEQC's part. It did not endear the Council to some members of CVCP. Overall, though, the Council took the view that there was more to be gained, in terms of protecting the UK's generally deserved reputation for quality, than to be lost in terms of competitor sniping. Not only have the overseas audits continued under QAA but some other regulatory authorities have followed suit. Some of the American regional accrediting associations, particularly the Middle States, New England and Southern Association, have begun to look at institutions' overseas operations as part of their accreditation process. Some of the specialist accrediting bodies have been even more active, notably in business management and in engineering technology. The new Australian Universities Quality Agency (AUQA) includes offshore provision in its audits, with visits to operations in Singapore, Malaysia, Thailand, Vietnam, Hong Kong and China (David Woodhouse, personal communication to the author).

Learning from Audit 2

Learning from Audit 2 (HEQC, 1996c) summarized the findings of the next 48 reports completed up to July 1995. (There was no *Learning from Audit 3* because of the demise of HEQC and the higher priority given to other things by the new agency.) By this time institutions being audited were being asked questions designed to establish how they defined and determined their standards, what comparators they used to ensure their standards were broadly in line with those of other institutions, and how they ensured that their standards were in fact being maintained. Unlike the first *Learning from Audit* (HEQC, 1994d), which was almost entirely about the pre-1992 universities, *Learning from Audit 2* covered a wide range of institutions including seven colleges of higher education (the HEQC Board having agreed that these should be audited in their own right and not via their validating or accrediting university). The findings were not therefore fully comparable with those of the first *Learning from Audit* or the AAU report. Nevertheless it was possible to draw some general conclusions, and these were highlighted in the Introduction by the Director of Quality Assurance.

This drew attention particularly to the design and review of programmes and the use of external examiners as areas where real progress had been made. But some of the matters highlighted previously remained. In particular, the tension between the demands of quality assurance and available teaching resources 'appears to be no less acute than hitherto'. One of the reasons for this tension was the continuing baleful influence of research selectivity:

> Not least of these [competing pressures upon managers] is the increasing emphasis on the production of prestigious academic research output and the consequent demand made upon institutional behaviour by a competitive research funding system. The resulting conflict between the costs of high quality teaching and research, which was noted in 1991 in the AAU report is even sharper now. All the big prizes are given for

research achievement: high quality teaching and learning continue to receive scant recognition either internally or externally, even though the task of providing it is getting more and more challenging each year.

(HEQC, 1996c: 4)

Finally, the decentralization of responsibilities for quality and standards from the centre to schools or faculties continued to exercise audit teams:

The current group of reports show clearly the dilemma of reconciling the fact that quality can only be truly assured by those responsible for the delivery of programmes of study, with the equally important consideration that it is the institution that ultimately guarantees the quality and standards of an award and must therefore have some means of verifying and approving decentralised practices.

(HEQC, 1996c: 4)

We shall come back to the centralization issue in Chapter 4.

There were also a number of important new issues. First, following the greater emphasis on academic standards, it was clear that institutions placed almost total reliance on the external examiner system as the guarantor of standards. However given the general audit findings, as well as HEQC's own investigation (see next section) only limited reliance could be placed on external examiners for this purpose. The second new issue was that of modular approaches to programme structure and the implications for exam boards. Whilst the jury was out as to whether this had any ultimate impact upon standards, it did mean that questions that might have remained unasked for a long time within single subject honours degree schemes, such as the security of the tacit assumptions shared by peers, had suddenly started to demand attention. Third, there was the enormous expansion of postgraduate students since 1989, which meant that nearly one in five students was now a postgraduate. This had brought a series of new concerns to the fore.

Continuation audit

By this time (March 1996) the first audit cycle was drawing to a close. The Council therefore faced the dilemma of all custodians of quality regimes, successful and unsuccessful: what to do for an encore? Matters were further complicated by the progress towards a single quality system (see Chapter 5). Nevertheless, given the uncertainties over the timescale and implementation of a new system, the Council decided that it should press on with what was by now a tried and tested approach.

The Board decided that the future focus of audit should be narrowed and that the nature of the enquiry should shift from the direct examination of institutional documentation to the verification of institutions' claims, which would be concentrated into an 'analytical account'. Most of the evidence needed should come from existing internal and external review processes, including external assessment and accreditation, rather than be generated for the purpose. In this way the burden on institutions would be reduced, and the prospects of closer integration with other quality processes (such as assessment) increased, without diminishing the potential power of the audit method.

The four areas chosen for scrutiny were divided into two 'major' and two 'minor' ones. The major ones were the institution's strategy for achieving its educational objectives (its 'quality strategy'), and its policies for maintaining and improving the quality and standards of programmes and awards. The two minor aspects were the institutional learning infrastructure, and internal and external communications.

The other major innovation with continuation audit was that in addition to the one-year-after inquiry about the follow-up to the audit, which had been introduced in 1993, there would be a 'review meeting' between audits to review progress and discuss future plans. (A six-year audit cycle was envisaged, starting in the summer of 1997 with some of the universities audited by the AAU.) The meeting might involve a one-day visit by an auditor and an HEQC officer. The form of the meeting would reflect the nature of the judgements contained in the audit report.

Once again, the process would begin with a pilot. The first pilot audit reports were being published just as HEQC was going out of existence. Regrettably, there is no published summary of the findings.

Enhancement

Enhancement was the obvious corollary of audit, and much of its strength came from the evidence base provided by audit. *Quality Enhancement within HEQC 1995–96* (HEQC, 1996d) described the Quality Enhancement Group (QEG) as having five objectives:

- Identifying and investigating issues of national concern or interest in order to inform national and institutional planning and policy-making;
- Identifying and codifying good practice and quality management in higher education;
- Creating and supporting developments which inform and challenge current practice and stimulate change where necessary;
- Establishing national networks which facilitate the exchange of ideas and practice between colleagues who share responsibility for quality assurance and enhancement;
- Developing active links with a wide range of external constituencies in order to avoid duplication of effort, share scarce resources and build upon and learn about their expectations and experiences of quality assurance and enhancement.

(HEQC, 1996d: 2)

At its maximum the QEG comprised 11 professional and four administrative members of staff. The group also ran the national Quality Assurance and Enhancement Network, a valuable grouping of quality assurance practitioners in institutions, which ran conferences and seminars and facilitated communication with the institutions. This continued after HEQC's demise until support was withdrawn by QAA.

Good practice guidelines

As already noted, HEQC inherited good practice guidelines from both CNAA and CVCP. One of the first tasks therefore was to produce an integrated set. *Guidelines on Quality Assurance 1994* (HEQC, 1994c) was the outcome, overseen by a working party chaired by Dr Ann Wright, Vice-Chancellor of the University of Sunderland. As well as covering the main areas (overall quality framework, entry, quality of student experience, student outcomes), the *Guidelines* contained an overall checklist, a review of alternative or supplementary approaches to quality (Investors in People, BS5750, Total Quality Management) and local examples of good practice known to the council, with contact points. A revised and expanded version, mapping more closely onto the areas now covered by audit, was published in 1996. Other HEQC guidelines covered credit-based learning, guidance and learner support, and postgraduate research degrees. This was in addition to the guidance produced specifically for auditors (HEQC, 1995g).

Research reports

The HEQC produced a series of reports on various aspects of teaching and learning. Some of these were the results of research carried out by, or under, the aegis of, QEG; others were more in the nature of 'think pieces' to which colleagues in the sector contributed. The former included reports on performance indicators for academic programmes (a project inherited from CNAA and carried out by Professor Mantz Yorke), FE/HE links in both England and Scotland, *Managing for Quality* (departmental case studies on aspects of quality assurance and enhancement), modularity, and strengthening self-regulation (HEQC, 1996a). The latter – called the *In Focus* series – included papers on guidance and counselling, external examining and vocational qualifications. All were very professionally produced by Bridget Rogers (now Lady Nixon) and her small publications team.

Liaison with other quality agencies

A major issue was (and remains) the demands on institutions arising from different, sometimes competing and often conflicting external quality processes. HEQC made contact with some of the organizations concerned to explore whether there was common ground.

The most important of these was a project, led by Professor John Hilbourne, entitled *Improving the Effectiveness of Quality Assurance Systems in Non-Medical Health Care, Education and Training* (HEQC, 1996b). The project was sponsored by the NHS Executive, HEQC and the Yorkshire Regional Health Authority (subsequently North and Yorkshire RHA).

Cooperation between regulators sometimes involves one regulator agreeing to use for their purposes material prepared for, or by, another. This project went wider and proposed a single quality specification covering those areas where the principal parties – in this case the higher education institutions, the relevant professional bodies and the NHS, with the HEQC acting as broker and facilitator – had a shared need for evidence. This specification, which was fleshed out in the final report, would be incorporated into the quality documents that were already used by institutions in developing and monitoring courses. The institutions and the external bodies would then use these documents as the primary evidence base in their interactions about quality. The external bodies also agreed to use these documents as a means of communicating more effectively between themselves in sharing judgements and opinions about the quality of courses and programmes. The final report of the project, published in September 1996, was endorsed by myself and Ken Jarrold, NHS Director of Human and Corporate Resources.

External examining

External examining was on HEQC's agenda from the outset. This arose from three main sources: a concern about the process expressed by the Minister for Higher Education in his letter of March 1992 about establishing HEQC (Chapter 2), the messages emerging from the early audit reports and crystallized in the AAU report already mentioned, and the fact that the council inherited a remit (and some money) from CNAA to investigate the feasibility of a national external examiner database.

It is fair to say that these concerns were of long standing. The Lindop Committee that reviewed CNAA between 1983 and 1985 had referred to 'the original functions of the external examining system' as being to assure the broad comparability of standards between institutions and to ensure that judgements were fair and impartial (Lindop, 1985). The same year the Department and CNAA commissioned an investigation, under the aegis of the Economic and Social Research Council (ESRC), into the role of external examiners for undergraduate courses. The report of the investigation – by a team from the Institute of Education, University of London and Cambridgeshire College of Arts and Technology – was never published, and in fact the last two chapters were withdrawn at the behest of the sponsors. However, some flavour of what it might have concluded can be obtained from the presentation one of its authors – Professor David Warren-Piper – made, at my invitation, at an HEQC conference on external examining and graduate standards on 30 March 1995 (Warren-Piper, 1995). Like his book *Are*

Professors Professional? (1994), this drew on research both in Britain and in Australia (where David became Director of the Tertiary Education Institute at the University of Queensland).

David (who, after returning from Australia, was to become a colleague of mine at Southampton Institute) argued that the fundamental difficulty with any system of external examining lay with the foundations on which it was based, that is, the quality of the internal assessments and the extent to which these were monitored and assured by the institution through exam boards and other means. He referred both to a long and fairly consistent literature and to his own researches as demonstrating a continuing lack of rigour in university assessment, to which double-blind marking would, if it were applied sufficiently, be only a partial but significant antidote. Clearly, if there is no real comparability between students within an institution it is very hard to have meaningful comparability on a wider basis, even if it is desirable and can be done in a cost-effective way.

The introduction of modular courses made things even worse, because it was extremely unlikely that any one internal examiner would have an overview of all the candidates' work:

> This can mean that the external examiner is the only person in a position to make an overall judgement of a candidate's performance. However, if external examiners are appointed for only parts of a degree then no one body is overlooking the total results, except, possibly, the collective body of the Examining Board.
>
> One of the consequences of adopting a modular degree structure is that the work of external examiners is more complex. Harold Silver (Silver, 1993) has pointed to the problems with time, with sampling scripts, with being briefed, with judging appropriate standards, and with writing reports. These problems appear to be getting worse. There is a greater volume of work, procedures are more mechanical, there are more examiners relating to each other through the system of examining boards and sub-boards.
>
> We have perhaps already passed a point where the external examiners can no longer fulfil their traditional functions as described by Lindop. The gap between examiner and candidate widens, fewer external examiners actually see any students and are inexorably pushed towards judging the teaching and examining systems and away from judging the candidates. This is an unplanned shift to a meta-level of quality assurance – an incidental effect of adopting modular degree structures and the progressive move to mass higher education.
>
> [In sum] the effect of a more complex degree structure is not just to give external examiners more work; it requires them to do a different type of work as the emphasis on a single discipline recedes, so does the reliance on an examiner's specialist subject knowledge as it is replaced by a need for expertise in the processes of examination. As discipline

fades as the organising of principle of examinations calls for regulations in exam rules move to the fore.

(Warren-Piper, 1995: 11)

The HEQC's first project on external examining was to look at a possible national database which the Council might hold or commission someone to hold on its behalf. This was seen as desirable since it would offer institutions access to a wider pool of examiners, avoid possible overload on individuals, and develop reciprocity between institutions. However, the consultation response was mixed. While the majority of institutions – nearly all of them post-1992 ones – favoured this, a significant minority – all of them pre-1992 universities – did not, particularly in the light of the resources, at both institutional and national level, that might be required. HEQC therefore abandoned work on it pending its wider review of the practice.

This began with a mapping exercise carried out on the Council's behalf by the Quality Support Centre of the Open University (Silver, Stennett and Williams, 1995). Drawing upon this report, audit reports and other sources, a consultation document was circulated. This outlined a number of distinguishable roles (the 'additional' examiner, the moderator, the calibrator and the consultant) and invited institutions to comment on which they preferred and how (if at all) the roles might be combined. The report *Strengthening External Examining*, published in June 1996, was the outcome (HEQC, 1996e).

Strengthening External Examining was influenced not only by these specific inputs but also by the early outcomes of the Graduate Standards Programme (see next section). These were very much in line with the Warren-Piper thesis. We were therefore very tempted to recommend the abolition of external examining in its present form as not being a good use of resources. However, by this stage (summer 1995) the single system debate was well launched and we were concerned not to leave the field clear for the assessors. We were also aware, from the various consultation exercises, of how attached institutions were (and are) to their externals, 'keep a hold of nurse for fear of worse' being a phrase that comes readily to mind in this context.

The report was therefore a compromise. Instead of the heroic role of assuring comparability historically allotted to them, external examiners were now seen by the Council as having a more limited and realistic remit:

- To assist institutions in the comparison of academic standards across higher education awards and award elements;
- To verify that standards were appropriate for award or award elements for which the external examiner took responsibility;
- To assist institutions in ensuring that the assessment process was fair and was fairly operated in the marking, grading and classification of student performance.

(HEQC, 1996e: 11)

As we shall see, however, this reformulation was very far from being the end of the matter.

The Graduate Standards Programme

Following Mr Patten's Keele speech, discussions took place between John Stoddart and the CVCP Chair, Dr Kenneth Edwards (Vice-Chancellor of Leicester) about how the sector should cope with the new Ministerial interest in standards. A statement was cooked up which stated that, in a diverse system, 'broad comparability' could best be achieved through the assurance of threshold (minimum acceptable) standards: 'CVCP and HEQC would develop definitions of threshold standards and mechanisms for providing assurance about their achievement. HEQC would then establish, on an institutional basis, whether such standards were being maintained' (Edwards, 1994).

The QEG therefore started work on an exhaustive programme of research and analysis, including no fewer than ten specific investigations. Some were based on fieldwork, others on documentary and statistical analysis. The main findings were:

- With certain exceptions, institutions treated academic standards as implicit in the methods they used for the design and approval of courses and the assessment of students, rather than as explicit.
- The notion of comparability had become increasingly problematic.
- Where classified honours degrees predominated, the concept of threshold standards was unclear and tended to be defined in somewhat negative terms.
- It was not yet obvious whether it would be feasible to establish threshold standards at the level of broad subjects: it might be possible to do so with specialisms within them.
- The most promising approach to establishing shared, explicit standards seemed to lie in exploring the generic qualities that might be expected in any graduate in any subject – what came to be called 'graduateness'.
- There was confusion and ambiguity in the use of award titles. The distinction was not clear, for example, between 'honours' degrees on the one hand, and 'pass', 'ordinary' and 'unclassified' degrees, on the other.
- Nevertheless, in all parts of UK higher education, there was an increasing desire to find ways of articulating, in explicit and publicly accessible terms, the basis, standards and criteria for judgement of programmes of study, for the benefit of intending students, employers and society at large.

These findings, which were broadly confirmed by subsequent work, were outlined by Robin Middlehurst at the vice-chancellors' residential conference in Belfast in September 1995 (the interim report was published in December).

The author was present, and it can truly be said that you could have heard a pin drop as Robin made her presentation. The 'black box' of academic standards was at last being opened!

As the GSP findings began to emerge within the Council, there was a good deal of discussion about how they should be followed up. Thinking crystallized when Robin, Peter Williams and I found ourselves together, unusually, at a conference in Utrecht in May 1995. We happened to be dining together at a restaurant that used paper tablecloths. As our discussion proceeded, we were able to sketch various possibilities and their interrelations. By the end of the evening we had identified what we saw as the key elements in a more secure standards network (I still have the tablecloth). These were:

- whether it would be possible to develop agreement on the qualities expected of graduates, including generic attributes and skills;
- the development of a convention about the use of degrees and other award titles;
- the strengthening of the system of external examiners to underpin standards;
- the identification of what might constitute threshold standards for degrees and diplomas.

On these issues the conclusions in the final report published, after consultation, in December 1996, were:

- The notion of 'graduateness' was not yet sufficiently robust to be used to define the nature of the UK degree or to offer a threshold for all degrees, although it might serve as the basis for establishing the range of expectations that UK degrees now encompassed.
- There was considerable support for the development of a convention or set of guidelines governing the structuring and nomenclature of awards and the levels at which they were offered.
- The new external examining framework (see above) provided a basis for strengthening the system, but only if the expectations in it were realistic: that is, the limitations to comparability were acknowledged and explicit benchmarks were developed.
- While in due course it might be possible to establish 'direct' threshold standards (specified attributes, the possession of which could be demonstrated to a sufficient extent through assessment) in some specialisms or sub-disciplines, in the immediate future the best approach across the sector as a whole would be an 'indirect' one, creating the conditions within which such standards could be established.

The report also stated the Council's view that the dominance of the classified honours degree, and the values and practice embodied in the classification process, hindered the establishment of positive thresholds of achievement for first degrees. More generally, the report concluded that the dominance of honours-level degrees (rather than a balance between ordinary and honours-level degrees) seemed out of line with the needs of an expanded HE system (HEQC, 1997b, 1997c).

One of those who was most interested in these questions was Sir Ron (now Lord) Dearing, who came to see me as soon as he was appointed to head his inquiry into higher education (February 1996) and who subsequently received, and clearly appreciated, presentations on our progress. I deal in Chapter 5 with what his committee actually did with our work. For the moment there are just two points.

First, it cannot be emphasized too strongly that it was the Council's view that ultimately academic standards were institutions' business. HEQC's aim throughout was to strengthen the institutional capacity for self-regulation by offering some benchmarks and tools as a means for institutions to analyse, benchmark and strengthen their provision. By contrast, the effect, if not the aim, of the Dearing Committee (and subsequently, I believe, the QAA) was to create a framework through which institutions' compliance with collectively agreed benchmarks could be monitored and regulated externally. The difference between these two positions may be subtle, but it is certainly profound (Brown, 1998a).

Second, the implications of the GSP went well beyond standards, important though these were. If institutions could be more secure in their knowledge and transmission of their standards, less attention could be paid to how those standards were achieved. There could then be an end to, or at least a radical scaling down of, external assessment. Other external regulatory processes – such as those associated with the professional and statutory bodies, the NHS and the Teacher Training Agency – could also be simplified since these also focused on standards, or at least claimed to do so. The Dearing Committee recognized this, but as we shall see, its recommendations were disappointingly cautious.

Regrettably, with the demise of HEQC, the adoption of the Dearing recommendations (which were, almost but not quite unaccountably, warmly welcomed by the very same vice-chancellors who had initially been somewhat resistant to our proposals), the handover to QAA and the loss of Robin and a number of other key personnel following the agency's relocation to Gloucester, these cues were never really picked up. Assessment continued as before, and compliance and games playing became even more the order of the day. However this agenda remains (HEQC, 1997c; CVCP/HEFCE, 2000).

Other functions

Although audit and enhancement absorbed the bulk of the Council's resources, a number of other functions were important both in their own right and in complementing these core ones. Unfortunately considerations of space preclude all but the briefest account.

After audit and enhancement, perhaps the most important of HEQC's functions was advising the Department on applications for degree-awarding powers and university title, because this involved the Council playing a gatekeeping role on behalf of the entire academic community. The Council considered 15 applications for taught degree-awarding powers, five for research degree-awarding powers and two for both. In all cases its advice was accepted. It also considered one application for university title. During this period the Government 'raised the crossbar' for applicant institutions, mainly by introducing a three-year delay before they could apply (this was another outcome of the Patten speech).

As already noted, HEQC inherited from CNAA responsibility for the arrangements underpinning the quality assurance of recognized Access Courses, a responsibility discharged mainly through the periodic review of the 40 or so consortia that actually validated the courses. The value of this work, in the capable hands of the late Philip Jones, was confirmed by an independent review in October 1994.

Another CNAA inheritance was the promotion of credit accumulation and transfer, although the separate CATS arm was disbanded when Harry Mitchell left. A project led by Professor David Robertson at Liverpool John Moores University investigated ways in which the wider development of such learning could be encouraged. The resultant reports *Choosing to Change* (HEQC, 1994a, 1994b, 1995a) called for a national credit framework based on a structure of levels of attainment, a common unit of credit and credit currency, agreed interim awards (an Associate Degree), and a shared approach to definitions of achievement. However the response from the sector was mixed, and with the wise and careful advice of the late Alan Crispin, the Council decided to confine its future role to scrutinizing the quality assurance aspects of credit-based learning (HEQC, 1995c).

Unlike the assessment units, HEQC was of course a UK-wide body. The Council's Scottish office, under the shrewd leadership of Norman Sharp, liaised with the Scottish Higher Education Funding Council and discharged some functions specific to Scotland, notably in support of the Scottish Credit Accumulation and Transfer Framework (SCOTCATS). Mike Williams, the former senior Treasury official in charge of degree-awarding powers, also acted as the council's Officer for Wales. In this way the Council built up a useful local rapport.

International links

Finally, Carolyn Campbell, as the Council's International Officer, liaised with various international organizations and kept herself informed about various international developments in quality assurance. For much of this period she was on part secondment to the ERASMUS Bureau in Brussels (in return for reimbursement of salary and expenses), where she was mainly engaged in administering the European Credit Transfer System (ECTS), of which she was subsequently appointed a Promoter. To assist with this the council occupied a room in the British Council's Brussels office for a nominal rent for a while. Carolyn's knowledge of developments overseas, and her range of contacts, contributed directly to much of what HEQC achieved, as well as to the fact-finding project on international quality frameworks, carried out under the aegis of the Dearing Committee (NCIHE, 1997).

Envoi

By the autumn of 1994, and after a slow start, HEQC had the wind in its sails. As well as the modification and extension of audit and the first GSP studies, the Council had published the first *Learning from Audit* and the first *Guidelines on Quality Assurance*, was overseeing the production of *Choosing to Change*, was working on future guidelines for external examining, was about to conduct the review of the Access Course Recognition arrangements, and was discussing with the Department modifications to its approach to degree-awarding powers. Relations with the Scottish and Welsh Funding Councils had improved greatly, as they had with HEFCE. The Council was also beginning to make real headway in its work with 'cognate bodies' with a view to streamlining arrangements. It was therefore singularly unhelpful that just at this point Mrs Gillian Shephard, John Patten's successor as Secretary of State, chose to throw the vice-chancellors a bone by asking the HEFCE Chief Executive to review the quality arrangements.

This decision, and the agreement between the parties nearly a year later about the way forward on a single regime, inevitably changed the context of HEQC's work. It is greatly to the credit of my former colleagues that the quality (and quantity) of that work was maintained, and that so many of them stayed until the bitter end. The CVCP Chief Executive Baroness Warwick's letter of appreciation on behalf of CVCP – delivered with a nice sense of timing just before the final HEQC Board in July 1997 – offered only partial compensation.[2]

Notes

1 Enterprise in Higher Education was a government initiative under which selected universities received grants to develop enterprise skills in the curriculum. £10 million was allocated in total over the five years from 1989. It was modelled on the Technical and Vocational Education Initiative.
2 Baroness Warwick of Undercliffe became CVCP Chief Executive on 1 September 1995.

4 Assessment

It might be said that the ultimate goal of quality assessment is to contribute to the enhancement of institutional quality assurance processes until such time as the institutions can demonstrate rigorous and effective self-regulation.

(Milton, 1996: 4)

Introduction

This chapter describes the evolution of assessment between 1992 and 2002. It mostly concerns assessment in England but there are separate, shorter sections on Scotland and Wales (Northern Ireland followed England).

One issue that immediately arises is what exactly is meant by 'assessment'. Like audit but to a much greater extent, assessment was subject to both major and minor changes, with the main one in 1995 to the universal visiting of providers and the adoption of a graded profile of performance in specified aspects of provision. Some of these changes were overt (and included in the published methodology), others were covert (for example, the increasing priority given to student assessment). The first part of this chapter outlines the principal features of assessment and how these were modified; it also summarizes the overall outcomes.

Assessment proved much more controversial than audit. The second and main part of the chapter looks at the chief claims made for and against assessment. While many of the charges against assessment are either unfounded or wide of the mark, and that while assessment, like audit, has almost certainly had a positive impact on quality, as a process it offered increasingly poor value as the decade proceeded, and should have been discarded much sooner than it was.

One reason for this was the way in which institutions managed to anticipate what was looked for by assessors, leading to a wholesale inflation in scores, which ultimately made them nearly meaningless. This – and many of assessment's other problems – was basically due to the authorities' insistence that the methodology had to provide a basis for discriminating between institutions, an insistence that remained even after the link to funding announced in the 1991 White Paper was in effect removed in 1994, and which goes back to the 'efficiency from above' rationale underlying the process which we encountered in Chapter 1.

The assessment method

The requirement that assessment had to provide a basis for differential institutional funding was repeated in the initial letter of guidance which the Secretary of State sent the new funding council in June 1992:

> It will be for the Council to determine the assessment approach to be adopted, in consultation with institutions and drawing on experience from the pilot assessments already completed or under way. The Council will need, in particular, to ensure that the outcomes of assessment visits are in a form which can be used to inform funding allocations. Reports of visits should be published. The Council should seek to ensure that serious shortcomings identified in reports are addressed by institutions, and monitored by the Council.
>
> (DES, 1992)

Circular 3/93

Circular 3/93 outlined the purposes and features of assessment. These were:

- to ensure that all education for which the HEFCE provides funding is of satisfactory quality or better, and to ensure speedy rectification of unsatisfactory quality
- to encourage improvements in the quality of education through the publication of assessment reports and an annual report.
- to inform funding and reward excellence.

> (Circular 3/93, paragraph 5: HEFCE, 1993: 4)

These were to be fulfilled through a process under which academic peers would assess the quality of provision in particular subjects ('units of assessment') and produce published reports categorizing such provision as 'excellent', 'satisfactory' or 'unsatisfactory':

> Excellent: Education is of a generally very high quality
>
> Satisfactory: This category would include many elements of good practice. Aims and objectives have been met and there is a good match between these, the teaching and learning process and the students' ability, experience, expectations and attainment.
>
> Unsatisfactory: Education is not of an acceptable quality: there are serious shortcomings which need to be addressed.
>
> (Circular 3/93 paragraph 15: HEFCE, 1993: 9)

The starting point would be a self-assessment giving the aims and objectives of the provision concerned and the 'subject provider's' view of how far these were being achieved. In effect, therefore, the assessors' report would indicate, explicitly or implicitly, how far they concurred with the view taken of itself by the provider. There were to be two reports, one published and one confidential to the institution, both containing the assessors' judgment.

One cardinal point was that the judgment was to be made by reference to the provider's aims and objectives: as with audit, a 'gold standard' was officially eschewed:

> The quality of teaching and learning in a diverse sector can only be understood in the context of an institution's own aims and objectives. . . . The Council believes that an approach to quality which encompasses the breadth and depth of student achievement and learning experience, based on an institution's own aims and objectives, will allow for a consistent and rigorous quality assessment process respecting diversity of institutional mission.
>
> (HEFCE, 1993: 8)

As Peter de Vries (1996) pointed out, there was already a fundamental contradiction between the intended use of intrinsic criteria – the subject provider's own aims and objectives – and the fundamental purpose of ensuring that all education was of satisfactory quality or better, which must imply some common meaning of 'satisfactory'. As Simeon Underwood has commented, this became even more self-contradictory as the interest in standards as measured by student assessment increased over time (personal communication to the author).

Institutions should decide whether to claim 'excellent' or 'satisfactory' for their provision. Assessors would visit all providers where a 'prima facie' case for excellence had been established or where there were grounds for concern that quality might be at risk. In addition, the Council would visit a sample of institutions where a claim of 'satisfactory' was being made. In the event 553 of the 972 completed self-assessments in England were the subject of a visit. In respect of the remaining 419 the grade of 'satisfactory' was allocated without a visit (HEFCE *Report on Quality Assessment 1992–95*: HEFCE, 1995).

Assessment was conducted according to Circular 3/93 from 1992 to 1995. Fifteen subjects were assessed across 144 institutions (England and Northern Ireland). 26.6 per cent of subject providers were found to be 'excellent', 72.1 per cent were found to be 'satisfactory', 1.3 per cent were found to be 'unsatisfactory' (Cook, personal communication to the author, November 2002; cf HEFCE, 1995). But as we shall see these findings were very far from being distributed uniformly across either subjects or categories of institution (see Tables 4.1 and 4.2).

As the tables show, the percentages varied dramatically. Nearly 77 per cent of anthropology departments were rated as excellent against just under

Table 4.1 Percentage spread of grades by subject 1992–95 (covers England and Northern Ireland)

Subject	Grade			
	Excellent	Satisfactory	Unsatisfactory	Grand total
Anthropology	76.92	23.08	0.00	100.00
Applied social work	20.00	78.67	1.33	100.00
Architecture	33.33	66.67	0.00	100.00
Business and management	18.00	81.00	1.00	100.00
Chemistry	22.03	77.97	0.00	100.00
Computer science	10.64	87.23	2.13	100.00
English	34.88	61.63	3.49	100.00
Environmental studies	21.15	76.92	1.92	100.00
Geography	33.33	65.33	1.33	100.00
Geology	51.43	48.57	0.00	100.00
History	21.18	78.82	0.00	100.00
Law	31.82	66.67	1.52	100.00
Mechanical engineering	12.16	86.49	1.35	100.00
Music	45.76	52.54	1.69	100.00
Social policy and administration	42.42	57.58	0.00	100.00
Overall	26.58	72.13	1.29	100.00

Source: Personal communication from Roger Cook, Napier University, to the author, 7 November 2002
(Reproduced with permission)

Table 4.2 Percentage spread of grades by institutional type 1992–95 (covers England and Northern Ireland)

Type of HEI	Grade		
	Excellent	Satisfactory	Unsatisfactory
Old	46.94	52.81	0.24
New	11.21	87.36	1.44
College	9.66	86.93	3.41
Overall average	26.58	72.13	1.29

Source: Personal communication from Roger Cook, Napier University, to the author, 7 November 2002
(Reproduced with permission)

11 per cent of computer science departments. Similarly, nearly 47 per cent of departments in the old universities obtained an excellent as compared with 11 per cent in the new universities. This discrepancy reduced over time, reflecting the changing subject sequence (and the fact that the older institutions were scoring so highly they could go no higher). The old universities

nevertheless outscored new universities and colleges right through the process. We will explore why later.

Circular 39/94

Circular 3/93 was published in February 1993. Sixteen months later, in June 1994, the purposes of assessment were reformulated following Mr Patten's April speech (see Chapter 3). 'Value for money' and 'quality improvement' remained, but providing 'effective and accessible public information on the quality of education' became the third purpose, instead of informing funding and rewarding excellence. (Circular 39/94, paragraph 23: HEFCE, 1994: 7).

This modification reflected the Government's decision in late 1993 to apply the brake to the late 1980s/early 1990s expansion by introducing a maximum number of funded places for each institution. This meant that one of the main reasons for the link to funding – to reward 'excellent' providers with extra student places – was no longer relevant. Nevertheless the emphasis on being able to discriminate between providers, now primarily to inform the 'market', remained, as did the warning that sub-threshold provision might not continue to be funded.

In his 1993 article on the causes of the great quality debate to which we will refer in Chapter 5, Leslie Wagner pointed out that under its then existing funding methodology, HEFCE's scope for linking funding to assessment outcomes was anyway limited. The Council funded teaching in 11 'programme areas' yet carried out its assessments in subject groups that formed only part of each area. Moreover most of the judgements were expected to fall in the 'satisfactory' category. He concluded, 'There is a danger that the costs of the whole exercise to the system, both to the Funding Councils and to the universities, will exceed the funds affected by the outcome' (Wagner, 1993: 281). This did of course prove to be the case![1]

The CHES evaluation

In late 1993, when assessment was still barely a year old, HEFCE commissioned an evaluation by the Centre for Higher Education Studies at the Institute of Education, University of London (CHES). The overall finding was that while there was 'a strong view in institutions' that in principle assessment was 'a justifiable undertaking' that was already producing benefits, there was also a widespread belief that the current system could be improved (CHES, 1994: 5). The evaluators therefore made a number of recommendations essentially to increase the fairness of the process and to increase its potential contribution to quality improvement.

Under the former heading, they recommended that the visits should be extended so as to cover all departments and programmes, since otherwise institutions not visited would continue to be unhappy with the judgements arrived at. Under the latter, they suggested that the judgmental component should be modified, essentially to indicate whether the provider concerned was operating at a threshold level of provision. Alongside this there should be a 'profile' of strengths and weaknesses which might form a basis for further quality improvement. There was no mention of the profile being graded, and indeed the report made it clear that such profiling was intended to be developmental, identifying both areas of strength and areas where there was scope for further strengthening.

As a result of the evaluation, and subsequent consultation with institutions, the council decided to move to universal visiting and to replace the aggregate scale of three judgmental points (excellent, satisfactory, unsatisfactory) by a profile of judgements against each of six 'core' aspects of provision. For each of these 'aspects judgments' there was however to be a four-point numerical scale (1 being the lowest, 4 the highest), together with an overall summative judgement using a two-point scale ('approved' or 'not approved', where a score of 1 on any aspect would automatically mean the provision being 'not approved'). In addition the practice of having separate reports was brought to an end.[2]

Both changes (universal visiting and graded profiles) stemmed from the continuing requirement for assessment to be able to discriminate between providers. As David Watson has said, 'the CHES approach would not enable [the Committee] to reach safe and defensible comparative judgements' (personal communication to the author, May 2003). Yet the council's decisions enormously increased the scale of the whole enterprise *and* the difficulties of getting consistent judgements across subjects and institutions.

Subsequent changes

Various secondary changes were made to assessment between 1996 and 2001 which it would be tedious to enumerate in full, but there were two significant ones. In November 1998 the QAA introduced, without consultation or explanation but almost certainly in response to Departmental prompting, a new rule under which departments which scored three or more grade 2s went 'on report' and had to provide an action plan one year on (*Subject Review Handbook October 1998 to September 2000*: QAA, 1997d). The agency also sought 'follow-up reports' from institutions that had generated this profile in earlier rounds!

Second, in March 1999 in a letter to heads of institutions, John Randall suggested a possible conversion scale to enable the grading scale to be expressed as a single number, in which grade 2s became, in effect, the bottom level. The sector opposed this and the conversion formula was not proceeded with.[3]

We turn now to the arguments for and against assessment.

Assessment: for and against

The claims for assessment

In an address at the University of Newcastle-upon-Tyne in 1994 the then HEFCE Director of Assessment, Dr Paul Clark, set out what he saw as the benefits of the process, the basic purpose of which was, in his view, to stimulate 'the further development of a critical and analytic attitude with respect to teaching and learning in higher education on the part of those actively engaged in those activities' (Clark, 1994: 2–3).

Dr Clark referred to the benefits adduced in the CHES evaluation. Moreover, informal feedback told the Council that:

> much useful information is being derived from the process and many changes have been made as a result. One can also simply observe the number of universities that, over the last two years, have put into place internal quality assessment operations at the departmental level, some of which involve external peer review, that mirror the HEFCE processes of quality assessment. . . . the quality assessment process is having an important developmental impact on the thinking and the practices of the English academic community.
>
> (Clark, 1994: 8)[4]

One clear consequence was that 'substantial numbers of academics (700 so far) are taking the opportunity to step out of their own departments, and their habitual ways of thinking regarding the teaching of their subject, and are putting their minds to the understanding of how two or three other departments approach this process and with what aims in mind' (Clark, 1994: 8). Similarly Professor Watson, writing in the *Higher Education Quarterly* the following year, stated:

> As a result of assessment there is strong evidence of more serious and systematic scrutiny of teaching and learning performance, of greater attention given to the professional development of lecturers and other learning support staff, and of consideration of how the infrastructure of universities and colleges can best meet the needs of students. The need for formal articulation of these priorities has been resented, but privately almost all involved agree that the discipline has been valuable.
>
> The experience of being an assessor has also been valued, and has in some ways made up for the loss of the subject-based professional networks which were a feature of the CNAA regime. Further, institutional managers have been quick to react to the marketing potential of high ratings (See annual reports and newsletters). Perhaps most importantly, action has been prompted in those few cases where peer assessment has

concluded that students were getting a demonstrably unsatisfactory deal.

(Watson, 1995: 335)

It is interesting that neither Dr Clark nor Professor Watson mentioned the public information argument, possibly because this had been introduced only recently. However others would make this claim. For example:

Quality assessment yields many benefits. The published reports on provision in named institutions are a source of reliable and independent information for potential students and their advisers, and employers of graduates . . . (Sizer 1993).

(Gordon, 2002: 204)

I believe the reports of individual assessments, together with the overview reports, will provide a valuable resource for students, staff and others who wish to obtain a current picture of the quality of provision in Scottish higher education institutions (Clark, 1998).

(Gordon, 2002: 204)

A wealth of information for prospective students.

(Sir Brian Fender quoted by Underwood, 2000: 86)

Reliable and independent information is also needed to widen participation in higher education.

(Randall, 2001: 5)

A great deal of information and evaluative comment has been made available to all those with a stake in higher education. I hope that anyone choosing a university course will take advantage of this unique set of information which is made freely available to them.

(Williams, 2002)

Criticisms of assessment

In his 1995 article Professor Watson attempted to identify and rebut the 'main charges' against the process. These were:

- excessive demands on institutions;
- violation of academic autonomy and freedom, linked to the fostering of a 'compliance culture';
- creation of 'hard managerialism' and managerial intrusion in academic matters;
- damage to Britain's hard-won reputation for quality.

(Watson, 1995: 328)

Other main charges have included:

- the failure of the process to meet basic tests of validity, reliability, consistency and transparency;
- a tendency to reflect and reinforce conventional notions of academic hierarchy and resourcing rather than the resource-blind institutional diversity arguably more appropriate to a mass or semi-mass system.

(Brown, 1999c, 2000b)

A final charge is the increasingly marginal impact and value of assessment, as institutions learnt to 'play the game', applying to the improvement of their scores the intellectual resources that might have been deployed in raising the quality of their teaching. (This is linked in part to the compliance culture charge.)

Benefits to teaching and learning

Evidence in support of the main claimed benefit – that institutions were improving their teaching – comes from evaluation reports, from some knowledgeable 'critics', and from the upward trend in scores.

In July 1997 HEFCE published two reports by the Quality Support Centre of the Open University (now the Centre for Higher Education Research and Information). The study covered the 15 subjects assessed during the first two assessment rounds undertaken between 1993 and 1995. The Centre was originally commissioned to analyse the extent to which the recommendations for quality improvement made by subject peer assessors had been acted upon. With HEFCE agreement the study was extended to consider the impact upon institutions not just of the reports and follow-up actions, but of the whole of the process: the anticipation, the preparation of the self-assessments and the experience of the visits as well.

It is important to appreciate that the study covered only the impact of the first two assessment rounds under the old pre-1995 methodology. Nevertheless it is worthwhile not only for its scope and impartiality, but also because it can be argued that the positive impact of assessment was possibly greatest at the start of the process. The overall conclusion was:

> There is little doubt that quality assessment has had an impact upon institutions of higher education in England. On the downside, it has used up a lot of time and resources and caused some stress. More positively, it has provided an impetus for institutions to give more attention to the quality of their teaching. The form which this has taken has varied between institutions and between subject groups within institutions. We have seen more importance being attached to the work of staff developers, to the formalisation and documentation of procedures, to surveys of student opinion, to peer observation of teaching. And 66% of the specific recommendations made by assessors led to some form of action.
>
> (Brennan, Frederiks and Shah, 1997: 74)

At the same time, the report raised one issue, which also applied to audit, namely the apparent pre-occupation with 'forms':

> While there is much support across higher education for the concep-
> tions of teaching quality which underpin quality assessment, there are
> also many people who are doubtful about the emphasis which they
> perceive to be placed on presentational and procedural matters, possibly
> at the expense of matters of intellectual substance. Whether the latter
> are properly the concern of the funding council and whether they can
> be addressed by quality assessment in anything like its present form –
> a process described as 'inspection' by large numbers of the people we
> interviewed – are matters for debate. Their omission from the assess-
> ment process limits the educational and intellectual significance of quality
> assessment to many academics, though its political significance cannot
> be disputed.
>
> (Brennan *et al*, 1997: 74)

HEFCE also commissioned an evaluation of the experiences of subject specialist assessors. This was carried out by Liz McDowell of the Centre for Advances in Higher Education at the University of Northumbria at Newcastle in 1996/7. Virtually all the academics who responded indicated that being an assessor had exerted a positive influence on their educational practices. Like Brennan and his colleagues, however, McDowell found that the benefits to other academic staff were far from being automatic. A lot depended on attitudes, with some staff seeing assessment as part of a general compliance culture. Availability of time was another factor. Yet another was the stance taken by the department: 'Some departments try to use the opportunity of quality assessment to review and improve their practices but in others the aim of their discussions and development was to maximise the results, operating strategically with little intention to make real changes' (McDowell, 1998: 3–4). McDowell also refers to the literature on 'deep' and 'surface' learning to illustrate how such differing strategies paralleled students' approaches to learning/assessment (McDowell, 1998). Other factors constraining benefits were the local context (including, yet again, in de-partments with a strong research focus) and the actual conduct of the assess-ment itself. Some assessors also made this criticism. Gordon (2002) also emphasizes the importance of the receiving department having the right culture if the messages from assessment and other exercises are to be absorbed effectively.

Other writers and commentators have also mentioned the benefits to teaching. The Dearing Committee said in its report:

> Teaching Quality Assessments . . . have raised the profile of teaching
> within institutions and have served a useful purpose. But, given that the
> vast majority of outcomes have been satisfactory, we are not convinced

that it would be the best use of scarce resources to continue the system in the long term. Moreover, we believe that it is exceedingly difficult for the TQA process to review the quality of learning and teaching itself, rather than proxies for learning and teaching, such as available resources or lecture presentations. The utility of such a system is likely to wane as institutions 'learn' how to achieve high ratings.

(NCIHE, 1997: paragraph 10.68)

Other authoritative commentaries that mention the benefits are those of Cook (2001), Drennan (1999), Fry (1995), Gordon (2002), Moran (2002) and Underwood (2000). A number of subject associations expressed support for the process, though usually with qualifications (Underwood, 1998). Finally there was the upward trend in average scores, not all of which can be put down to game playing.[5]

Public information

The best critique of the other main claim for assessment – that it provided valuable information for consumers – can be found in Simeon Underwood's scholarly discussion (Underwood, 2000; see also Jenkins, 1997). In summary, the problems were:

- the currency of the data. Most assessment reports were out of date by the time they were published and some were very old. Even within one two-year round there could be severe problems of comparability and fairness between providers assessed at different times;
- the robustness of the data;
- the vulnerability of the reports to simplistic or selective interpretation (mostly by the newspapers but also by institutions themselves and even sometimes the agency);
- report style.

Simeon refers to a survey by the consultants Segal Quince Wicksteed of stakeholder use of the reports. This found that the most influential sources of information in relation to quality and standards were the institutions themselves, league tables and schools careers advisers. Only 12 per cent of respondents considered QAA reports to be the single most important source of information about quality. The impact on employers was even more limited (Segal Quince Wicksteed, 1999, quoted in Underwood, 2000).

However Simeon pointed out that the various sources of information are not wholly independent of one another, 'indeed it could be argued that the league tables would not exist without the data provided by TQA results' (Underwood, 2000: 87). Moreover the QAA website was then receiving 12–15,000 hits per week, including many from overseas, which suggested a high level of public interest.

The author's personal view is that the audience for the relatively fine-grained information about quality and standards of the sort contained in QAA subject review reports is quite limited, and may remain so. In 1994/5 HEQC and the Universities and Colleges Admissions Service (UCAS) discussed the scope for publishing institutional quality 'profiles' incorporating general information about institutions alongside information about quality and standards, the intention being to use only publicly available material. However pilots that were carried out with sixth formers and college students suggested that the audience would be too limited to make it a worthwhile economic proposition. It is therefore ironic that the Government has in the January 2003 White Paper announced that the NUS will be taking a lead in producing a 'comprehensive survey' of institutions (DfES, 2003a: 7). Some of this will come from the expanded amount of information that institutions will be making available about quality and standards, which was recommended by the Cooke Committee on information (HEFCE, 2002), and which was an important part of the quid pro quo for dropping universal subject review (see Chapter 6).

The claims for assessment: conclusion

There seems little doubt that assessment helped to improve the quality of student learning and achievement after 1992. There can also be little doubt that assessment helped focus attention on student learning, encouraged departments to set up systems to demonstrate this, and increased or improved efforts to obtain feedback from students on their experience. There remains plenty of evidence, however, to suggest that research – and particularly research within the dubious Research Assessment Exercise – even now enjoys greater esteem than teaching, particularly when it comes to promotion (Drennan, 2001). Finally, there can be little argument about the benefits, in terms of staff and professional development, to those who acted as assessors (and, through them, their institutions, departments, subjects, professional groups and so on). Whether this was the best use of those staff development resources is another matter. The public information claim is more questionable. The issue is really whether equal or greater benefits could not have been achieved, and at least some of the detriments avoided, if HEFCE had followed the CHES advice about a more formative method. We now review the criticisms of assessment, some of which were of course acknowledged in the evaluations.

The demands on institutions

This was by far the most important and persistent complaint about assessment. It is what eventually led, in March 2001, to the demise of the process in its revised form as Academic Review (see Chapter 6). The burden on institutions arising from assessment, audit and other similar processes must by now indeed be nearly as famous, or infamous, as the Burden associated with the White Man in the days of the Empire. What is quite astonishing, however, even to someone like the author who has witnessed the whole sorry saga, is that only at a very late stage was any serious attempt made to compute the costs of the process, and even now no really systematic assessment has been done.[6] Indeed not the least of the criticisms that can be made of the sector since 1992 has been the failure to produce a really convincing, detailed critique of the distortions and costs, in either the narrow or the broad sense, of external quality assurance.

The author is aware of only two reasonably serious attempts to compute the costs of assessment. The first was made by the CVCP office in September 1993. On the basis of returns from institutions, this estimated an average combined cost of assessment and audit each year for each university of about £150,000, compared with an average annual teaching block grant of £16 million (thus, less than 1 per cent of expenditure on teaching) (CVCP, 1993: 2). This was just brushed aside by the vice-chancellors.

The second was made by PA Consulting in August 2000 in, ironically, a report on accountability commissioned by HEFCE. This found the average annual cost of audit and assessment together to be £120,000 to £150,000 for the University of Leeds and £160,000 to £280,000 for Leeds Metropolitan University. The difference was partly accounted for by the different curriculum structure of the two institutions. The main cost drivers in each case were the numbers of staff involved. Based on these estimates the extrapolated annualized costs for the sector were thought to be at least £30 million (PA Consulting, 2000: 20). The PA report mentioned unpublished research by the Association of University Teachers which found costs at about the same level (ibid: 21). As we shall see in Chapter 6, this report was almost certainly one of the main factors that led to the March 2001 announcement, as was QAA's failure to respond to it (at least publicly). Such figures do of course have to be placed in the context of average annual public expenditure on teaching in higher education of £6 billion over the period 2001/2. The issue is not so much the total amount as to whether much greater value could not have been obtained from these sums.[7]

Violation of academic autonomy and the creation of a compliance culture

A number of commentators (eg Russell, 2001) have criticized assessment as representing an interference with academic freedom whereby the government, through the Funding Council, attempted to substitute its preferred, economically relevant, academic standards and criteria for those which the academic community, left to itself, would have used (cf Roberts, 1997). A leading exponent of this view, and a scathing critic of assessment, is Professor Geoffrey Alderman. Like Tapper and Salter, Alderman saw assessment (and the Student Charter) as a vehicle through which higher education could be made to contribute to national economic well-being:

The government put 'quality' on the national agenda. It did so partly because it wished to be able to reassure the public that when the elite system of higher education was transformed into a mass system, 'standards' would not fall along with the unit of resource. But it also wished to use the weapon of 'quality' in order to bring about fundamental changes in the character of British higher education, replacing an elitist view of higher education (internalised accountability, knowledge for its own sake) with one orientated towards serving very practical and, I should stress, utterly legitimate national ends – primarily the education of a skilled workforce.

(Alderman, 1995: 7)

Accordingly, following the 1991 White Paper, 'HMIs were to be transformed into a new mechanism of control exerted by the Higher Education Funding Councils . . . created by the 1992 Further and Higher Education Act' (ibid: 9). Alderman contrasts the old universities' characteristic concern for the quality and intensity of the 'internal dialogue' (between teacher and student, and between student and student) with the Government's preference for economic relevance:

Polytechnics might become universities, but the last thing the government wanted was for the polytechnics to embrace collegialism and to bask in the academic autonomy of the old regime. On the contrary the old universities were to be remoulded, along with the new, into an entirely new shape. They were all to become elements of the national production process, and to be judged, and so funded accordingly. Government hoped that the statutory assessment visit carried out under the 1992 Act would act as a powerful engine for change in this direction.

(Alderman, 1995: 11)

There are clear echoes here of some of the writers we examined in Chapter 1. Alderman shows how economic relevance – in the form of things like the involvement of employers in the curriculum, graduate employability, the inculcation of key skills – was included in the criteria used by assessors to score institutions' self-assessments, using criteria that were not publicly available. Peter de Vries, in his analysis of the first 134 assessment reports in 1993–94, found assessors using private criteria which included 'relevance' as a major category, alongside depth of knowledge, breadth of subject coverage, learner autonomy, learner progression and curriculum cohesion:

The ivory tower image of higher education is not sustained in the assessors' statements in the reports; on the contrary, there is a very strong emphasis throughout most of the reports on curricula and teaching being relevant, in the main, to future employment, but also to further study and research. Assessors were looking for strong liaison between employers and academics especially in the applied disciplines; for curricula and materials to be orientated to the world of work; and for teachers to have some experience of employment through their research and consultancy. They were concerned about the contextualization of the curriculum and the materials in work practice so that the HEIs could 'produce graduates that would match industry's requirements'. Mechanisms were suggested for achieving the required synergy, such as liaison, meetings, involvement of outsiders in the subject areas, work placements.

(de Vries, 1996: 202–3)

In his response to this criticism David Watson wrote:

The prime focus of the processes is testing fitness for purpose. The institutions retain almost untrammelled responsibility for determining their own aims and objectives, or fitness of purpose. In these circumstances the appeal against external peer review from the basis of 'academic freedom' can appear hollow and tactical rather than principled. Even the most extreme statements of academic freedom do not remove the obligation to explain, especially to peers.

(Watson, 1995: 329)

It is possible to sympathize with both positions. There can be little doubt that the economic relevance criterion would not have been part of the original approach to assessment were it not for the government's general higher education policy (see Chapter 2). However it is also true that the criteria underlying assessment have for the most part been those devised by the academic community, and that most of those applying them have also come from that source. It is also of course the case that direct economic relevance is one of the things that many students are seeking, rightly or wrongly, in their courses and awards, and which top-up fees (see Chapter 7) will reinforce.

Perhaps a more serious criticism is the one made by a number of critics but most eloquently in the CHES evaluation, namely the confusion at the heart of the process between a fitness for purpose and a fitness of purpose view of quality, and the associated lack of an underlying theory of quality. Hence the evaluators' very first recommendation was:

That, in the light of experience of the first months of quality assessment in this report, the Quality Assessment Committee, the Quality Assessment Division and the Lead Assessors – perhaps in a residential meeting and possibly with some external input – might clarify the general approach to quality that should inform quality assessment. In particular, the relationship between an institution's aims and objectives and the fulfilment by institutions of any common sets of aspects of course delivery identified by the Council should be made more explicit. In turn, the operational consequences of any such clarification would need to be worked through in the training programme and in the various elements of the assessment methodology.

(CHES, 1994: 8)

HEFCE's response was to introduce the six core aspects of provision to 'provide a common structure for the main features of the quality assessment method – the self-assessment, the assessment visit, the assessment judgement and the assessment report' (Circular 39/94, para 24: HEFCE, 1994: 8). In addition, in the *Report on Quality Assessment 1992–95* the Funding Council listed a number of characteristics that peer assessors had associated with 'excellent' education across the sector and subjects (HEFCE, 1995, paras 82–84) While these changes must have helped both assessors and institutions, questions of consistency and fairness between providers and subjects remained, as will shortly be seen.

Hard managerialism

In a trenchant critique published in 1994, Martin Trow saw both research and teaching assessment as symptomatic of what he called 'hard managerialism'. While 'soft managerialism' saw managerial effectiveness as an important element in the provision of higher education:

> the hard conception elevates institutional and system management to a dominant position in higher education. . . . In this conception management would provide this continuing improvement in quality and efficiency (ie cost) through the establishment of criteria and mechanisms for the continual assessment of the outcomes of educational activities, and the consequent reward and punishment of institutions and primary units of education through formulas linking these assessments to funding.
>
> (Trow, 1994: 13)

In Trow's view such an approach reflected both:

> the withdrawal of trust by government in the academic community, and in its capacity to critically assess its own activities and improve them; and its need to find or create a 'bottom line' that performs the function of a profit and loss sheet for commercial business. This 'bottom line', if it could be found or created, would allow top managers in government departments and funding agencies to identify and assess the strengths and weaknesses of an enterprise (a university), its strong and weak units, and serve as an analytical tool for the continual improvement of the product and the lowering of unit costs.
>
> (Trow, 1994: 14–15)

The 'paradoxical result' of such an approach:

> may well be that vigorous efforts by agencies of central government to assist the quality of university work lead to its decline, as more and more energy is spent on bureaucratic reports, and as university activities themselves begin to adapt to the simplifying tendencies of the quantification of outputs. Our research suggests that departments and individuals shape their activities to what 'counts' in the assessments, to the impoverishment of the life of the university, which is always more complex and varied than assessment of 'outputs' can capture.
>
> (Trow, 1994: 41)

In his response to Professor Trow, published alongside this critique, Dr Paul Clark stated that in his view some form of external evaluation was necessary to ensure trust between higher education and its stakeholders. Assessment was a process of peer review. Through the self-assessment, and other means, the aim was to avoid the creation of a single, standard teaching style. Professor Watson was somewhat less measured: 'One of the phenomena the processes of audit and assessment have uncovered is the belated discovery of responsibilities for quality by managers and senior managers. This has sometimes been followed by an attempt literally to 'paper over' cracks and to scapegoat the external agencies for the deficiencies they have found' (Watson, 1995: 329).

There seems to be little doubt that, along with the RAE, audit and other pressures, assessment has increased the attention given to management and administration within higher education institutions. The QSC evaluation report mentioned, as one consequence of assessment, a trend towards centralization in most of the institutions studied. This, with some important exceptions, was also a feature of the six institutions (four old universities, two new ones) featured in Henkel and Bauer's comparative study of the impact of quality assurance in England and Sweden (Bauer and Henkel, 1997). Another familiar feature was the proliferation of cross-institutional and non-disciplinary academic support units, often with strong connections and roles in quality policies (some academic staff development units of course existed prior to 1992). Partly as a consequence, 'new coordinative, planning, administrative and even management responsibilities' were falling on deans and heads of department. Both assessment and internal quality systems had not only substantially increased the demand for conventional administrative skills and values. They had also raised the profile of administration and the ability of administrators, if they wished, to 'open the black box' of academic decision making and see to it that academics could justify the procedures (or lack of them) that they had.

There are echoes here of a conversation the author had with the vice-chancellor of an old university around the time that assessment was introduced in 1993. When asked why the old universities had not reacted more vigorously to the introduction of assessment, his answer was, 'Previously I wasn't even allowed in my chemistry department. Now through assessment I know just how good they are.'

A lot of what has happened on quality assurance since 1992 can be seen in terms of the internal decision-making structures of institutions. At the same time it is much harder for a vice-chancellor to explain away an audit report, covering as it does the whole institution!

In a series of studies Dr Jethro Newton has looked at the impact of assessment and audit in a large higher education college. This was a college that had done well in both audit and assessment (by SHEFC). However while all concerned agreed that external and internal accountability requirements had been successfully met, there were strong internal divergences of view:

> A variety of factors have been shown to combine to lead front-line academic and academic support staff to take a different view from academic managers and external quality monitoring bodies on the achievements of the quality system. These factors led staff to view the system as more 'accountability-led' than 'improvement-led'. They combined to reduce the level of positive engagement with the system, producing a tendency for procedures to be used instrumentally to 'keep the system running', or ritualistically 'feeding the beast' as one external observer expressed it. In this sense quality assurance systems may become a shield for the purposes of addressing external accountability requirements rather than providing a basis for quality development.
>
> (Newton, 1999: 231; see also Newton, 2000 and 2001, for a detailed view of academics' perception of quality assurance)[8]

Damage to Britain's international reputation for quality

In a speech after the opening of Hong Kong's British Education Exhibition in early 1994, Dr (now Sir) Clive Booth, Vice-Chancellor of Oxford Brookes University, argued that the introduction of a grading system under which only a small proportion of courses were found Excellent would damage Britain's ability to attract overseas students. In response Professor Watson argued that the quality assurance arrangements were 'a lost marketing opportunity': 'All departments are systematically scrutinised by academic peers, points of high achievement are identified, and action taken when they are not performing adequately' (Watson, 1995: 330).

On the basis of the experience with the introduction of the overseas audits (see Chapter 3), the author is inclined to agree with Professor Watson. However Dr Booth also drew attention to the fact that the process by which the various judgements were arrived at had been the subject of widespread criticism. This was less easily dealt with.

The quality of the process

As we have already seen, assessment suffered from two main sets of contra-dictions: one, between its various purposes, notably between accountability (to the funding councils and other external stakeholders) and improvement (a conflict which contributed to the 'ownership' issue); and two, within its accountability purpose, between a fitness for purpose and a fitness of purpose approach. These fundamental contradictions were exacerbated by the Fund-ing Council's decision to retain a graded, rather than a threshold, scale. The general problems of attempting to measure quality of teaching and learning, whether through quantitative performance indicators or grading scales, have been well set out in an important article by Sharp (1995). After comparing scales with two points with those with more than two points, he concluded: 'the result of including a summative quantitative judgement will be that attention will be directed to the very part of the assessment which is least worthy of it, with all this implies for the credibility of the assessment in the eyes of the assessors, the assessed and the consumers of the report' (Sharp, 1995: 314). This is of course exactly what happened!

The differences in outcomes between subjects and institutions that we observed for the 1992–95 period continued, as Table 4.3 (on pp 92–3) (covering England, Northern Ireland and Scotland) shows.

Roger Cook (2003) attributed these to the type of institution where the subjects were chiefly taught (which takes us to the next criticism – see below). He also found a marked underperformance in joint (as opposed to single) subject visits, where subjects were aggregated together (as where business and management were linked with hospitality and tourism). There is a parallel here with the RAE, both exercises confirming the continuing dominance of single discipline values and interests on the part of academic staff, a striking feature of British higher education institutions compared with many American ones.

As regards variations between institutions, Underwood (1998) reviewed complaints from the English Association (1995), the Association of Uni-versity Professors and Heads of French (1995), the Chemical Engineers (no date) and the University Council of Modern Languages (no date). The Funding Council's defence to these inconsistencies was to blame peer review. Here is Dr Clark:

> The third and last question to be highlighted here is the relationship of consistency of judgement to the process of peer review. At the heart of peer review, either in research or in teaching and learning, is the ultimate appeal to the experience and judgement of the people selected as peers, and, therefore the existence of a limit to which any system of peer review can be governed or controlled by a set of rules. A consequence is that there is a limit to the degree of consistency between judgements of different academic programmes in a given

Table 4.3 Grades by subject since 1995

Round	Subject	Average score by type of HEI			
		Pre 92	*Post 92*	*College*	*Average for subject*
1995–6	Chemical engineering	20.67	17.50		20.29
	Dutch	21.00			21.00
	French	20.43	20.80	17.50	20.30
	German and related languages	20.67	18.80		20.31
	Iberian language and studies	20.44	19.20		20.14
	Italian	20.54	19.50		20.40
	Linguistics	20.42	21.00	20.67	20.67
	Modern languages	19.56	19.19	17.67	19.13
	Russian & Eastern European lang. studies	20.27	19.33		20.07
	Scandinavian studies	21.50			21.50
	Sociology	20.85	19.42	19.75	20.09
1995–6 average		**20.50**	**19.45**	**19.13**	**20.06**
1996–8	Agriculture	21.50	19.17	20.57	20.42
	American studies	22.36	20.67	18.60	21.05
	Art and design		21.00		21.00
	Building	20.00	20.64	18.10	19.93
	Chemical engineering	19.33			19.33
	Civil engineering	20.62	20.33	20.00	20.49
	Communication and media studies	21.38	19.68	18.25	19.57
	Drama, dance & cinematics	22.39	20.20	19.71	20.74
	East & South Asian studies	22.29	23.00	20.00	22.11
	Electrical engineering	21.74	19.31	18.33	20.24
	European languages	21.43	19.67		20.90
	Food science	21.00	19.00		19.55
	General engineering	21.47	18.67	16.75	19.89
	History of art	21.74	20.54	21.00	21.22
	Land and property management	21.40	20.63		20.92
	Materials technology	21.32	19.75	21.20	20.91
	Mechanical engineering	21.20	20.25	18.67	20.53
	Middle Eastern and African studies	21.33	22.00		21.43
	Modern languages	20.00			20.00
	Planning and landscape	19.67		17.00	19.00
	Town and country planning	21.83	21.07	17.67	20.83
1996–8 average		**21.47**	**20.02**	**18.99**	**20.43**
1998–2000	Anatomy and physiology	22.64	21.83	22.00	22.38
	Art and design	21.83	21.38	19.95	20.62
	Dentistry	22.73	21.00		22.58
	Mathematics, statistics and OR	21.91	20.86	21.00	21.51
	Medicine	21.50	16.00	20.67	21.14
	Molecular biosciences	22.50	21.65	19.00	22.08
	Nursing	20.90	21.79	21.14	21.37
	Organismal biosciences	22.87	22.50	21.60	22.37
	Other subjects allied to medicine	22.27	21.69	21.10	21.81
	Pharmacology	22.77	22.67	23.00	22.75

Table 4.3 (con'd)

Round	Subject	Average score by type of HEI			
		Pre 92	Post 92	College	Average for subject
	Physics and astronomy	22.82	22.50		22.78
	Psychology	22.71	21.58	20.71	21.88
	Veterinary medicine	23.67		24.00	23.75
1998–2000 average		22.31	21.57	20.54	21.71
2000–1	Archaeology	22.58	22.00	24.00	22.62
	Business and management	22.40	21.86	19.94	20.51
	Celtic studies	23.33		21.00	22.75
	Classics and ancient history	22.72			22.72
	Economics	22.75	21.81		22.46
	Education	23.04	21.81	20.69	21.83
	Hospitality and tourism	22.18	21.56	19.80	20.71
	Librarianship and information man't	22.25	20.60		21.33
	Philosophy	23.48	22.90	23.00	23.31
	Politics	23.14	22.00	21.00	22.68
	Theology and religious studies	22.50	22.17	21.58	22.14
2000–1 average		22.85	21.86	20.18	21.63
Overall average		21.90	20.82	19.97	21.12

Source: Cook, 2001 and 2003
(Reproduced with permission)

subject, much less across subjects, that can be expected of a peer review system. All that can be expected is that the assessment process is carried through in a consistent manner for each provider and that the point is clearly identified where the rules stop and the appeal is made to peer judgement.

(Clark, 1996: 8)

The Funding Council and QAA did in fact introduce a number of mechanisms to increase consistency beyond those already mentioned (the six core aspects and the summary in the *Report on Assessment 1992–95* of the features of 'excellent' provision). These included increased assessor training and guidance, the creation of a new category of reporting assessor (to take charge of assessment visits and to run several assessments in the same subject), and the introduction of an 'institutional facilitator' (a staff member from the same institution, but not an academic from the same subject, as was being assessed) as part of the assessment team. But in contrast to the contemporaneous inspection of FE colleges, there was no systematic moderation of judgements so that, as Simeon Underwood wrote, 'There is no guarantee that an aggregate score or an individual aspect score will have the same value from one visit to the next' (Underwood, 2000: 85)[9]

Table 4.4 Average score per round

Round	Type of institution			
	Pre-1992	Post-1992	College	Grand total
1995–6	20.50	19.45	19.13	20.06
1996–8	21.47	20.02	19.00	20.44
1998–2000	22.31	21.57	20.52	21.70
2000–1	22.85	21.86	20.18	21.63
Overall average	21.90	20.82	19.97	21.12

Source: Cook (2003)
(Reproduced with permission)

Institutional bias

Chapter 2 mentioned the debate in the CDP in 1991 between Professor Watson and Dr Booth, with the former attempting to persuade the Committee that the assessment of teaching would give the polytechnics an edge over the universities and a means of compensating for their lack of competitiveness in research funding. As we saw, however, from 1992 to 1995 the old universities outscored the new universities, which in turn outscored the higher education colleges. This continued after 1995, as Table 4.4 (covering England, Northern Ireland and Scotland) shows. The old universities also gained by far the highest proportion of Excellents and 24s.

In seeking an explanation for the discrepancy in the earlier period, the HEFCE *Report on Assessment 1992–95* looked at three possible correlates with Excellents over the period: high quality research (as measured by the RAE), size of provision, and institutional prosperity (as measured by total income per student). The findings were:

- Over the eight subjects in the first two assessment rounds, 11 per cent of this sample had an RAE rating of 5. Of these (the 11 per cent), 71 per cent achieved a grading of Excellent in TQA. In the third round, 15 per cent of the sample had an RAE rating of 5; of these 97 per cent achieved a grading of Excellent in TQA. Indeed in six of the seven subjects all of the RAE grade 5s achieved a grading of Excellent. In short, a department with a 5 for research appeared to have an extremely good chance of getting an Excellent ranking for its teaching (HEFCE, 1995: 33).
- While subject was important, there was a tendency for excellence to correlate with size: over 55 per cent of the judgements of excellent quality across the eight subjects in the first two rounds were made in respect of provision in the largest 40 per cent of providers (HEFCE, 1995: 34).
- Excellent quality was concentrated in the relatively prosperous institutions. In the first two assessment rounds, 45 per cent of the assessments

carried out in the 20 per cent of institutions with the highest resource levels (measured by total income per student) led to judgements of Excellent. Only 2 per cent of assessments in the 20 per cent of institutions with the lowest resource levels led to judgements of Excellent. In the third round of assessments the broad pattern was maintained (HEFCE, 1995: 35).

Correlation with research performance

The analysis in the HEFCE report used scores from the 1992 RAE. The British Educational Research Association (BERA) has confirmed a broad correlation in the 2001 exercise in England (BERA 2003: 17). Lynn Drennan has confirmed the correlation in Scotland up to and including the 1996 exercise (Drennan, 1999).

HEFCE itself admitted, in giving evidence to a government review of higher education in 1995, that 'There is some evidence from the quality assessment reviews carried out so far that departments most successful in research, and therefore attracting the most research funding, are among the most successful at teaching' (HEFCE, 1995, quoted in Alderman, 1996: 7). Whether the older institutions scored more highly because of the direct link from research in terms of better teaching, or whether the link was indirect, through the fact that institutions more highly rated for research tend to be better resourced (including through the resources won for research, which can then be used to improve the teaching environment – better libraries, better laboratories, better staff–student ratios and so on) we do not know. We seem to have a new version of the three Rs – research, resources and rhetoric.[10]

It is interesting that while the published assessment reports quite often refer to the importance of research to high quality teaching, statements of specific linkages are actually quite hard to find. The *Report on Assessment 1992–95* itself mentions three factors: impact on the curriculum; the likelihood of there being a greater number of staff in the department/school, and the impact this has on tutorial and small group teaching; and the impact of research funds on the depth and quality of library provision and equipment. The last two of these are of course resource-related.

Roger Cook's 2001 analysis of assessment scores between 1998 and 2000 supports the resourcing argument, as does his study of academic review scores in Scotland. As regards the former, all institutions appeared to have weaknesses in Teaching, Learning and Assessment and Quality Management (which tends to be a ragbag category, often used to deflate the overall score). But two of the three largest differences between the pre- and post-1992 universities were in the areas where the absolute level of resources was important – Student Progression ('where they pick the best students' to quote Cook) and Learning Resources (Cook, 2001). As regards the latter, Table 4.5 (on p 96) (covering England and Scotland) is surely conclusive.

Table 4.5 Percentage spread of grades in new Academic Review method

Aspect	Grades	Old	New	College	All
Standards	Confidence	100.0	100.0	92.0	95.2
	No confidence	0.0	0.0	8.0	4.8
Teaching and Learning	Commendable	93.8	76.5	56.0	69.1
	Approved	6.3	23.5	44.0	30.9
	Failing	0.0	0.0	0.0	0.0
Student Progression	Commendable	93.8	52.9	51.0	63.6
	Approved	6.3	47.1	48.0	35.8
	Failing	0.0	0.0	1.0	0.6
Learning Resources	Commendable	95.8	64.7	28.0	51.5
	Approved	4.2	35.3	72.0	48.5
	Failing	0.0	0.0	0.0	0.0

Source: Cook, R (personal communication to the author, May 2003)
(Reproduced with permission)

This shows even more strongly the link between resourcing and grades: 96 per cent of visits to pre-1992 universities produced a 'commendable' for resources, against only 28 per cent of visits to colleges (in this table, mainly FE colleges). Moreover the differences between types of provider are really stark: 83 per cent of pre-1992 institutions got the highest grade possible, compared with 41 per cent of post-1992 institutions and only 16 per cent of colleges.

Correlation with unit size

Some years ago Ron Johnston (1996) demonstrated a strong correlation between size of department and RAE score. Roger Cook, looking at the 2000–2 assessments, found only that very small departments (less than 50 students) tended to be weakest:

> This seems to be mainly related to the grades awarded for Teaching, Learning and Assessment and it may be that the main reason lies in a reliance in informality for such small departments. If this means that they have not developed the structured approach to assessment that is now the expectation then they would have been marked down. However, as it stands, performance by size is also linked to differential subject grades and there is a need for a more detailed statistical analysis to disentangle these various effects.
>
> (Cook, 2003: 100)

Correlation with institutional prosperity

It is interesting that the HEFCE analysis quoted above does not say anything about the Unsatisfactory category. According to Geoffrey Alderman

(1996), a phrase to the effect that the tiny amount of Unsatisfactory 'lies in the lower ranges of AUCF (Average Unit of Council Funding) and institutional income' was included in a draft of the report but omitted in the final version. He also pointed out that when the process was revised, expenditure per student was dropped from the list of statistical indicators used without, apparently, any explanation.

Some time ago David Watson and Rachel Bowden showed the clear and strong correlation between institutional prosperity (again, income from all sources per student) and *The Times* League Table position (the league tables of course rely heavily on RAE and TQA scores) (Watson and Bowden, 1999, 2001). As Dr Peter Knight, Vice-Chancellor of the University of Central England, has said, 'it seems extraordinary that the Funding Council has to have a separate process in order to tell it where its money is spent'.

Value for money

We turn finally to what is perhaps the strongest criticism of assessment, value for money. In his 2002 article, Cook showed how average scores per round increased continually between 1995 and 2001 for those institutions that had been subject to the process throughout. There had also been an increase in the proportion of visits awarding the top grade (24) and a fall in the proportion of grades 2s awarded. The result of this was that 18.5 per cent of providers in the final (2000–1) round got a 24. At the old universities the percentage was 36.4, and a further 30 per cent got a 23. (Cook, 2003: 94; see also Cook and Underwood, 2002).

When challenged on this from time to time, government spokespeople have claimed that the improvement in average scores (from 20.06 in 1995/96 to 21.63 in 2000/01) (21.7 in 1998/00 for all categories of institution) reflects ever-improving quality. While there can be little doubt that assessment has raised quality, there can also be little argument that increasing familiarity with the process has enabled institutions to exploit it.

If any doubts remain on this score, the case of the FE colleges should dispel them. Initially these institutions performed poorly because they were unfamiliar with the process, and many of them were small providers. However scores have gradually risen as they have learnt to play the game (Roger Cook, personal communication to the author, November 2002).

This improvement in quality has been achieved at a price, though. Out of 3,311 assessments, there have been only 35 published fails (Cook, personal communication to the author, May 2003). Was it worth all this effort to gain such an outcome? Alternatively, could such an outcome – that virtually all of the provision in the sector is of acceptable quality – not have been obtained more economically? Could the resources expended not have been put to better use? The answer to both questions must surely be 'yes'. As this book shows, quality assurance in UK HE since 1992 has had many ironies. Not the least of them is that a process which was basically about improving efficiency in the use of resources should itself have been such a poor use of resources!

For a last word on assessment, let us refer again to Simeon's 2000 article:

> A third conclusion is that the Funding Councils, who are the primary stakeholders in the sense that they are paying for the exercise, are probably getting least out of it. The stated purpose which is most closely associated with them is the one which is furthest from being met. They would be justified in asking whether they are getting value for money from the exercise; the government would be justified in asking whether they are meeting their statutory obligations.
>
> A fourth conclusion is that the institutions and the academic staff within them, who are the most hostile to the exercise, are, paradoxically, probably benefiting from it the most. The exercise itself and the enhancement it is effecting are giving the institutions material with which to counter criticisms of the quality of their provision. This may also put them on a better footing to deal with the growth in complaints and litigation which may follow from the new student consumerism.
>
> (Underwood, 2000: 88)

Graded assessments at subject level were to continue until Academic Review was swept away by Mr Blunkett's announcement in March 2001. Even with the benefit of hindsight it is extraordinary that the Funding Council (and behind it the Department) clung so tenaciously and for so long to such a limited process. Even now its shadow lays over the new quality framework, rather like that of Count Orlok's in the original *Nosferatu*, as we shall see in Chapter 6.

Assessment in Scotland and Wales

Although it was the Government's original intention that assessment should proceed on broadly the same lines in each part of the UK, divergence inevitably, and quickly, took place.

Like England, Scotland went for a three-point graded scale at the outset, then (from 1993–4) for a four-point scale. Unlike England there was an explicit link with funding. The same bias in favour of the older institutions was apparent as in England. However the problems of quality, and especially consistency in judgements between providers, were not as severe north of the border. This was partly because of the much smaller scale, which meant that the same panel could be used for each review, with members dropping out when their own institutions were being assessed. Also there was much less willingness to criticize the Funding Council as being a newly Scottish creation. It is therefore paradoxical that the Scots should most recently have embraced what is described as an 'enhancement-led' assurance process (see Chapter 7).

In Wales too the scale of the provision made it much easier to manage the process. However what was distinctive in Wales was the much greater emphasis given to quality improvement and to a genuine partnership at all levels, something largely lacking in England. From the outset the Funding Council sought to involve institutions in the design of the process. Some attempts were even made to get away from a single summative judgment about the quality of provision, but the Higher Education Funding Council for Wales (HEFCW) retained the descriptors 'Excellent', 'Satisfactory' and 'Unsatisfactory' so as to keep in step with England. Evaluations by Lewis Elton (1996) and Jethro Newton (1997) both commended aspects of the Welsh process, and particularly the attempt to get away from sharp, absolute judgments towards seeing quality in qualitative terms. Sadly, the success of the Welsh approach had little impact elsewhere, as we shall shortly see.

Notes

1 Whereas in Scotland institutions obtaining 'excellent' in the subject area received an additional 5 per cent of funded student places for the successful department, in England the only explicit use that was made of assessment scores was in relation to the Fund for the Development of Teaching and Learning from 1995, where the lead department in a consortium had to have an excellent. (The irony of institutions that were already highly rated getting additional funds to improve still further will be apparent.) This was not repeated when the Teaching Quality Enhancement Fund was established in 1999. The main reason for this coyness was lack of confidence in the robustness of the judgments.
2 The six core aspects were to be:

   - curriculum design, content and organisation;
   - teaching, learning and assessment;
   - student progression and achievement;
   - student support and guidance;
   - learning resources;
   - quality assurance and enhancement [later changed to quality management].

                                      (Circular 39/94, para 29: HEFCE, 1994: 9)

3 The Agency realized that the numbers were simply being totalled and the full profile ignored. The graded profile proposed would also have enabled it to show slightly more 'failing' provision (Simeon Underwood, personal communication to the author).
4 Another view would be that institutions were simply replicating external processes internally.
5 One other benefit was to highlight certain less well-regarded aspects of provision. For example, a correspondent at the University of the West of England Bristol has commented how the inclusion of student support and guidance raised the profile of this activity (personal communication to the author, November 2002).
6 When reporters for the *Times Higher* asked about the costs of the new Academic Review process when this was unveiled in February 2000, a QAA spokeswoman replied, 'Oh it is much too early to be talking about that'.
7 Following the PA Consulting report, HEFCE established a forum to discuss ways of streamlining institutions' accountability. This work was eventually taken

over by the Better Regulation Review Group (see Chapter 6). A more legitimate institutional complaint has been the direct and opportunity costs and distortions and indeed wasted work arising from the conflicting claims of the various cognate external quality assurance processes: not only audit and assessment but also professional bodies of accreditation, the Teacher Training Agency, the NHS and so on. As we shall see, HEQC, HEFCE and QAA all made efforts in this area, but so far the results have been relatively meagre, mainly because of the reluctance of the agencies concerned to pool their sovereignty.

8 Morley (2003) makes a similar point in her study of quality and power in HE, where she uncovers the ways in which quality is experienced by academics and managers. There seems to be a general agreement that overall external quality assurance has led to greater centralization of power within institutions. There is less consensus on whether this is a good thing (Brown, 1998b). The quality agency itself is not entirely consistent. John Randall (QAA Chief Executive from 1997 to 2001 – see below) was fond of quoting Loughborough as an example of a successful university in quality terms, and indeed its assessment scores reflect this, with the fifth highest aggregate score (22.69), reflecting high scores in each round. Yet the continuation audit report in 1998 questions the decentralized structure that produced these results (personal communications with Simeon Underwood and Roger Cook, May 2003).

9 Similar points about lack of consistency are made by Allen (1993), Larrington and Lindsay (2002), and Cockrell (personal communication to the author, November 2002). Underwood also made the point that:

> just as the gradings are not moderated, the textual material in the report is left very much up to the teams themselves, with a small amount of help from the QAA office in final drafting and preparation for publication. An immediate result of this is that the data which appear in the reports, for example on progression within and withdrawal from programmes, are not necessarily consistent from one report to the next. Again there is a contrast here with the further education inspection reports, which produce data on the institution concerned to a standard format in a final annex.
>
> (Underwood, 2000: 85)

10 In a paper presented to the Eighth International Conference on Assessing Quality in Higher Education in 1996, Geoffrey Alderman commented:

> Assessors from the old universities reacted against the culture of compliance with which the HEFCE had confronted them; instead, ignoring what had been said in the self-assessments, they made judgements based on the reputations of the teachers in each institution visited, the resources which the institution was able to deploy, and the extent to which students were exposed to the research undertaken by their teachers. Assessors from the new universities – the former polytechnics – cast approving eyes over the generous resources they observed in the old universities, and the research-led teaching which they witnessed. They reacted not with jealousy as much as with admiration.
>
> (Alderman, 1996)

5 The creation of the single system

In his opening remarks the Chairman referred to the burden of accountability now placed on higher education institutions suggesting that this had gone too far and that current arrangements for audit and assessment were an example of this. He challenged the Group to see the task before it as devising machinery which could be in place in 10 years time and would stand to the credit of the Group.

(Introduction by Sir William Kerr Fraser,
Chairman of the Joint Planning Group: JPG, 1996a: 1)

Introduction

Almost as soon as the Further and Higher Education Act 1992 was on the Statute Book, concerns were being raised by the sector about the new quality arrangements. In December 1992 the *Times Higher Education Supplement* declared that 'quality assurance arrangements are going wrong' (*THES*, 11 December 1992). The *Higher* began what it called the 'quality debate'. In January 1993 it published the results of a survey of vice-chancellors in which 82 per cent of respondees condemned the new arrangements as 'too bureaucratic' (*THES*, 1993).

It is hardly surprising therefore that in discussion at the vice-chancellors' residential conference in September 1993 there was some support for a move towards a single system of quality assurance: a single quality process administered by a single agency. Just over three years later, in December 1996, the Joint Planning Group (JPG) reported on how such a system could be established. The Quality Assurance Agency for Higher Education (QAA) was incorporated on 27 March 1997 and took over HEQC's functions on 1 August 1997. The assessment staff of the English and Welsh Funding Councils were transferred on 1 October 1997. This chapter describes how all this occurred.

There were four main phases:

* between September 1993 and December 1994, when the Secretary of State agreed to a review of the 1992 arrangements;

- between December 1994 and September 1995, when agreement was reached between the main parties on the way forward;
- between September 1995 and December 1996, when the JPG final report was published;
- between December 1996 and August 1997, when the QAA was established and the Dearing Committee reported.

September 1993 to December 1994

Reference has already been made to Leslie Wagner's contemporaneous analysis of the reasons for the vice-chancellors' revolt, and in particular his point that it was difficult to see how the fundamental purpose of assessment – to relate funding to quality – could be achieved. However in Leslie's view the revolt also reflected the cost and complexity of the new arrangements:

> Compared to what they had experienced prior to 1992 or were anticipating, their perception of agreed complexity and cost to themselves was correct. Most of the older universities had not yet experienced an audit from their own Academic Audit Unit and had no experience of HMI or other assessments other than that of the professional bodies. The ex-polytechnics thought they had seen off the CNAA in receiving their new titles and degree-awarding powers. Most had received the visit which led to accreditation in the late 1980's and CNAA involvement in their affairs had fallen away in the early 1990's. Her Majesty's Inspectorate still carried out subject visits but these were sporadic and also began to recede following the 1991 White Paper. The PCFC made quality judgements but they did not involve visits or the submission of any significant paperwork. For both old and new universities therefore, the arrangements introduced in 1992/93 came as a major shock.
>
> (Wagner, 1993: 280)

Moreover:

> While the cost to institutions of the new arrangements has increased significantly the cost to the government has been reduced. The CNAA, in its final year, had an annual budget of some £7 million. The Higher Education Quality Council will receive £2.5 million of these funds as a contribution to its work. The remainder of its funds will come from contributions the old universities previously made to the Academic Audit Unit and income for services for example, on advising the Government on Degree Awarding Powers. Its total budget is less than half of that of the CNAA. No figure has been published for the cost to the Funding Councils of their quality assessment work but it is unlikely to be more than the cost of the former HMI system which has now been abolished

for higher education. In effect therefore, the costs of the quality assurance arrangements have been transferred from the government and its agencies to the universities.

(Wagner, 1993: 280–81)

As we saw in Chapter 4, the overall cost of the new arrangements was actually tiny in relation to the total expenditure on teaching. Nevertheless the new arrangements were proving to be very controversial. Not surprisingly therefore the September CVCP residential conference at Leicester had, as one of its main agenda items, 'accountability for teaching quality'. As background there were two briefing papers, one prepared by the CVCP office highlighting the issues, and drawing on a survey of 64 institutions (this has already been referred to in Chapter 4), the other on Total Quality Management (TQM) by Sir Frederick Crawford, Vice-Chancellor of Aston University and a noted authority on quality.

The office paper put the concerns about the costs of quality assurance into perspective but stated, 'Where institutions have commented on the future shape of external quality assurance arrangements, opinion is divided between those who wish to see an enhanced role for HEQC, operating significantly developed procedures, together with Funding Council activity responding to public concerns, and those who believe that a single body would be preferable on cost grounds' (paper for main committee meeting 21–23 Sept 1993, para 27: CVCP, 1993: 7). Sir Frederick's paper (written in 1991) advocated the adoption of TQM at all levels in the universities as being preferable to an attempt to link institutional funding to quality assessment outcomes.

At the conference vice-chancellors divided into groups to discuss the issue. The report of the discussions to the plenary session indicated 'a strong preference' for audit and assessment to be carried out by a single agency: 'Coordination of the two processes within a single agency should minimise duplication, costs and disruption caused by separate processes of audit and assessment, and possibly also of accreditation. Many departments and institutions have cyclical internal reviews; it would be helpful if external audit and assessment could be synchronised with them' (CVCP, 1993: 5).

Opinion at the plenary was less clear cut. Whilst some vice-chancellors spoke in favour of a single body, others worried about the possible implications for institutional sovereignty. For example, the Director of the London School of Economics, Professor John Ashworth, said that while a single agency was logical, universities must distrust any single body dominated by government or its agency. The funding councils implemented government policy. There could be a loss of control over the institutions' major professional responsibility and concern: 'governments always play politics with such things'.

Summing up the discussion, the new Chair, Dr Kenneth Edwards, Vice-Chancellor of Leicester, who had earlier spoken of 'the strong support for a single agency', said (according to the author's notes) that there was agreement that the universities should look for a single agency but with considerable input from institutions. The idea should be worked up in more detail, taking account of the separate evaluations then in progress of both audit and assessment (see Chapters 3 and 4). The Vice-Chancellor of Aston would be asked to lead a task force for this purpose.[1]

The Crawford group included vice-chancellors representing both the funding councils' assessment activities and HEQC. There were a series of reports to the main committee, the first identifying a number of principles that quality assurance should meet, the second commenting on how various existing processes scored against them. This report set out very clearly some of the strengths and weaknesses of the existing arrangements, but did not offer a means of combining them, mainly because it seemed clear that the Funding Council was not prepared to relax its control over assessment, or see any significant changes to the process.

In any event the group's work was overtaken by the renewed interest in academic standards shown by the Secretary of State in the spring of 1994, which culminated in his speech to the HEFCE conference at Keele in April (see Chapter 3). Dr Edwards, who was already losing patience with the Crawford group, felt strongly that CVCP must be seen to be responding vigorously to the Government. In his letter to the Secretary of State in June 1994, after outlining the various steps the sector (in practice HEQC) would be taking to clarify the position on standards, Dr Edwards stated, 'The aim in the medium term shall be to create a single agency with responsibility for all aspects of quality assurance; this could be a reconstituted HEQC so that the interests of appropriate external stakeholders are represented (Edwards, 1994).[2]

In the meantime, the letter proposed an audit-based quality process whereby, where an HEQC audit gave rise to concerns about standards at an institution, there would be a follow-up assessment on a subject/programme basis in which the Funding Council would normally be involved. The distinction between quality and standards that underlay the post-1992 arrangements was already becoming blurred.

December 1994 to September 1995

Although the June statement took account of the Crawford group discussions, it was essentially the work of Dr Edwards. His efforts were rewarded when the new Secretary of State, Mrs Gillian Shephard MP, announced to the CVCP Committee on 2 December 1994 that she had asked the HEFCE Chief Executive, Professor (now Sir) Graeme Davies, to report to her on ways in which audit and assessment might be brought together to create a single system, taking account of the views of the representative bodies. The speech specified a number of requirements of any system of quality assurance that would be acceptable to the Government.

The main ones were to provide 'assurance that standards of degrees are maintained and are broadly comparable – which does not mean identical – and also that the quality of teaching and learning is such that students have the best opportunity of reaching those standards'. The Government also wanted the process of external quality assurance to be 'transparent so that it can assist in enabling choices to be made':

- choices by universities and colleges themselves in deploying their resources in full knowledge of their strengths and weaknesses;
- choices by potential students about university and course;
- choices by employers in recruiting graduates;
- choices also in the deployment of public funds both by the Government and the Funding Council.

There were 'of course' other requirements as well. External quality assurance arrangements 'must respect academic autonomy while having an external element. It must respect academic diversity and freedom while at the same time addressing value for money and public accountability. It should encourage the enhancement of quality and the dissemination of good practice. Last but not least, it should be cost-effective and avoid unreasonable burdens on institutions' (Shephard, 1994).

It is still not entirely clear what led to this concession, since hitherto the Government had stood firmly behind the dual system, indeed Mr Patten's Keele speech earlier in the year had talked of 'the prime purpose of having your own organisation in place to safeguard academic standards' (were the vice-chancellors listening?). Among the factors that almost certainly played a part were a wish by the government to be conciliatory towards the sector, as part of the general move to pacify the entire education system following the turbulence associated with Mrs Shepherd's predecessor (which reached its climax with the revolt over the Key Stage 4 English tests); increased recognition of the demands that the various external accountability processes had placed upon institutions; and the fact that assessment linked to funding had been conceived before the era of consolidation (see Chapter 4).

Early in February 1995 Professor Davies sent the CVCP chair and vice-chair an initial, confidential draft of ideas for creating a single system, and this was discussed at a private meeting in mid-February. The paper proposed that there should be no second round of institutional audits: 'monitoring of audit processes' would be incorporated within assessments. Assessment should continue unchanged until 2000 but before then discussions could commence about eventual 'internalisation'. The meeting was quite heated. The CVCP representatives expressed very strong reservations and the document was formally withdrawn: it was agreed between those present that there had been no paper and no meeting!

A month later Professor Davies produced a second draft. This became known as the 'Options Paper' because it set out a number of ways in which a single system could be created. Six of these were assessment-based, one audit-based. The paper considered that if a proper level of public accountability and information was to be achieved through quality assurance, only an assessment-based option would do. The paper did however indicate a willingness to consider some internal membership of assessment teams and to operate assessment with a 'lighter touch' (as far as can be discovered this was the first time that this fateful phrase was used). After the current round, institutional audit would only occur where a pattern of weaknesses was identified through assessment, or at the request of an institution.

The Options Paper was circulated to CVCP Council members, some of whom welcomed HEFCE's willingness to embrace greater internal involvement in assessment. It was discussed at a meeting with CVCP officers (Chair and Secretary) at which, at the Funding Council's suggestion, John Stoddart and the author were also present. Considerable reservations were registered by both HEQC and CVCP, but it was left that the Committee would submit a detailed critique and possibly counterproposals. In the event the CVCP main committee a day or so later decided that there should be a more firmly rejectionist stance. The CVCP critique, and some counterproposals drafted in the office, were therefore never sent. The author's main recollection of the meeting is surprise and dismay at the lack of trust, bordering on contempt, that the Funding Council representatives appeared to have in the institutions.[3]

Because of the late arrival of the HEFCE document it had not been possible to circulate it to vice-chancellors. CVCP was therefore rejecting a paper that only a minority (the Council members) had seen. So CVCP requested that the paper should be circulated to all institutions and that time should be found to discuss it at the HEFCE conference early the following month. This was agreed.

The conference (at Warwick) was mainly notable for two things. First, the Department showed its hand publicly for the first time, with the Minister for Higher Education (Mr Boswell) warning that the consequence of failure to agree on a new system would be the continuation of the present one. It was in this speech that he made a mocking reference to the inability of some of the best minds in the country to reach agreement on a matter of such great importance to them. Second, the discussion revealed the very considerable gulf between the Funding Council and many vice-chancellors. Some of these criticized, in trenchant terms, not only the proposals but also the way in which the consultation had been conducted by the Funding Council. The HEFCE subsequently circulated its proposals for general comment. A wide range of responses was received. It was becoming clear that while some institutions, mainly the older ones, could 'live with' assessment if it was modified to allow for a greater degree of internal involvement, other institutions, mostly the newer ones, favoured a process based much more directly on the internal processes they had developed under CNAA.

Dr Edwards was not present at the conference. However he subsequently wrote to the Funding Council with fresh proposals. These were for subject-based evaluations of teaching quality conducted by institutions, with external members accredited and approved by a single agency. The agency would be jointly owned by institutions and external stakeholders (of whom the chief would be the funding councils) together with independent members.

In putting these ideas forward, Dr Edwards made it clear that he was acting in a personal capacity. Nevertheless, although one or two members were unhappy, the CVCP Council at its next meeting on 12 May endorsed them. The HEFCE Quality Assessment Committee also reacted positively. On 24 May CVCP and HEFCE jointly issued a press release announcing that the funding council at its meeting on 17 May had welcomed the proposals, and had agreed that they provided a basis for further discussions.

It was therefore widely expected that the Funding Council's formal sub-mission to the Secretary of State, originally expected by the end of March but now planned for the end of May, would either incorporate these ideas or at least make a substantial move in their direction. But the document that resulted, while it contained some moves in CVCP's direction, notably a recognition for the first time that the Funding Council could contract out the management of assessment to another agency (as was anyway clearly envis-aged in the Act), was fundamentally unchanged in rejecting institutional control of assessment. Nevertheless Dr Edwards was prepared to recommend acceptance of the proposals to the main committee. The briefing note that the CVCP office prepared for the chair's use at the meeting mentioned the names of one or two supportive vice-chancellors and suggested calling them early in the debate. In the event, after the chair's introduction every vice-chancellor called to speak spoke strongly against the document. Indeed but for the presence of one or two vice-chancellors who were also members of the Funding Council, the proposals would have been rejected unanimously. The Committee agreed that the time had now come for CVCP to put its own ideas forward.[4]

The HEQC's position

Discussions had been going on within HEQC from November 1994 on-wards on ways in which audit and assessment could be combined so as to meet the requirements for a single process laid down in the Secretary of State's speech. The main conclusion was that, to create an effective single process, it would be necessary to get behind the existing ones, and to design a genuinely new mechanism, one which would better fulfil the underlying objectives and purposes which each of the existing processes was intended to serve.

In February 1995 the HEQC Board received a report on developments. Formally the matters under discussion were outside the Council's remit because they concerned the policy 'envelope' within which the council was working: this was, strictly speaking, a matter for the parent bodies. Nevertheless the HEQC was legally independent, and there were concerns that since the discussions would almost certainly affect the Council's future, the parent bodies should at least be fully aware of the range of matters with which the council now dealt. The result was a specially prepared briefing paper for CVCP and SCOP setting out the details of the Council's work up to that point.

The Board's next meeting at the end of April took place almost immediately after Dr Edwards' personal initiative. By now the Board, and particularly its independent members, were beginning to be seriously concerned at the direction the debate was taking. Quite apart from the possible implications for HEQC, the Board was concerned, first, at the way in which the discussion of new supervisory arrangements was already running ahead of the discussion of process; and second, at the extent to which institutions' internal arrangements for quality assurance were being discounted. The board therefore decided that the Council should set out its own thoughts about the issues to be taken into account in designing a single system, drawing on the Council's experience. This document was sent to the parent bodies, the Funding Councils and the relevant government departments in early May. It was never acknowledged.

The main point in the Council's document was that the most important test of any external approach to quality assurance was the extent to which it led to improvement. Since there were anyway certain matters that could only be resolved by the academic community, the basic approach could only be self-regulation but with some degree of external oversight. At the same time institutions should publish sufficient information about the quality and standards of their provision to enable students and others to make informed choices about the courses and awards on offer. Such information should include the stated objectives for learning achievement or programme results, and the nature and level of the associated awards (this reflected the Graduate Standards Programme findings). A single system should monitor the accuracy of this information and of the claims based upon it. At the same time, it was not necessary, desirable or even feasible for the activities of a single process to extend to every individual course, award or unit. The underlying concept was that a single system should bring together the main elements of external quality assurance – institutional review, the evaluation of teaching and learning, enhancement and networking – into an integrated whole. This has of course still to be achieved!

By the time of the next board meeting, in early July, matters had moved on again. HEFCE had published proposals, on which the Council had not been consulted, which involved the transfer of functions, staff and resources from HEQC. The Board took the view that since HEQC was now directly affected by the discussions, whether it liked it or not, it should go a step further and publish its own proposals. There was also at least the implication not only that CVCP was not giving sufficient support to the HEQC, but that it was not sufficiently appreciative of – perhaps had even overlooked – the purposes for which HEQC had been established by the CVCP, CDP and SCOP, namely to provide a vehicle for the *sector* to exert collective control over quality and standards as a way of protecting institutional autonomy from the government and the funding council.

The council's proposals were published on 14 July 1995. They envisaged a tiered system of internal reviews of programme providers, each involving two external assessors appointed or approved by an external agency alongside internals, together with external reviews of institutions, leading to a published institutional quality profile. In other words, institutions would conduct their own internal assessments, with external inputs, and the agency would then review the effectiveness of those processes via periodic institutional review. The assessments would cover academic standards but would not lead to any gradings. This is more or less what has now been agreed in Scotland! (See Chapter 6.)

A week later CVCP published its formal proposals. These were for a dual process of institutional audit and subject assessment, where the assessments would be carried out by teams drawn from both within and outside the institution. These would be carried out by a new agency which should have 'demonstrable independence' from the government and its agencies and be 'led by the sector'. To ensure comparability of outcomes, the Funding Council could require the setting of the framework for negotiations with individual institutions over the cycle of reviews, allowing as much flexibility as possible over the precise timing and form, leading to a published, graded quality profile. Having contracted the task of assessment to the agency, the Funding Council would retain the right and capability to carry out its own scrutiny if it were not satisfied with the outcome of a single process in any institution. The agency would also have 'a comprehensive remit' to carry out the wider functions currently performed by HEQC, including quality enhancement.

The covering letter to the Secretary of State stated:

> It is common ground between CVCP and HEFCE that there should be a genuine partnership in designing and conducting a single process reaching to the point of delivery of programmes and courses; that this should be closely coordinated with professional accreditation where relevant, and preferably integrated with it; a single agency; a combination of internal and external reviews; flexibility in respect to the precise timing, and the definition, of the subject or programme areas to be assessed; and some form of joint planning group as the best way to carry these ideas into effect. . . . We believe that our proposals form a basis for a single review within institutional subject or programme areas which meets both internal and external needs.
>
> (Edwards and Roberts, 1995)

In September 1995 Mrs Shephard wrote welcoming CVCP's proposals and accepting that they could form the basis for an agreed solution. It would be important to establish the costs and benefits of the proposed arrangements, and to compare those with present costs and benefits. However while there were advantages in basing quality assurance on measures taken by individual institutions, 'in respect of assessment at least, I could not contemplate a solution which relied mainly on self-regulation'. There was also 'a particular concern' about linking quality assessment with the cycle of reviews for each institution, if this meant that the assessment of particular subject areas would take place over a lengthy cycle. 'That would not offer the benefits of comparability for the Funding Council, potential students and employers and hence would weaken accountability. To that end I believe that the cycle for individual subjects should not exceed two years in length' (Shephard, 1995).

This continuing mistrust of institutional quality control, together with the overriding preoccupation with comparisons between institutions (an issue already highlighted in the discussion of assessment in Chapter 4), would necessarily place a severe constraint on the ability of a single system to integrate audit and assessment, as will shortly be seen.

September 1995 to October 1997

The Joint Planning Group (JPG) was established by CVCP and HEFCE. Its main job was to develop detailed proposals for a new agency and to produce an agreed implementation plan, the aim being to establish the new agency by January 1997. The group was required to have regard to a range of reference material (ironically, and insultingly, this did not include the HEQC proposals). The group had an independent Chair, Sir William Kerr Fraser, former Vice-Chancellor of the University of Glasgow and previously Permanent Secretary at the Scottish Office. It otherwise consisted of representatives from CVCP, SCOP, HEFCE, COSHEP, the Northern Ireland Higher Education Council and the Higher Education Funding Council for Wales. The Scottish Higher Education Funding Council provided an observer (who subsequently played an important part in the discussion). To keep an eye on things there were also assessors (arguably, minders) from the relevant government departments.[5]

HEQC was not represented in its own right, but John Stoddart was one of the CVCP representatives and HEQC provided a member of the joint CVCP/HEFCE Secretariat. However, neither Dr Clark nor the author was ever invited to attend any of its meetings, although Dr Clark was a member of a sub-group (see below). HEQC's role and expertise was further downgraded by its being listed among the 'other groups' with whom in its initial terms of reference the group might consult 'as seems appropriate' (and after a whole swathe of other, and less relevant, bodies). So much for the

Council's efforts to implement and defend self-regulation on behalf of the sector!

The group's first meeting was in January 1996, its last meeting in November 1996. These were preceded by preparatory meetings, a so-called 'quality forum', between CVCP and HEFCE (represented by their respective chair and chief executive) on the one hand, and the individual agencies on the other, notably HEQC and the HEFCE Assessment Division. It was not clear to the author then, and it still is not clear now, what purpose these meetings achieved beyond prolonging the agony for all those involved. Surely CVCP and HEFCE already knew, or should have known, all that their respective organizations were doing, and could have shared this knowledge if they had wished?

The JPG's first meeting had before it a paper commissioned from Dr Clark and myself in effect proposing an agenda for its work: as just indicated, this was almost the extent of our direct involvement in the group's discussions! As the extract from the minutes of the start of the chapter shows, the Chair challenged the group to see the task before it as devising machinery that could be in place in 10 years' time and which would stand to its credit. The piquancy of this will rapidly become apparent. Most of the discussion then concerned the structure, funding and role of the new agency, and the transfer of existing staff to it.

The second meeting in February had two papers about process. The first, by the Secretariat, outlined an 'integrated' quality assurance process. There would be two elements. The first was subject/programme area review much along the existing lines but extended to cover how the department/unit concerned identified and confirmed the achievement of appropriate standards of attainment for the relevant awards (pending sector-wide agreement on benchmarks). The second was institutional review (that is, audit). The second paper, by the Director of Quality Assessment for Wales, had more of a developmental flavour and favoured internal reviews of areas determined by institutions being conducted by mixed teams of assessors from within and outside the institution, leading to jointly signed-off, published reports; institutional reviews would continue as before. The group was quite taken with the idea of mixed teams, and there was also support for the idea of looking at greater flexibility of timing (within the two-year period laid down by Ministers) and at the aggregation of subjects for review.

The third meeting in March was again mainly concerned with the new agency. It was agreed that it should be a company limited by guarantee with the representative bodies as the members: the legal advice at that stage was that the funding councils could not be members because the agency's functions would go beyond their statutory powers. (This subsequently changed.) The board should consist of 15 directors: in addition to the chief executive, four directors should be selected from nominations made by the representative bodies acting together, and four from nominations by the participating funding councils and Department of Education for Northern Ireland (DENI) acting together. The balance would be provided by six 'independent' members (persons knowledgeable about issues of quality and standards and not currently holding remunerated posts in any higher education institution) (JPG, 1996a: para 3.3.f). After the first board subsequent appointments should be made by the Board itself, including the chair. The agency would be funded through a combination of institutional subscriptions and Funding Council grants. A proposal from John Stoddart that to save time and money the agency might be created by simply adapting HEQC was rejected. Finally, the meeting agreed to establish a working party under Professor David Watson to work up some ideas about the new process to build on the discussion at the February meeting. The working party would include some colleagues from the sector chosen on a personal basis as well as Dr Clark and Peter Williams, Director of Quality Audit at HEQC.

In the meantime, and following discussion at its fourth meeting in April, the group published its first report. This proposed that the purposes of quality assurance in higher education should be to:

a.   Facilitate quality improvement through the sharing of good practice and innovation.
b.   Enable the higher education funding bodies and the institutions to discharge their statutory responsibilities for public accountability.
c.   Provide timely and accessible public information, on a consistent and comparable basis, on the quality and standards of the educational provision for which each institution takes responsibility.
d.   Ensure that any unacceptable provision is speedily addressed.

(JPG, 1996b: 4)

There then followed a description of a process very much on the lines of the Secretariat paper but with the following potential benefits as compared to the status quo:

a.   Engagement with a single agency and a consistent contact point, reduction in 'transaction costs'.
b.   One published external programme and timetable, allowing institutions to plan more effectively over a longer time period, and allowing for the maximum coordination with internal processes (for example, departmental reviews).
c.   The greater part to be played by institutional self-evaluation.
d.   The participation of an institutional observer or institutional members in the work of external review teams.
e.   Subject/programme area review data providing the basis for institution-wide review, maximising the quality enhancement potential.

f.   The potential for increasing the existing scope for negotiation with institutions (for example, team composition, timing of reviews, aggregation of subjects).

g.   The explicit integration of standards issues with quality issues, thus resolving an area of some confusion and uncertainty in current external subject review.

(JPG, 1996b: 8)

Institutional reactions to the report were almost universally critical. Many felt that the basic issues had been ducked, and that there was little prospect either of reducing the quality assurance burden or of getting better value from the resources invested. Despite the rhetoric there was no sign of greater weight being given to institutional self-evaluation. There was also concern that although the single agency's remit included the scrutiny of institutional standards, the funding councils would be represented on the board while institutional representatives were in a minority. There were also criticisms of the procedure for finding the first chair (which one institution described as 'undemocratic'), and for appointing board members subsequently. Finally, questions were raised by one or two respondents about the agency's account-ability: to whom would it be accountable?

Reflecting on these responses at the fifth meeting in May, the Chair outlined a process whereby heads of institution would agree with the agency the units for review in their institution. The head would appoint teams composed of internal and external assessors to review each unit, and the teams would report to him/her. The report would be sent on to the agency, with the institution's comments. The agency would then decide whether the report was adequate. If it judged that it was not, it could choose to send in its own team. At the end of the subject/programme review cycle there would be an institution-wide review. But the Chair accepted that while this could reduce burdens and cost, it would be unlikely to deliver the consistency of process and comparability of differentiated outcomes that was needed by the funding bodies to allocate funding. It was not therefore pursued.

Professor Watson then reported on the work of his sub-group. This had come up with the idea of a six-to-eight-year institutional quality assurance 'plan', agreed between each institution and the agency. This would give a measure of control to institutions in the planning, timing and number of reviews, within a published national framework. There might be roughly the same number of units for assessment as hitherto, but subjects would be brigaded in two-year blocks so as to facilitate grouping and aggregation. Institutions would map all their provision onto the overall structure and timetable, and would agree this mapping with the agency. This would enable subject/programme reviews to reflect internal structures and priorities. As regards mixed teams, the group favoured having internal observers rather than internal members. Finally, institutional review would focus on an institution's management of quality, with subject/programme area review reports as the main source of evidence.

The working party's report was a major item for discussion at the sixth meeting in June. The report was generally welcomed, although the departmental assessor said that the Department would have reservations about a substantial reduction in the intensity of visitation by external teams because it would affect the value to students of the comparative information on provision. (Chapter 4 offered an appreciation of this 'value'.) The group also had before it a letter from Professor (now Sir) Gareth Roberts (a member, Vice-Chancellor of Sheffield and by now CVCP Chair). This expressed concern that institutions would fail to find the reassurance on costs and burdens that they sought. A 'strong signal' was needed, such as a reduction in the number of units for assessment to, perhaps, the 12 academic subject categories used for funding purposes. Professor Roberts was also concerned that institutions should see a greater degree of management of the process in their own hands, for example by selecting the members of the review team from an approved list. He also sought a broader, if less intensive, institution-wide review which would focus on the general educational health of the institution. The group then moved on to identify the main issues that would need to be addressed in its next report.

The group's next meeting was on 19 July. Prior to that meeting the CVCP Chief Executive, Baroness Warwick, concerned like her Chair about the institutional reaction to the group's proposals, took a personal initiative with a small group of vice-chancellors on or close to the group. The basic idea was that as well as negotiating with the agency how their sub-institutional provision should be assessed, institutions should have the option to go for a self-managed assessment process, as an alternative to an externally managed one, if the agency agreed. She also expressed doubts about the arguments in favour of institution-wide review. If such review was needed at all it could be done by private consultancy firms or the British Standards Institute, while HEQC's enhancement role could be taken forward by CVCP outside the quality assurance arena!

Accordingly the main paper for the July meeting contained no reference to the new agency's enhancement function, and asked whether institution-wide review should be universal or optional, and whether it could not be carried out by agents other than the new agency. John Stoddart, who was unable to get to the meeting, protested vigorously that these questions went against the group's agreement at a much earlier stage that the new agency should take over all of HEQC's functions, and that institutional-level review was essential if the new process was to scrutinize standards. Nevertheless most of those present at the meeting agreed that institution-wide review might not need to be undertaken on a universal basis. (The Scottish Higher Education Funding Committee (SHEFC) 'observer', Professor John Sizer, had already spoken strongly against audit at an earlier meeting.)

There then followed an intensive behind the scenes lobbying exercise in which a letter from Professor Peter Bush, Deputy Vice-Chancellor of Glasgow Caledonian University and the Northern Ireland Higher Education Council representative on the group, was particularly influential. This expressed strong doubts as to whether subject/programme-level review could embrace the wide range of matters covered by audits, such as off-campus provision. But in any case, institutional-level scrutiny was needed because it was institutions that awarded degrees, not departments or subjects.

As a result of this lobbying by Peter and others, the draft final report which was circulated to institutional heads in September contained the statement that 'a substantial majority of us consider that all institutions should be subject to an institution-wide review once in each eight year cycle'. It also proposed that 'all' of HEQC's functions should transfer to the new agency. The introduction contained the following statement:

> We are sensitive to the criticism that what we propose might be rep-resented as simply a continuation of audit and assessment but under a single body. We do not believe this to be the case: the new agency will operate an integrated process of quality assurance covering the totality of each institution's provision, wherever and however delivered and however funded, with significant benefits for institutions. Our proposal can and should eliminate areas of overlap and duplication in current quality assurance arrangements; be sufficiently flexible to accommodate a wide range of academic structures; involve discussion between the agency and each institution concerning the number, scope and timing of reviews; enable the agency and each institution to harmonise internal and external review arrangements; and involve the head of each institution in the selection and composition of review teams.
>
> (JPG, 1996c: 8)

While the report contained no estimate of the relative costs and benefits of the new process and the existing ones, it did point to potential savings through there being institutional reviews only every eight years (as opposed to the current six), through 'the elimination of the current duplication between audit and assessment' (though the group had found none), and from there being fewer subject reviews after aggregation.

At the CVCP Residential Conference in September the report was broadly welcomed, although a number of vice-chancellors expressed disappointment at the continuing absence of any costings or savings. In a measure of desperation the Committee agreed that the new agency's total budget should be 80 per cent of the total current cost of HEQC and the quality assessment divisions. In the subsequent consultation with institutions many of the earlier concerns both about the new process and about the new agency's constitution resurfaced. Nevertheless most of the institutions that responded (49 universities and 12 colleges) agreed that the report was the best that could be achieved in the circumstances. There can be little doubt that war weariness, and the Funding Council's unwillingness to concede on the fundamentals of assessment, not to mention the setting up of the Dearing Committee in February just as the group was getting down to its task, played an important part in all of this: after all the 'debate' had by now been going on for more than three years!

The JPG's final meeting, in November, looked at some of the issues that had been raised in the second consultation. It was decided to rename the proposed institutional quality assurance plans 'programmes'. It was agreed to stick to the eight-year review cycle. As regards the 20 per cent cut, the group took the view that cash limiting was consistent with the broader funding of UK higher education, and that it was for the agency itself to produce a detailed business plan to show how it would achieve the functions and tasks identified within the funding envelope provided. If funding was insufficient, or if new tasks could not be achieved within the funds provided, it was for the agency to raise the issue with its customers. It was the group's judgment that the proposed functions could be achieved within this budget constraint. So much for the leadership of the sector!

As regards the agency board, it appeared that the funding councils had now received legal advice to the effect that their membership would be possible! The HEFCE Board wished the Funding Council to be a member of the company since otherwise it would have insufficient control (sic). The group agreed that this was a major change late in the day which would not be well received by institutions. It might be best to defer it until the Memorandum and Articles of Association were being drawn up.

Finally, the Chair reported that, following private soundings, he had identified two possible candidates for the Chair's post. In sending the group's final report to the Secretary of State he was able to say that Mr Christopher Kenyon, Chair of William Kenyon & Sons Ltd, had agreed to serve. Christopher Kenyon was at the time Chair of the Council of the Victoria University of Manchester, of which institution the then Chair-Designate of the CVCP, Professor (now Sir) Martin Harris, was Vice-Chancellor.[6]

In the meantime work had commenced on establishing the new company which was incorporated on 27 March 1997. The costs were met largely by the HEFCE, presumably in pursuance of its duty to secure provision for assessment. The QAA Board met for the first time on 16 April. On that day the Head of Professional Services at the Law Society, John Randall, was appointed Chief Executive, the advertised salary for the post being £60,000, a salary level nearly £20,000 below the author's then salary, for a job embracing a much wider range of responsibilities!

On 1 August 1997 QAA took over HEQC's functions and all of its staff apart from its Chief Executive, who became redundant. By this time the quality agenda had been considerably expanded as a result of the report of the National Committee of Inquiry into Higher Education chaired by Sir Ron (now Lord) Dearing.

The Dearing Commitee

The National Committee of Inquiry into Higher Education was appointed by Mrs Shephard in February 1996 to: 'make recommendations on how the purposes, shape, structure, size and funding of higher education, including support for students, should develop to meet the needs of the United Kingdom over the next 20 years, recognising that higher education embraces teaching, learning, scholarship and research (NCIHE, 1997: 3).

The Committee was established to find a way out of a conundrum which has faced every government since 1945, how to contain the costs of an expanded system within what the taxpayer and the customer together are prepared to support. The Committee's solution, in its report *Higher Education in the Learning Society* (NCIHE, 1997), was to recommend a non-means-tested flat-rate tuition fee accompanied by means-tested maintenance grants, a solution which was immediately rejected by the Government. However, the Committee's proposals on quality were more successful.

Like HEQC the Committee saw the clarification and maintenance of the standards associated with institutional awards in a large and diverse system as being the central issue facing the sector. Also like HEQC, Dearing saw the key to this as being through the creation of a national qualifications framework together with the development of benchmark information on standards. But whereas HEQC saw these as a means primarily of assisting institutions in determining the appropriateness of their awards by strengthening peer review (as noted in Chapter 3), Dearing saw them as a means whereby an external agency could 'ensure that diversity is not an excuse for low standards or unacceptable quality' (para 10.8: NCIHE, 1997: 143).

Accordingly, the subject benchmark information 'should be used by external examiners to validate whether programmes are within agreed standards for particular awards' (para 10.67: NCIHE, 1997: 157). QAA should work with universities and other degree-awarding institutions 'to create, within three years, a UK-wide pool of academic staff recognised by the QAA, from which institutions must select external examiners' (Recommendation 25: NCIHE, 1997: 373).

As regards quality assurance, while the Committee saw a continuing role for periodic, perhaps five-yearly, institutional reviews to test adherence to codes of practice (what HEQC had called 'guidelines'), it was as we have already seen sceptical about assessment (see Chapter 4):

Finally, the Committee was critical of the priority that many institutions gave to research over teaching, when both were needed, at a high level of quality, if the system was to meet all the demands likely to be made on it in future. Part of the key lay, in the Committee's view, in putting higher education teaching on a more professional basis. It therefore recommended that the representative bodies, in consultation with the funding bodies, should 'immediately' establish a professional Institute for Learning and Teaching in Higher Education. The Institute should accredit training programmes for teachers, commission research and development in learning and teaching practices, and stimulate innovation. The need for such activities was of course one of the reasons why CDP had insisted upon the Department's original quality assurance proposals being modified to give the new sector-owned quality agency (HEQC) an enhancement function! This aspect of the Dearing Report is picked up again in Chapter 6.

The new agency's inheritance

Higher Education in the Learning Society was published in July 1997, just as the new agency was getting going. In contrast to the critical reactions that the overseas audits and the initial Graduate Standards Programme report, not to mention HEQC's single-system proposals, had all received from CVCP, the vice-chancellors welcomed the Dearing proposals, although in the wake of them they made a final, and unsuccessful, effort to curtail assessment.

The new agency therefore faced a difficult inheritance, with the institutions wanting, and anticipating, a less demanding external regime, the Government expecting to see a closer degree of scrutiny of institutions' academic standards, and the Funding Council determined to hang on to assessment in its existing form for as long as possible (Brown, 1997b). Internally, the Agency faced the challenge of assimilating several groups of staff with very different backgrounds and cultures, and also of deciding what role HEQC's Enhancement Group, which had no counterpart in the funding councils, should play. All this was to be done within a smaller funding envelope and under the leadership of a chief executive from outside higher education. How far it succeeded we shall see in Chapter 6.

Notes

1 The minutes merely say that it was agreed to establish an ad hoc group with as chair the Vice-Chancellor of Aston to prepare for an early debate in the main committee.
2 At the September conference a number of vice-chancellors had suggested that instead of creating a wholly new body, HEQC might be modified. The CVCP Council subsequently agreed that any single body should be under 'strong institutional ownership'.
3 This is well reflected in the paper of 30 October 1996 by the late Dr Peter Milton, Dr Clark's successor as head of the HEFCE Assessment Unit, from which the quotation at the start of Chapter 4 is taken.
4 Sir William Taylor, who had attended many such meetings as the head of several universities, caused great amusement by commenting that he had never seen such a degree of agreement among the vice-chancellors and wondered whether, for the first time ever, the minutes could report that the committee was 'unanimous' in its view.
5 One of the JPG members recalls that the JPG 'listened extremely carefully' to the assessor's comments. The group appreciated that there was considerable ministerial interest in what was going on and that there was a need to keep the Minister 'on board' (Peter Bush, personal communication to the author, January 2002).

6 At a conference held by Goldsmiths College University of London on 20 March 1997, Professor Roberts took credit for steering the discussion to that point and complimented Sir William Kerr Fraser for having brought the JPG to a 'brilliantly successful conclusion' (author's note dated 21 March 1997).

6 The Quality Assurance Agency 1997–2002

> The Quality Assurance Agency is the last and only chance to have a quality assurance regime that is owned by the higher education sector – and at the same time to develop a system which will meet the expectations of other audiences, notably students, employers and the Government.
>
> (Randall, 1997: 1)

Introduction

This chapter looks at the work of the Quality Assurance Agency (QAA) from August 1997, when it took over HEQC's functions, to August 2002, when the *Handbook for Institutional Audit* setting out in detail the quality process agreed in March 2002, was published. As with the chapter on HEQC, it begins with an overview of the Agency's work followed by sections covering the main issues with which it dealt.

By far the longest section concerns the development of a quality process to incorporate the recommendations of the Joint Planning Group and the Dearing Committee. This section also looks (briefly) at the parallel development of the post-HEQC quality enhancement agenda. Other sections deal with the creation of the quality infrastructure (the set of precepts and guidance on which quality assurance was to be based), work with the professional and statutory bodies and the NHS, and degree-awarding powers and university title. There are also short sections on subject review and institutional audit (including the Thames Valley affair). In the main however the chapter looks at those aspects of the Agency's work that were either wholly new, or that represented a significant departure from previous policies.

Overview

In June 1997, even before it had assumed its functions, the new agency issued an information bulletin. This was almost certainly the work of the new CEO. The bulletin, the substance of which was reproduced in the first edition of the Agency's newsletter *higher quality* (*HQ*) the following month, acknowledged institutions' hopes that the new framework would reduce the duplication between the various existing external quality processes, and embrace to a greater extent than hitherto institutions' own quality processes. It continued, 'However, the Agency also recognises, very much as did the Joint Planning Group, that new, robust quality arrangements will require a balance to be established between, on the one hand, the desirability of developing a partnership with institutions and on the other, the need to deliver well founded judgements on the quality and standards of higher education and its programme awards' (QAA, 1997a: 2). Few could miss the implication – that a partnership with the institutions was at least potentially inimical to 'well founded judgements'!

The other main leitmotif was the agency's 'independence'. This was exemplified when, in March 1999, as recommended by the Dearing Committee, a student observer was invited to attend the Board. The Board also acceded to the Government's request that a Departmental observer should attend its meetings, while rejecting a request from the representative bodies that they should send observers, as had been the practice with the HEQC.

In its first couple of years – beyond establishing itself in its new offices in Gloucester (mainly financed from the reserves that HEQC had built up, which had been passed on) and securing continuity of functions – the Agency's two main tasks were to devise the new quality process and to develop the infrastructure of guidance on which it was to be based.

The first commenced with the issue in March 1998 of a consultative paper. It was not until January 2000, however, that the final important element – the way in which the outcomes of the learning opportunities aspect of the subject review element of the new process should be reported – was settled. The new process ('Academic Review') came into effect in Scotland that October, more than three years after the handover from HEQC. Yet in little over a year, in March 2001, the Agency was in effect told by Ministers to dismantle the new process in England, where it was due to come into force in October 2001. It was from this point that the Agency appears to have lost control of proceedings. The agency's newsletter *higher quality* reflects this, with no issue between January and November 2001, and no reference in the November 2001 issue to John Randall's resignation in August 2001! Even so, it took another year for yet another new process – based, like HEQC's rejected July 1995 proposals, on institutional audit – to emerge.

Although it was not without controversy, the Agency was more successful with the quality infrastructure, though even here most of the groundwork had been done by HEQC and important parts of it, notably the Qualifications Framework, were developed by former HEQC staff. Even so, it was not until January 2000 that the Qualifications Framework was finally published. This partly reflected the intellectual challenges of turning HEQC's concepts into administrative instruments, and partly the need to consult with the sector whilst this was being done. The other main areas where the agency took things further were in its work with the professional bodies and the NHS, and on degree-awarding powers and university title.

As part of the transfer of functions, QAA took over HEQC's Enhancement Group under Robin Middlehurst. In *HQ* issue 2 in November 1997 (QAA, 1997c), Robin described its programmes under three headings: coordinating and supporting the Agency's development work; maintaining and supporting practitioner networks such as the Quality Assurance and Enhancement Network; and learning from the Agency's quality processes. However Robin herself left the Agency the following year, and her former staff focused mainly on the new quality infrastructure. The Agency discontinued its support for the network (which the HEQC had seen as a valuable adjunct to its work and an effective way of tapping into institutions) and the *Learning from Audit* series effectively ceased. The enhancement baton passed elsewhere.

The new chief executive

Soon after John Randall was appointed he came to meet the HEQC staff in London, and afterwards we had a drink at a local wine bar. Although it had not yet been published, John was clearly seized with what he saw as the main message from the Dearing Committee: the need for closer attention to be paid to institutions' academic standards. I said that the problem as I saw it was that insufficient groundwork had been done on this and other aspects, and that in particular insufficient agreement had been reached between the key parties on what should be the priorities in the new process. This reflected the basic difference of view about quality assurance which has been one of the main themes of this book. I was not therefore over-optimistic about the chances of success.

However it soon became clear that John saw things very differently from me, advocating a strengthening of the regulation of the sector, and seeing the new agency as key to this. John set out his views on this at various times and in various places. One important statement is the essay 'A profession for the new millennium?' (Randall, 2000) which was included in the book *Higher Education Re-formed*, published in 2000 and edited by Peter Scott. The essay charts the development of externally controlled self-regulation in a number of professions and considers how, if it is indeed to be regarded as a profession, university teaching should be regulated. John saw the Agency's quality infrastructure as providing the codes that should govern university teaching:

> Subject benchmark information, programme specifications that spell out the outcomes to be achieved, and a qualifications framework based on clear and explicit descriptors of level are the new means of defining standards in higher education. Together, they have a function similar to that of a code defining professional standards, in that they tell the

individual client (the student) and the wider interested public (especially the employer) what they can reasonably expect from a professional service. Universities and their teachers must deliver to those standards if they are to convince the world that they are true professionals.

(Randall, 2000: 166)

The essay concludes with the statement, 'Institutions that behave professionally, and which promote professional standards amongst their staff, will be treated as having earned the right to play a part in the regulation of their activities. . . . Models of professional regulation that assume a producer-defined service offered by self-employed sole practitioners no longer accord with reality.' (Randall, 2000: 168).

This is some way from the HEQC's approach.

The new quality process, March 1998 to December 2000

The initial consultation

The March 1998 consultative paper essentially set out the framework within which the new quality process would operate. The purposes were to be much the same as before, but with a greater emphasis on academic standards:

- to assist institutions in enhancing the quality of their provision;
- to *promote public confidence*, at home and overseas, in higher education and the standards of awards [present author's emphasis];
- to enable the Funding Councils to fulfil their statutory responsibilities;
- to generate reliable public information that is helpful to potential students, employers, parents, Government, Funding Councils and the institutions themselves;
- to ensure that there is clarity and transparency about the purposes of programmes and the meaning of awards;
- to provide a measure of accountability for the resources provided by the public purse and individuals to fund institutions.

(*HQ*, no 3, QAA, 1998a, para 14)

The basic notion was that in future institutional quality assurance would be judged against a number of frameworks: one or more qualifications frameworks, 'benchmark statements of subject threshold standards' and codes of practice. These sector-wide frameworks would be supplemented by local specifications setting out the intended purposes and outcomes of each programme of study and by 'progress files' recording individual students' achievements.

A key role in this was to be played by the notion of Registered External Examiners (REEs). The justification for this was set out in the following paragraph:

In framing its proposals for the future, the Agency intends to build on the HEQC Guidelines and the Recommendations in the Dearing Report. This would have the effect of moving the HE sector from a position in which academic standards are determined by each institution acting independently, and verified in part by individual external examiners, to a system in which there are consistent mechanisms demonstrating some collectivity in the definition and setting of standards, which would then be verified and calibrated by the REEs. The proposals would:

- give external examiners an explicit role in public assurance of quality and standards;
- create a national framework within which external examiners will operate;
- require external examiners to be registered and competent;
- create mechanisms which enable institutions to compare their academic standards in a more systematic and informed way.

(*HQ*, no 3, QAA, 1998a: part VI, para 11)

For this purpose, the consultative paper suggested that for each of the subjects where benchmark information was available, institutions with relevant provision would nominate two or more of their experienced examiners who would report to the Agency as REEs, be included on the Agency register, and be remunerated by the Agency for this work. However the consultative paper also included, as an alternative, the possibility of simply strengthening the external examiner system without the requirement for examiners to be registered with the Agency and to report to it.[1]

The consultative paper also tried to take forward the Dearing notion of 'a lighter touch':

The key to this lies in a reduction in duplication of effort. In part this will come through better coordination of external scrutinies that are now separate, by building on existing collaboration, using common timetables, paperwork and personnel. It will also come through a better inter-relationship between external and internal scrutiny processes at institutional and programme levels. There could also be greater differentiation in external scrutiny in general with provision previously judged to be good being subject to review on a longer cycle, or at a reduced intensity (using) the evidence of quality audit and quality assessment so far and the evidence to be generated by the Agency's assurance processes. Criteria for using this evidence to determine future review arrangements will need to be developed.

(*HQ*, no 3, QAA, 1998a, part I, paras 16 and 31)

It is a fact that no such criteria were ever developed, nor did the Agency ever say precisely how review at institutional and programme levels would be integrated. The two processes, institutional review and subject review, continued to run in parallel until the new audit-based quality framework was introduced in early 2003. So much for one of the main reasons for creating the new agency!

Reporting on the outcome of the consultation, John Randall wrote in October 1998, 'the Dearing proposal that external examiners should report directly to the agency met with real concerns that the independent role of the external examiner as "critical friend" would be undermined, with a loss of frankness in reporting. We are not proceeding with that proposal' (QAA, 1998b: 1). However, 'on other matters' – notably subject benchmarks and programme specifications, where similar concerns about autonomy and diversity had been expressed – 'we have concluded that it is the view of the external stakeholders [employers and students] that must prevail'.

The second-stage consultation

HQ issue 4 (October 1998) launched the second stage of the consultation on the new framework, concerning the actual quality process. This would have two elements: institutional review and programme review. Institutional review would focus on:

* the effectiveness of the exercise of the awarding function (or, where the institution does not award its own qualifications, the effectiveness of its academic management system); and
* the effectiveness of institutional management of the support of student learning.

(HQ, no 4, QAA, 1998b: 4)

It would lead to the same types of judgment as continuation audit: areas for commendation, concern or need for urgent action. It would draw on the outcomes of both existing subject reviews and future programme reviews.

Programme review would have two elements: outcomes (standards) and the quality of learning opportunities. The former would cover:

* The extent to which students' attainment matches any applicable subject benchmark standard, qualification definition and/or level descriptor in the qualifications framework.
* The extent to which students are achieving the objectives set out in the programme specification (including any relating to key skills);
* The effectiveness of the design, content and organisation of the curriculum in delivering the intended outcomes; and
* The appropriateness of student assessment methods as instruments for measuring the intended outcomes.

The latter would cover:

- teaching and learning;
- student support and guidance;
- learning resources;
- quality management and enhancement

(HQ, no 4, QAA, 1998b: 6)

It was not yet clear what kinds of judgement would be made. Certainly for outcome standards a threshold judgement would seem logical. However, 'The Funding Councils have made clear that in principle they consider it highly desirable that the QAA assessments should include summative quantified ratings as well as narrative descriptions of strengths and weaknesses; and that that is particularly important to underpin any link between funding and quality of the sort currently used in Scotland and Wales' (*HQ*, no 4, QAA, 1998b: 8).

Following prolonged and difficult negotiations between the Agency, the Department, HEFCE and the representative bodies, a compromise was eventually reached in January 2000 whereby:

- For **programme outcome standards** (sic) there would be a threshold judgement establishing (a) whether the intended programme outcomes were appropriate and (b) whether the actual outcomes delivered were consistent with those intentions. Where the standards were being achieved but there were doubts about the ability to maintain them, a judgement of 'limited confidence' might be made.
- For **learning opportunities** there would be a graded judgement for each aspect (commendable/approved/failing). Within the 'commendable' category reviewers would identify any specific aspects that were 'exemplary'. If provision was found to be failing in any aspect of quality, or if reviewers had no confidence in the standards attained, the provision would be regarded, overall, as 'failing'. All provision that was not 'failing' would be regarded as 'approved'.
- **Institutional management of standards** (assessed through institutional review) would be subject to 'an overall judgement of confidence' with the report identifying matters in respect of which it was essential, advisable or desirable that the institution should take action. (This followed the practice with continuation audit.)[2]

It was clear to everybody that the new process was more comprehensive than those it had replaced not only in terms of coverage – in broad terms, quality, standards and quality assurance were all now firmly embraced within the external regime – but also in the specificity and expectations of the regulatory framework: qualifications frameworks covering every award, programme specifications for every course, benchmark statements for every main subject, not to mention codes of practice for every aspect of quality assurance. Moreover the new regime was being administered by an agency which, at least in its language, had already shown itself to be less sympathetic to the institutions than HEQC. What then was the quid pro quo for the institutions? The Agency's answer lay in 'lightness of touch' and 'differential intensity of scrutiny'.

Lightness of touch was to be secured in two ways. First, institutions would be able to negotiate with the Agency when in the proposed six-year review cycle their programmes should be evaluated so that, for example, such a review could coincide with an internal review or validation event. Institutions could also seek to have programmes aggregated. This was the outcome of the JPG's institutional quality assurance plans. However for purposes of comparability each subject would be allocated to one of two three-year semi-cycles, 'thus ensuring that [the resultant information] is not so old as to invalidate comparability'. Review times could also be negotiated with professional bodies.

Second, instead of set piece events, reviewers (who would be known as Academic Reviewers) would form their judgements by observing the institution's programme validation and review events, by drawing on the findings of external examiners, by seeking feedback from students, staff and employers, and by scrutiny of some 'overall institutional processes' (*HQ*, no 4, QAA, 1998b: 5). In other words, institutions would not have to assemble large amounts of information just for external review, and the external review could take place when information was already available from internal processes rather than specially prepared. That at least was the theory.

Variations in the intensity of scrutiny would be in the extent of engagement with internal processes:

> If in a subject area, there is a high level of confidence, the involvement of Reviewers is likely to be concentrated on the latter stages of the internal revalidation exercise, with reliance being placed on evidence gathering and evaluation carried out earlier by the institution itself. Pending the establishment of that level of confidence, Reviewers would be more directly involved in those earlier stages, and, for the purposes of quality reviews, would scrutinise a higher proportion of the provision within the subject area . . . Evidence for a high level of confidence would come from the Agency's experience of working with internal processes, and from earlier assessment and audit reports. Conversely, if there is a low degree of confidence in internal procedures it may not be possible to rely on them at all. In that event, the Agency would have to carry out directly full reviews of provision at subject level.
>
> (*HQ*, no 4, QAA, 1998b: 7)

The Agency would prepare institutional 'profiles' based on previous assessment and audit reports (John Randall referred to these as 'profs', thus creating a second use of the term in higher education). These would be shared with the institution concerned but not published. On the basis of the profile, together with previous subject review reports, other relevant and available information such as professional body or accreditation reports and, subsequently, the academic reviewers' analysis of the self-evaluation document (which was the trigger for the review), the Agency would determine, after discussion with the institution, the overall approach to academic reviews (that is, the intensity of reviewer effort) for the three-year period.

While the Agency was at pains to emphasize that this would not be a matter of 'simple grading', what was in effect being developed here was a form of institutional accreditation not dissimilar from that which CNAA had developed or, indeed, from that which the Agency itself applied in relation to applications for degree-awarding powers.

The new methodology was set out in detail in the *Handbook for Academic Review* (QAA, 2000). In an article in October 2000 (Brown, 2000c; cf Brown, 1999d), the present author reviewed this and considered particularly the likely effectiveness of the new process in terms of the demands on the institutions, information for third parties, and feasibility. As regards the demands on institutions, the article noted three main issues (beyond the extension of coverage to standards already agreed in the JPG):

- The amount of effort institutions would need to make to gear themselves up and their internal processes for the new regime, both initially and in keeping themselves up to date.
- The relative lengths of the old and new cycles. The first cycle of assessment in England was to last ten years. The new cycle was intended to last six. Even if the amount of contact time for individual visits was less – and it was unlikely to be so for all institutions, since otherwise the phrase 'varying the intensity of scrutiny' had no meaning – it was hard to see how the annual claims on an individual institution would be lower.
- The efforts that institutions would undoubtedly continue to make to rehearse and prepare for reviewer engagements.

The article also pointed to the clear risk of duplication between the roles of academic reviewers and external examiners (cf Swain, Tysome and Baty, 1999). It was also sceptical of the claims made for the informational benefits of the new process. It asked:

- is it clear that what is proposed by the Agency will provide what is wanted by external stakeholders?;
- is it worth doing if the process by which the information is arrived at is itself of questionable quality, at least in the absence of means by which the Agency itself will ensure the reliability and validity of its judgements?

- do the costs justify the effort, particularly bearing in mind the fact that by the time the reports appear they are well out of date?
- will the act of providing the information itself lead to other detriments, in particular unhelpful effects on institutional behaviour as institutions do what is necessary to get a better 'score' rather than improve quality – perhaps the acid test of any evaluation regime?
- will the information actually be used by stakeholders or will the fact that it can still be fairly easily reduced to numerical scales mean that it will continue to be used mainly for 'snapshot' purposes by people who should know better?

(Brown, 2000c: 335)

However the main doubts concerned feasibility. The article contrasted the Agency's approach to the institutional profiles with its advice to Ministers about the future handling of applications for degree-awarding powers, where it had emphasized the need for more explicit and transparent criteria (see below):

Degree awarding powers of course concerns only a handful of institutions. Varying intensity by definition applies to all. Judgements will be made by Agency officials (not themselves peers), using reports which were written for a different purpose, which are at best historical, and many of which anyway fail quite basic tests of validity and reliability because of the absence of any serious mechanism to moderate variations either between review teams or between subjects. Why should these judgements be any more reliable than those made previously by Funding Council officers about 'satisfactory' provision under the first assessment method which was subsequently abandoned? Moreover these judgements will not become public, unless an institution chooses to make them so. Nor does it appear that there will be any appeal against the judgements, though there will no doubt be a good deal of bilateral 'give and take'.

Whatever approach is adopted, it is difficult to see how varying the intensity of scrutiny can be combined with the avowed need for reliability and consistency, a need which is reinforced by the continuation – regrettable in the author's view – of graded judgments for the three aspects of learning opportunities. If it is difficult to have comparable and defensible outcomes when the reviewer input is relatively constant, how will it be possible to achieve this when the reviewer input varies? Variability of scrutiny cannot logically support consistency and reliability of judgment or valid, comparable information for stakeholders, especially for prospective students. This is another basic tension in the whole framework.

(Brown, 2000c: 338)

What this approach *would* do was to focus attention on those who made the judgments, on their accountability to the Agency, and ultimately on the agency's own accountability for those judgements. This was indeed to become clear within months of the article being published.[3]

The new quality process, January 2001 to August 2002

On 21 March 2001, apparently without any warning to the Agency, the Secretary of State for Education and Employment, David Blunkett, announced a 40 per cent reduction in the volume of external review activity. Universal assessment was to be abandoned. Departments that had achieved 'good scores' in the current round (due to end in December) would be exempt in the next one, 'apart from a small proportion which will be sampled by agreement and [which] would provide the necessary benchmark of good practice'. By 'good scores' was meant at least three scores of 3 and three scores of 4. HEFCE would discuss proposals for achieving this with QAA and the representative bodies. The announcement made no reference to Academic Review.

It is still not entirely clear what precipitated this change. There were three possible contributory factors. First, there was the PA Consulting report of August 2000 (to which reference was made in Chapter 4) showing total annual costs to the sector of at least £30 million, mostly incurred in assessment. Second, in an article in *Education Guardian* on 30 January 2001 (Harrison *et al*, 2001), a group of economists at the University of Warwick (which had gained a 24 in a recent subject review) poured scorn on the exercise (to which the Agency was moved to reply). Third there was the lobbying of Number 10 by prominent Russell Group vice-chancellors including, it is believed, Professor Colin Lucas of Oxford University and Professor Anthony Giddens of the London School of Economics. It was possible that this was connected to the Government's announcement in February 2001 that top-up fees were to be ruled out for the life of the next Labour government (Beckett, 2001: 30).[4]

All these pressures were reflected in a House of Lords debate on 21 March 2001 initiated by Lord Norton of Louth, who as Professor of Government at the University of Hull was based in a department about to undergo assessment. Lord Norton made a general attack on the over-bureaucratic and over-complex regulation of teaching in higher education. He was joined and supported by a number of other noble Lords, including Baroness Warwick. It was perhaps fortunate for the Government speaker, Lord Davies, that he was able to refer to the Secretary of State's statement earlier in the day.[5]

Following the announcement discussions began between officers of the various bodies. The Funding Council was now in the driving seat in determining how the announcement was to be implemented, not the agency. It soon became clear that once the requirement for universal assessment was relaxed, programme review was not an adequate basis for a comprehensive regime. The consultation paper which – in agreement with the Agency,

UUK and SCOP – HEFCE issued in July 2001 therefore proposed that, while external subject reviews would continue 'on a highly selective basis', institution-level review 'conducted on audit principles' should be 'the basis of external review'. This was of course what HEQC had proposed in July 1995 after HEFCE (and the CVCP Chair) had plumped for an assessment-based approach! Moreover, the consultation paper emphasized that the objectives of quality assurance were 'secured primarily' by institutions' internal procedures, and that 'the purpose of external review is to validate the reliability and effectiveness of those procedures, without duplicating or distorting them' (HEFCE, 2001: para 8). Finally, although it no longer featured as an 'objective' of quality assurance, the document gave greater emphasis to enhancement:

> Through institution-wide audits . . . the QAA review teams will collect evidence about developing practice in teaching and learning. That evidence should be used to prepare, in collaboration with the Learning and Teaching Support Network (LTSN) and individual subject centres, periodic overview reports, at institution level (along the lines of the reports produced previously by the Higher Education Quality Council), or by subject area or theme. That . . . will ensure that the information gained is exploited to best effect. (HEFCE, 2001, para 36).[6]

But there was a price to be paid. First, certain 'subject areas or themes' would be selected for more detailed review 'on a purposive basis, focussed on programmes and institutions where there may be grounds for concern about the quality and standards' (HEFCE, 2001, para 10c). This would enable the audits to review not only institutional mechanisms and procedures, but also the outcomes delivered in practice – 'the quality and standards actually experienced and achieved by students' (HEFCE, 2001, para 10d). As part of each institutional audit, subject specialists would therefore review individual departments or programmes up to a maximum of 10 per cent of the institution's students. The QAA would aim to secure that 'a balance of provision was examined, across the whole sector, in each of the full range of 42 subject areas during a full five year review cycle' (HEFCE, 2001, para 26). The role of these subject specialists would be to:

> drill down to test, in the chosen area, how well the institution's internal quality assurance processes were working, the reliability of the information being provided, and the outcomes being delivered. . . . The results would form an integral part of the audit, and would be published as part of the audit report. So long as no areas of significant weakness in quality and standards were identified, that would complete the external review activity for the institution. There would be no separate programme of subject-level review.
>
> (HEFCE, 2001, paras 27–28)

However there could and would be 'follow-up' subject reviews where there were areas of concern. The conclusions of such reviews, and the institution's response, would be published together as part of the main audit report. Each report would include a statement of the confidence that could be placed in the institution's safeguarding of quality and standards, and in the reliability of the information published by it.

Second, there was a still greater emphasis on the role of external quality assurance in meeting public information needs, and indeed this was listed as the first 'principle' on which the new process was based. Accordingly, institutions would be required to collect and to publish more information about quality and standards. For this purpose a task group was to be established, under Professor (now Sir) Ron Cooke, Vice-Chancellor of the University of York, to identify the categories of data, information and judgments that should be available (see below).

Finally, the consultative document envisaged that there would be a five-year review cycle. However the first audits would take place over a three-year cycle, the reason being 'that the institution-level audit is the vehicle through which decisions are taken about the selective programme of reviews to follow up any areas of concern. It would not be acceptable for those institutions whose audit is scheduled to take place at the end of the audit programme to have no external review activity for as long as five years' (HEFCE, 2001, para 39).

For those institutions whose institution-level audit was scheduled for the second or third year of the initial cycle (to begin in the autumn of 2002) there would be a 'highly selective' subject-level review programme. This would cover subject areas not previously reviewed and new programmes; subject areas and institutions that, under the assessment method applying prior to 1995, were not visited but were self-assessed as satisfactory by the institution, or that were assessed as unsatisfactory; and/or subject areas in institutions that were identified as failing or requiring substantial improvement in the post-1995 review programme. The results of such reviews would be fed back to the institution, and the effectiveness of its response would then specifically be considered, and reported on, as part of its institution-wide audit.

There was then a period of consultation in the course of which John Randall resigned (see below). The document was broadly welcomed by the institutions but there were two major concerns: the apparent continuation of subject review by another name through the intention that sub-institutional subject scrutiny would cover a representative sample of subjects and provision, and the risk that the information proposals could actually represent an increase in the external regulatory burden.

The author commented on the proposals in a note for SCOP in July 2001. This described the competing views of quality assurance which have in large part been the subject of this book. The note concluded:

The tensions between these competing views are reflected in, rather than resolved by, the consultation paper, in two main ways.

First, in the tension between the emphasis on institutional procedures as the 'primary' means of securing the various objectives of quality assurance, on the one hand, and the emphasis upon meeting various public information needs, on the other. . . . Second, in the continuing role foreseen for Subject Review, albeit in a more limited role, alongside institutional level scrutiny. It is in the detailed working through of these tensions that the potential effectiveness, or ineffectiveness, of the new approach will be established. In the long run, only an audit-based approach, at either institutional or subject level, can provide the necessary stimulus to quality improvement which is the most basic justification of external quality assurance.

(Brown, 2001c)

Further negotiations took place between the parties. Eventually, on 20 March 2002, almost exactly a year to the day since Mr Blunkett's announcement, the Department announced the Minister's approval of the new process, the details of which were set out in the Operational Description (OD) published at the same time by the agency.

The OD did not differ in essentials from the consultative document but there was some modification of the subject-level proposals. What were now to be called 'disciplinary audit trails' would not routinely include subject specialists, nor did the process depend on this; 'Instead, it relies on audit teams making more generic judgements, informed by scrutiny of a sample range of discipline areas or themes, about quality and standards as delivered in practice' (OD, para 8; QAA, 2002a: 2).

Moreover, there would not for most institutions be further subject reviews during the transitional period; instead there would be 'a new, developmentally-focussed, form of engagement at the disciplinary level' ('developmental engagements'). The full cycle would now be six years rather than five.

The audits would look at the effectiveness of institutions' assurance structures and mechanisms, and ways in which the quality of programmes and awards were regularly reviewed and resulting recommendations implemented; the accuracy, completeness and reliability of the information (including programme specifications) that an institution published about quality and standards; and a number of examples of its quality processes at work at the level of the programme ('discipline audit trails') or across the institution as a whole ('thematic enquiries'). In the light of the information gathered, the audit teams would provide 'principal' judgements on:

- the level of confidence that can reasonably be placed in the soundness of the institution's management of the quality of its programmes and the academic standards of its awards; and, through direct scrutiny of primary evidence, whether the institution is securing acceptable academic standards and quality;

- the level of reliance that can reasonably be placed on the accuracy, integrity, completeness and frankness at the information that an institution publishes about the quality of its programmes and the standards of its awards.

(OD, para 18; QAA, 2002a: 4)

Audit teams would not make 'simple binary' judgements:

> Where they find institutions that are managing quality and standards soundly and effectively, and where the prospects for the future continuation of this appear good, they might be expected to express their 'broad confidence'. Where they have doubts, either about the current assurance of quality and standards, or about an institution's ability to maintain quality and standards in the future, they will make a judgement in a form that indicates whether their concerns are limited to a small number of matters or are more widespread, and whether or not these matters place academic standards at risk. In these circumstances a team might qualify its judgement of confidence. In all cases audit teams will be required to indicate clearly the areas of concern that have given rise to any limitation of confidence.
>
> (OD, para 20; QAA, 2002a: 5)

Following consultation with institutions, the *Handbook for Institutional Audit* was published in August 2002, the first audits commenced in February 2003.[7]

Scotland and Wales

Scotland and Wales followed broadly the same course as England but with some important modifications. In Scotland the opportunity was taken, following Mr Blunkett's announcement, to stand back and reflect on what had been learnt from past experience. For this purpose the Scottish Higher Education Funding Council (SHEFC) created a joint group with Universities Scotland, the QAA and the National Union of Students (Scotland). This led to a circular in December 2001 proposing that the existing combination of institutional audit and academic review be replaced, from 2002/03, by a new process with four main elements:

- institutional audits as in England but without disciplinary audit trails and with greater emphasis on quality enhancement and effective student feedback;
- public information that would not include the compulsory publication of external examiners' reports or summaries of such reports (see next section);

- an internal subject review process except where an institution had insufficient 'track record' of HE quality assurance or where there was evidence from other sources suggesting serious concerns about quality in specific subject areas;
- a separate quality enhancement process with specific engagements within sector-wide 'themes' with the overall aim of identifying and disseminating good practice.

This approach was incorporated, following consultation and detailed modifications, in the *Handbook for Enhancement Led Institutional Review: Scotland* published by QAA in April 2003 (QAA, 2003). As already noted, it bears an even more striking resemblance to the HEQC proposals of July 1995 than the audit-based method adopted in England.

As we saw in Chapter 4, Wales had always had reservations about the assessment approach in England, going back to circular W94/36HE of May 1994 (HEFCW, 1994). At the same time the Welsh Funding Council wished to synchronize its quality arrangements with those in England. There was therefore no subject-based activity in Wales from 1997 until the calendar year 2002, when the Agency introduced 'developmental engagements' that effectively acted as pilots for those introduced in England. Like the Scots, therefore, the Welsh Funding Council adopted an enhancement-based version of the English model without disciplinary trails or the requirement to publish external examiners' reports or internal reviews!

It is striking that, in spite of having exactly the same statutory duty to ensure that institutions are assessed, Scotland and Wales differed so much from England. Was this simply a flexing of the muscles or the result of more effective institutional representation is it that in each country there is a better appreciation of the value of higher education, and a greater degree of trust and respect for the universities, than in England?

The Better Regulation Task Force

Shortly before the *Handbook* emerged, the Cabinet Office's Better Regulation Task Force published its report on the regulation of higher education *Higher Education; Easing the Burden* (Better Regulation Task Force, 2002). It broadly agreed with the sector that it was over-regulated, with the areas of greatest concern being funding, quality assurance issues including multiple audits, and data collection. In the task force's view a major reason for this was the lack of coordination between the various regulatory agencies. Its main recommendation therefore was that the Funding Council's HE Forum (see Chapter 4) should be strengthened:

It should be supported by a Secretariat funded by DfES. It should, with the Minister responsible for higher education, agree an action plan to reduce burdens on HEIs. It should report on progress annually to both

the Minister and other stakeholders. The HE Forum should take on a gatekeeper role to prevent unnecessary new burdens being placed on HEIs.
(Recommendation 1; Better Regulation Task Force, 2002: 11)

The Government accepted this, and the White Paper on higher education in January 2003 announced the creation of a task force under the chairmanship of Professor David VandeLinde, Vice-Chancellor of the University of Warwick. This aim would be 'to take a hard look at bureaucracy across the sector, building on the work of the Better Regulation Task Force and going beyond it to cut back bureaucracy wherever possible' (DfES, 2003a: 79). The task force, retitled the Better Regulation Review Group, commenced its work in March 2003. The author is a member.

Information

The final report of the Cooke Committee on information was published in March 2002; an interim report had been published in November 2001. The Committee sought to steer a careful path between those, such as the Minister, the National Union of Students and others who wanted to see more information published, and the institutional representatives who were concerned about distortion, costs and utilities/demand.[8]

Needless to say, the report contained no estimates of the costs of its proposals, still less any evidence to justify its choice of proposals.[9] The report listed the categories of information that should be available in all institutions and that should be published. A summary is in Appendix 3.

The main area of controversy was the treatment of external examiners' reports. The Committee had proposed that external examiners should be asked to prepare summaries of their reports and to publish these 'as a new form of public information'. Full reports to the institution would continue to be confidential. This had been warmly welcomed by students' and employers' representatives but strongly opposed by the institutions, who feared that this could compromise the frankness of reporting and perhaps create an adversarial situation. The Committee stuck to its guns but decided to propose a template which would require external examiners to provide 'succinct commentary' for publication, as well as confirm that the standards elements had been considered and judged satisfactory 'by reference to the quality infrastructure' (sic). The details of the implementation of this are still under discussion at the time of writing.

Enhancement again

In March 2002 HEFCE, UUK and SCOP agreed to set up a committee, also under the chairmanship of Sir Ron Cooke, to look at the division of labour in the effort devoted to quality enhancement by the main national agencies – Institute for Learning and Teaching (ILT), LTSN, the Higher Education

Staff Development Agency (HESDA) and QAA. The Teaching Quality Enhancement Committee (TQEC) (of which the author was a member) produced an interim report in August 2002 (HEFCE/UUK/SCOP, 2002) and a final report in January 2003 (HEFCE/UUK/SCOP, 2003).

TQEC found that the differing roles of the various bodies were not well understood and that there was some duplication between them. They also identified a major enhancement agenda for institutions including, not least, the challenges presented by a much wider range of student learning needs. The Committee concluded that the best way of helping institutions to respond to this agenda would be to create a single agency, provisionally entitled the 'Academy for the Advancement of Learning and Teaching in Higher Education', which would incorporate ILT and LTSN together with the relevant functions of HESDA. This conclusion was endorsed by HEFCE, the representative bodies and the Department. Professor Leslie Wagner, Vice-Chancellor of Leeds Metropolitan University, was appointed to lead the new agency in May 2003 (HEFCE, 2003b).

Nearly six years after HEQC's demise, therefore, the sector had either in place or firmly in prospect two agencies, one concerned with accountability, the other with enhancement. The accountability agency was operating a process based on audit, was working to an agenda, the key elements of which had been created by HEQC, and was headed by the former head of the council's Quality Assurance Group. As the final TQEC report acknowledged, the enhancement agenda had been established by CNAA and HEQC. The way in which the enhancement agenda was proposed to be taken forward was, with one important exception (the introduction of what is in effect a professional qualification for lecturers), how HEQC would have taken things forward if it had had the chance (that is, on the basis of mandatory institutional subscription). What a waste.[10]

External examining again

On 16 May 2002 the then HEFCE Director of Institutions, Stephen Marston, wrote to Sir Ron Cooke 'following initial consultations with UUK, SCOP and QAA' to ask his committee to look at ways of promoting better training and development for external examiners, 'particularly through some form of accreditation [which] could usefully be devised to promote higher standards and to develop over time a form of 'college' or 'academy' of accredited external examiners' (Marston, 2002). The network could 'over time become an effective force in setting and promoting higher standards in external examining'. The letter did not of course refer to any evidence suggesting such a scheme was necessary, or even desirable, nor did it say how such a scheme might be likely to be received by individual examiners, nor was any reference made to the costs or who should bear them.

In response, the Committee gave its view that 'imposing compulsory accreditation on the system of external examiners risks losing the expertise and goodwill of a great many dedicated members of the academy, especially at this juncture when staff feel under considerable pressure. They also strongly advise against interfering with the nature of the contractual relationship between institutions and their appointed examiners' (Cooke, 2003). Instead, the Committee proposed 'improved institutional preparation' and 'the availability of a national development programme' for external examiners. The latter could be operated by the new Academy with effect from 2004–5 (the new agency having come into being in January 2004).

On 27 January 2003 the HEFCE Chief Executive, Sir Howard Newby, wrote to Baroness Warwick asking Universities UK and SCOP to inform the Council of the timetable and proposals for taking forward the recommendations (Newby, 2003). Lady Warwick replied on 13 February saying that the UUK Board had agreed to discuss with QAA a revision of the external examining code of practice (to include references to 'apprenticeship' systems); to invite ILT and LTSN to consider with QAA, UUK and SCOP a timetable and programme to implement the supporting of institutions in induction, a national programme for, or as part of, this and a programme for engaging the subject associations; and to invite the ILT to consider with QAA, UUK and SCOP a system of voluntary accreditation for institutions' systems of induction and support for external examiners and specifically to relate this to the element in the existing accreditation system for induction programmes for new teaching staff, and in any CPD proposals which they might currently be entertaining addressing assessment more generally (Warwick, 2003).

It is reasonable to conclude that the continuance of some form of subject review within or alongside the new quality process (at least until 2005), the stronger emphasis upon public information (whatever the evidence about costs and benefits), and the continuing interest in turning external examiners into a national cadre (in spite of the sector's reaction to QAA's registered examiner proposals) were all symptoms of the Department's disappointment at 'losing' subject review, yet again reflecting the apparent lack of trust in the institutions which has been one of the fundamental causes of all this instability in arrangements, and which has still not been overcome to this day.

The new process: envoi

On 20 May 2002 QAA held its annual subscribers meeting in Edinburgh. By now the new process had been agreed, and a mixture of relief and self-congratulation hung in the air as various aspects of the new arrangements were described. In a prepared speech the new Chief Executive, Peter Williams (who had been appointed in March, having acted in the role since John Randall's resignation) spoke of how, while the new process was undoubtedly an improvement on previous ones, the experience of the past ten years had proved worthwhile and essential ('a necessary journey has been undertaken'). As Peter Spoke I reflected that the relatively happy state of affairs which now prevailed was not due to any of those present, and that but for the Russell Group's putsch we should still be trying to hack our way through Academic Review.

It is now proposed to discuss much more briefly some of the QAA's other major activities.

The quality infrastructure

The national quality infrastructure consists of the *Framework for Higher Education Qualifications* (*FHEQ*), the 47 subject benchmark statements and the quality assurance *Code of Practice*. As already noted, these sector-wide documents are intended to be supplemented by local programme specifications and 'progress files' recording the achievements of individual students.

The *FHEQ* was published in January 2001. It consists of a framework for qualifications in England, Wales and Northern Ireland together with a credit and qualifications framework for Scotland to enable higher education to be incorporated into a comprehensive Scottish Credit and Qualifications Framework. The *FHEQ* divides the qualifications awarded by universities and colleges into five levels: Certificate, Intermediate, Honours, Masters, Doctoral. It contains a broad description of the academic expectations associated with the particular level of award, together with more detailed descriptors of the skills and competences associated with award holders.[11]

The first 22 subject benchmark statements were published in April 2000. A further 25 statements were published in March 2002. (A further statement, covering inter- and multi-disciplinary programmes was prepared but never published.) The statements were drawn up by groups of subject specialists selected by the Agency from across the sector. A full list is in Appendix 4. In addition, benchmark statements for the Department of Health/ NHS were produced in August 2001; statements for Masters in Business and Management in October 2002, Scottish benchmark statements in January 2003 and an Annex to Academic Standards – Engineering for MEng degrees was produced in March 2003.

The Agency originally asked subject groups to produce statements representing 'general expectations about standards at the threshold level for the award of honours degrees' in the subjects concerned. With such a broad steer, not to mention the greatly varying 'widths' of the subjects chosen, it was perhaps inevitable that the statements themselves should vary considerably in coverage and depth.

Most looked at the aims and purposes of programmes in the subject concerned. All set out the skills, abilities or competences to be developed in students. Some also made recommendations about curriculum content or knowledge. Most also proposed assessment procedures (often involving 'unseen exams') and/or performance criteria. Above all, the groups adopted a widely varying approach to 'threshold', with some not even using the term.[12]

Finally, the agency published, between January 1999 and September 2001, a *Code of Practice* or, to give it its proper title, the *Code of Practice for the Assurance of Academic Quality and Standards in Higher Education*; HEQC's comparable document had of course been entitled *Guidelines* (see Chapter 3). To quote the code's 'Overview', 'The Code is intended to help higher education institutions to meet their responsibilities for the assurance of academic standards and quality, by providing a framework within which they can consider the effectiveness of their individual approaches to a range of activities' (Overview, para 1).

The code is in ten sections covering postgraduate research programmes; collaborative provision; students with disabilities; external examining; academic appeals and student complaints on academic matters; assessment of students; programme approval, monitoring and review; career education, information and guidance; placement learning; student recruitment and admissions. Each indicates the 'key issues' to be considered by the institution in each case and is in two parts:

- precepts encapsulating the matters that an institution can reasonably be expected to address through its own quality assurance arrangements;
- guidance suggesting possible ways by which those expectations might be met and demonstrated.

(Overview, para 3)

Like the FHEQ and the subject benchmark statements, the code is intended to be updated regularly.

Institutions expressed various concerns about the different elements of the infrastructure, the main one being the potential threats to institutional autonomy, diversity and innovation, as well as the ever-present fear of 'bureaucracy'. However the central issue, which has still to be resolved, is how strictly external reviewers will adhere to these various documents as they evaluate quality, standards and quality assurance in institutions. It is not unfair to say that there is some ambivalence here.

At an early stage agency spokespeople certainly gave the impression that reviewers and institutions would be expected to follow the infrastructure fairly closely, and this was reflected in early versions of the code. For example, the draft code on collaborative provision spoke of the need for partner institutions' awards to 'meet any national benchmarks'. Subsequently, however, as the effect of the Dearing Committee wore off and the Agency was (very obviously) under new management, it began to adopt a more liberal stance. In *HQ* issue 9 (Nov 2001), Peter Williams and another former HEQC colleague, Peter Wright, argued that the infrastructure represented an 'expository' approach to standards, one that 'encourages the academic community into dialogue with itself and the translation of the traditionally implicit into a more explicit form'. This was as opposed to a 'prescriptive' approach which 'starts from an assumption of deficiency'. So the subject benchmark statements, for example, represent 'reference points' as opposed to required outcomes:

> A reference point is like a map: it links the particular with the general and throws more light on it; it says where we are and where we can go. Overall, the possession of a map widens your choice. In contrast, a required outcome is like an itinerary: it tells us where we should go, with little contextual information, and might have nothing to say about other possible journeys or options. Although an itinerary has its purposes and uses, a map increases possible choice or general awareness.
>
> (*HQ*, no 9, QAA, 2001b: 12)

It remains to be seen whether hard-pressed auditors and others will appreciate these subtleties. They may find that following the various codes fairly closely (where this is possible) is the only way to get the job done. In fact the worst outcome for institutions – and, ultimately, the Agency and all its stakeholders – is where auditors and others apply the infrastructure inconsistently. This would not have mattered so much under HEQC: it is the Dearing 'spin' on the infrastructure that has caused, or could cause, problems. One should not of course overlook the tendency with institutions for staff simply to adopt the external quality 'architecture' uncritically.[13]

Another major problem with the infrastructure was well put by David Dill in an article in the QSC Digest:

> the expected strong influence of codes of practice . . . is remarkably optimistic. For a country such as the UK, which has no written constitution, and has relied upon strong traditions rather than extensive rules and regulations to achieve academic coordination, to place so much stress on the value of written codes of practice is unexpected. The danger is that future institutional quality reviews will be directed at evaluating administrative documents and assuring that a broad array of administrative procedures conform with externally defined standards, rather than holding academic institutions accountable for the quality of their academic outputs. An emphasis on conformance to codes of practice may also retard innovation in academic and administrative processes.
>
> (Dill, 1998: 5)

And, one might add, further distance quality assurance from the everyday work and values of academic staff.

Referring specifically to the subject benchmark statements up to that point, John Brennan also drew attention to the risk that these would not reflect the values of the academic community as a whole:

Standards are to be assessed against national benchmarks with different subjects. Who will set the benchmarks? The majority (38 out of 58) of the members of the QAA's subject benchmarking groups are from 'old' universities. Only 13 are from 'new' universities. This suggests that the QAA is looking to define the standards in terms of the conventions of the pre-1992 universities. Concerns have been expressed about the applicability of subject benchmarking to modular and multidisciplinary programmes and a special advisory group has been set up by QAA to look into this. Recent HESA statistics indicate that a high proportion of UK undergraduates now enrol on such programmes. Multidisciplinary programmes are a particular feature of new universities and yet only two of the 15 members of the special advisory group are from such institutions.

(Brennan, 1999: 10–11)

There is also the whole issue of how the infrastructure can be kept up to date. This was well put by David Dill in another article in the same issue of the *Digest*:

A second critical point . . . is a rapid expansion and development of new academic fields. Traditional disciplines are fracturing into new sub-fields at a rapid rate, and whole new interdisciplinary subjects emerging. International academic competition will only speed up this process. In this context sorting academic work into 42 academic fields and sustaining a systematic external process for reviewing and comparing this as suggested in the new framework appears a hopeless task.

(Dill, 1999b: 10–11)

Perhaps the most succinct criticism of the quality infrastructure came in an article by Alison Wolf in the *Times Higher* on 22 May 1998 entitled 'Two sides of A4 will not do the trick'. This compared the quality infrastructure with other attempts to disseminate and guarantee standards through written definitions: 'The experience confirmed the tenets of assessment theory. Standards cannot, in fact, be disseminated or internalized in this way – they depend on tacit knowledge and socialization into assessor groups.'[14]

Professional training

As has been seen, one of the hopes of the JPG report was that an integrated quality regime might make cooperation with the professional and statutory bodies easier. HEQC's work with the NHS has already been mentioned (Chapter 3). The HEFCE Assessment Division had also made some progress. In the 1996 to 1998 assessment cycle, the Royal Institution of Chartered Surveyors relied on HEFCE assessment information to decide whether or not to make an accreditation visit, combined assessment and accreditation visits were undertaken with the Institution of Electrical Engineers and the Institution of Mechanical Engineers, and there were some parallel visits in civil engineering with some sharing of documentation. The new agency therefore took this up as a major challenge.

HQ issue 2 (Nov 1997) described discussions with a number of professional bodies in the medical and paramedical areas. Professional body representatives were, of course, to be heavily involved in subject benchmarking. *HQ* issue 6 (Nov 1999) reported that the agency was in discussion with the NHS Executive about the possibility of contracting with them for subject review using the new Academic Review method in England from 2001/2. *HQ* issue 8 (Jan 2001) announced that six prototype reviews of nursing and professions allied to medicine would take place between October 2001 and July 2002, with a full cycle beginning in October 2003. *HQ* issue 9 (Nov 2001) reported on the six institutions that had agreed to participate. Finally, the *QAA Evaluation Report*, published in November 2002, stated that a total of 70 programmes had been reviewed:

> The results of the evaluation indicated that the prototype method was successful in reaching judgements on academic and practitioner standards, and the quality of learning opportunities. . . . There was a high level of expressed satisfaction with the method from all those participating. . . . The review method offers a real opportunity to integrate and streamline quality assurance mechanisms in NHS-funded nursing, midwifery, health visiting, and allied health professions' educational provision.
>
> (QAA, 2002e: 4)

However, no references can be found anywhere to any headway being made with the Teacher Training Agency. It remains to be seen whether the Better Regulation Review Group will fare any better. HEFCE and the Teacher Training Agency do of course report to the same Secretary of State.

Degree-awarding powers and university title

In 1998 the Department asked QAA to review the criteria and procedures for degree-awarding powers and university title. It appeared to be quite clear from what was said to the author at the time by contacts at the Department that the underlying aim was to further restrict the number of institutions that could achieve a university title (with taught degree-awarding powers en route). This was subsequently confirmed by John Randall at a private meeting with a number of SCOP principals on 13 January 1999, at which the author was present, just before the revised criteria were announced; he did nevertheless emphasize that it was still intended to be seen 'as a developmental process'!

In summary, the criteria developed by HEQC – which had themselves been based on CNAA experience – were considerably expanded both 'horizontally' (to cover in particular governance and management, which were arguably more matters for the funding councils anyway) and 'vertically', to introduce greater specificity. The avowed intention was to produce greater transparency and consistency than was believed to have been the case under HEQC. At the same time the application procedure was made significantly more elaborate, with the introduction – once a prima facie case for serious consideration of an application had been established following a preliminary visit – of a year-long process of direct observation and engagement in institutional processes by Agency assessors. Only then would a scrutiny panel visit the institution.

The proposals put to the Department by the Agency were actually far more radical than those which were eventually agreed by ministers. In particular:

- Applications should not be considered until there had been 'a full appraisal of all the options available for the future of the institution'. This might include a merger or an association with an existing university.
- The powers, once granted, might be limited to particular subjects, levels or types of course.
- Only universities should be able to validate or accredit another institution's provision: university colleges (ie colleges with degree-awarding powers) should only be able to do so once they had a proven record.
- Most controversially of all, the QAA should be able to recommend the removal of degree-awarding powers from both university colleges and universities (Swain, Tysome and Baty, 1999; Tysome, 1999; Barron, 1999).

Even without these refinements, however, this is one policy at least that has achieved its objective: at the time of writing (May 2003) so far as the author is aware, since the rules were changed only one college has attained taught degree-awarding powers, one has achieved research degree-awarding powers, and one has attained a university title.[15]

Subject review and institutional audit

Chapter 4 described the main changes made to subject review under QAA: none of these was fundamental. Similarly, continuation audit continued without major changes. Sadly, no latterday equivalent of HEQC's *Learning from Audit*, setting out the overall findings and conclusions of the individual audits, has yet appeared although, like Billy Bunter's postal order, one is daily promised.

Similarly, the overseas audits continued on broadly the same lines as under HEQC. In 1997 there were visits to partnerships in Germany, Greece and the Netherlands. In 1998 Bahrain, Bulgaria, Dubai, Greece, Hungary,

India, Israel, Oman, Poland and the United Arab Emirates were visited. In 1999 Dubai, India, Ireland, Israel, Malaysia and South Africa; in 2000 China, Ireland, Israel and Spain; in 2001 China, Cyprus, Egypt and Hong Kong; and in 2002 Denmark, Greece and Singapore were visited.

In 1999 the agency published an overview report of the visit to Malaysia (reference is made to it in *HQ* issue 11, which also gives the Web site reference). *HQ* issues 8 and 9 carried brief accounts of some of the main findings from the visits, some of which tallied with those from the HEQC. *HQ* issue 10 (Jul 2002) went into greater detail about some of the 'headline messages' that had emerged from the preparation for the Israeli audits in 2001; many of these were of more general applicability. *HQ* issue 11 (Nov 2002) contained an update of the 1999 Malaysian overview report on the basis of a third round of visits there (in 2002). It also promised a Learning from Overseas Audit. The Malaysia report in *HQ* issue 11 found that local knowledge of previous audit reports was mixed.

The Thames Valley affair

In February 1998, at the institution's request, the agency conducted a 'special review' of the ways in which Thames Valley University assured the academic quality and standards of its provision. The precise origins of the review can only be a matter of speculation; there had been reports in the press in 1997 that a pro-vice-chancellor had ordered some assessors to turn fails into passes, which the university subsequently admitted. The importance of the review can be seen from the fact that the audit team included the Agency's then Director of Institutional Review as well as two of the Agency's (and HEQC's) most senior auditors. Clearly, no mistakes were to be made! The auditors concluded that there was no evidence that students had been awarded degrees they should have not received, or that standards had fallen. But the report did contain 'clear evidence' that the university was 'in a position where its academic standards and the quality of its students' experience, especially in its College of Undergraduate Studies, were and are under threat, and can now only be maintained by special measures'. The report was published on 12 November 1998 and the Vice-Chancellor, Professor Mike Fitzgerald, resigned the same day. It is fair to say that the affair sent shock waves through the sector.[16]

QAA 1997 to 2001

John Randall resigned on 21 August 2001 (QAA, 2001d: 17).[17] In various public statements he argued that the reduction in subject-level scrutiny to 10 per cent was 'a step too far'. In his view the July proposals left the universities facing too little scrutiny to ensure public confidence in standards, and students, employers and others with too little information with which to judge the quality of provision.

Like HEQC, the agency had effectively been sidelined. In the circumstances there was little alternative but for John Randall to go, as he confirmed: 'When the two biggest funders of the Agency (UUK and HEFCE) are going in a direction that is different from the one I would take, clearly it does become a difficult position. You can see the difficulty of holding the views that I do and taking the leading role in shaping the way forward' (Randall, 2001, quoted by Baty, 2001).

As should by now be clear, the basic reasons for the Agency's failure to come up with a credible and acceptable quality process were 'structural': the failure to achieve a lasting agreement on the purposes and forms of external quality regulation which has been the central theme of this book. But in my opinion matters were not helped by its Chief Executive's enthusiastic espousal of a 'tougher' regulatory regime when something more modulated was what was required, as will now be argued.

Notes

1 John Randall clearly believed Dearing had envisaged external examiners actually reporting to the agency (see Randall, 1998). Peter Wright recalls that there was general agreement among the 'professionals' at the agency that the Dearing proposals were unworkable, but the Agency could not be seen to be too obviously 'losing' them. Eventually the late Peter Milton suggested that the alternative might be put into the paper, suitably camouflaged, so as to offer the Agency a way out (Peter Wright, personal communication). More generally, Peter Wright does not agree with my thesis of a step change between HEQC and QAA, via Dearing. As a senior member of both HEQC and QAA, he sees a greater degree of continuity and consistency than the material quoted here might suggest. A possible resolution of this difference of view is the fact that the Agency often under its CEO used sharp rhetoric when the reality was much more moderate.
2 In November 1999 the agency had issued a consultative document proposing that there should be judgements on three aspects of Learning Opportunities: teaching and learning; student progression; effectiveness of use of learning resources. For each, there would be a judgement of 'excellent', 'approved' or 'not approved', depending on the extent to which each aspect contributed to the achievement of the relevant outcomes. In addition there would be a summary judgement on the provision as a whole, again using these terms but also taking into account the reviewers' confidence in the standards achieved. Following consultation the agency changed the terms to 'commendable', 'approved' and 'failing'. The judgements on the individual aspects were otherwise to be unchanged but the overall judgement would be either 'approved' or 'failing': that is, there was to be no 'exemplary' category for the provision as a whole. This was the only modification made and the only concession to the institutions, which had overwhelmingly wanted summative judgements to be replaced by a narrative style of reporting and 'graded action points' (which the representative bodies had also wanted). Students, employers and professional and statutory bodies however all favoured summative judgements (*THES*, 2000).
3 David Dill, writing in the Open University Quality Support Centre's *Digest* in Spring 1999, came to a similar conclusion: 'the overall framework is overly ambitious and unwieldy, requiring the development of many new procedures and processes foreign to the academic community, and potentially vulnerable to

the changing dynamics of mass higher education'(Dill, 1999a: 7). Elsewhere in the article David mentions how, as universities have internalised what might previously have been purely external review processes:

> critical academic decisions must now be defended within the university community itself. The growth of American Studies at a university now has to be justified, not just to the Funding Council, but also to the Faculty of Chemistry. In this new context of heightened financial accountability and university-based processes for evaluating academic programme investments, external reviews conducted by outside agencies on their own timetables and for their own purposes are increasingly perceived by the universities them-selves as a redundant irritant. While the QA is aware of this problem, I would suggest that the criticism will only grow more shrill as the manage-ment organisations of the universities mature. It will not only be Henry II who will mutter, 'Who will rid me of this meddlesome priest'.
>
> (Dill, 1999a: 6)

This comment turned out to be not merely astute but prophetic.

4 The Russell Group consists of the Universities of Birmingham, Bristol, Cam-bridge, Cardiff, Edinburgh, Glasgow, Leeds, Liverpool, Manchester, Newcastle upon Tyne, Nottingham, Oxford, Sheffield, Southampton and Warwick together with Imperial College, King's College London, the London School of Economics and University College London.

5 Another theory is that the reason for the Russell Group pressure was that some of them had not done all that well in assessment, and they wished to destroy a process that showed some of the new universities doing better than them: in other words, any process which showed new universities ranked above them was by definition flawed. This was a point actually made by Lord Parekh in the Lords debate. (Lord Parekh is another Professor at Hull but had previously been at the LSE where he is now Visiting Professor.) An article by Francis Beckett in *Guardian Education* on 1 May 2001 showed two new universities – West of England and Northumbria – in the top ten institutions in terms of the proportion of depart-ments scoring above 21; LSE was in eleventh place. See also O'Leary, 2001.

6 LTSN is a programme funded by the UK funding bodies. Its role, mainly discharged through university-based subject centres, is to support all institu-tions and all practitioners in learning and teaching, and to develop and dissem-inate good practices. It is answerable to a steering committee established by the funding bodies, and is located within the ILT as the host organization. The total grant cost of LTSN is approximately £40 million spread over five years. LTSN services are freely available to all in the sector (HEFCE/UUK/SCOP, 2003: 8). Using assessment evidence to support enhancement was of course what the HEQC had tried but failed to achieve with the HEFCE Assessment Unit (see Chapter 3).

7 One novel feature of the *Handbook* was the inclusion, for the first time so far as can be determined, of some 'organisational principle and process standards'. The *Handbook* goes on to say that the principles had been used to develop 'explicit service standards' for institutional audit, the details of which are published on the Agency's website (QAA, 2002f). As regards quality assurance, the *Hand-book* states:

> The Agency is committed to the regular monitoring and evaluation of its policies, procedures and processes, to ensure their ongoing credibility and to continuously improve its performance in response to the results. In respect of institutional audit, this commitment includes providing the

opportunity for participants in the process, including students, to provide structured feedback on their experiences.

(*Handbook*, annex J, para 5; QAA, 2002c: 36)

One other new feature of the expanded audit method was the more prominent position given to student representatives. Audit teams had for many years had meetings with students as part of the audit. However the Operational Description and the *Handbook* give student representatives the opportunity to provide information to the auditors at the start. During the briefing visit student representatives will have the opportunity to give their views on the choice of audit trails. Both students and staff will also have quite considerable opportunities during the visits to comment both on institutional quality assurance arrangements generally and on the matters raised during the disciplinary audit trails. As already mentioned in Chapter 4 the January 2003 White Paper (see Chapter 7) proposed that institutional information about quality and standards should be 'drawn together' by the NUS in 'a more comprehensive and easily accessible guide to higher education' (para 4.5; DfES, 2003a: 48). Clearly, NUS lobbying had paid off.

8 This difference was reflected in the 'unit' that was to be the basis of report. Student representatives wanted as specific a unit as possible (that is, a course), but the cost of this would have been disproportionate. Institutions wanted a much higher level of aggregation. The eventual outcome – dividing the curriculum into 19 areas – seems unlikely to satisfy either constituency.

9 The first meeting of the committee had before it the Segal Quince Wicksteed report mentioned in Chapter 4 showing that there was little evidence of demand for information of this kind from either students or others.

10 HEQC's impact has also been international. Within Europe generic descriptors for Bachelors and Masters degrees, known as the Dublin descriptors, are being developed under the Joint Quality Initiative. These are due to be ratified at the Berlin conference in September 2003, which is the next review of progress under the Bologna process. The descriptors are in terms of the demonstration of knowledge and understanding, not in terms of time or credits. There is also developing interest in national and international qualifications frameworks, with a seminar in Copenhagen later in 2003. Another development is the Tuning project which is looking at the desirability of some subject-specific descriptors or broad benchmark statements for degrees; the areas currently being looked at include history and business administration. Work is now going on to test the feasibility of these instruments as a basis for a European, trans-national scheme of evaluation at subject/programme level. There is also a developing interest in international standard-setting instruments in UNESCO. It is hard to believe that any of this would have happened without the Graduate Standards Programme.

11 The agency had wanted four undergraduate levels, with one level specifically for the new foundation degree and ordinary degrees. However the universities were strongly opposed to this, since most work to a three-level model. At a meeting at the Department in October 2000 the Minister told QAA that in view of the opposition from the sector it should drop its proposed four levels and accept three. In the event both qualifications were accommodated at Level 2.

12 What comes across most strongly from the statements is the sheer conservatism of the academic community. Innovative ideas about assessment in particular are almost entirely confined to 'new' subjects, likely to be taught mostly in post-1992 institutions.

13 I have already mentioned that Peter Wright takes a different view of the infrastructure – see note 1. Peter argues that because of its exclusionist nature

(Wright, 1989), reflecting, and reinforced by, institutional autonomy, English higher education is 'intrinsically more hostile than most to deliberate, self-critical, public reflection on standards, strengths and weaknesses'. What could be seen as 'opportunities to explain, gain support for and disseminate the purposes, values and aims of higher education are seen as threats to higher education' (personal communication to the author, May 2003; see also Wright, 1996).

14 Professor Wolf's study for HEQC about the scope for establishing threshold standards (HEQC, 1997a) should be read by everyone interested in the subject.

15 The 2003 White Paper (see Chapter 7) announced the government's intention to make yet further changes to the criteria for degree-awarding powers and university title. At the time of writing (May 2003) the details have still to be announced.

16 The *THES* claimed on 5 November 1999 that the QAA report was seriously flawed, and that the university contested matters of both fact and interpretation in 57 of the report's 77 paragraphs. The agency stood by its work (Baty, 1999). During the discussions about a new system in 1995, one of the points made by Professor Davies and others was that audit reports had not shown up quality problems uncovered through assessment. It is therefore interesting that the TVU audit report made no reference to any of the TVU's assessment reports. This was because they would not have alerted QAA to the issue, although a careful reading of the university's continuation audit report might have done.

17 According to the QAA's Annual Report 2000–1 John Randall received £61,787 compensation for loss of office, having been on a salary and benefits package of £102,028 (QAA, 2001c: 19).

7 UK quality assurance: past, present, future

> The crucial factor in a system of academic quality control, monitoring and improvement lies in efforts to create an institutional culture marked by self-criticism, openness to criticism by others, and a commitment to improvement in practice. This above all is the responsibility of institutional leadership.
>
> (Trow, 1996: 30)

Introduction

This final chapter summarizes what has happened to date and speculates on how the current quality arrangements may evolve.

The past

Purposes

As should by now be clear, the main reason for the changes to the various quality regimes since 1992 has been continuing disagreements between the key players – the Government, the Funding Council and the institutions through (mainly) their representative bodies – about the purposes, forms, coverage and ownership of quality assurance. The most important of these conflicts has concerned the best means of protecting the quality of student learning. In essence, the two views were as follows.

First, quality is best protected by institutions competing against one another for students and income. The crucial information about quality is the information that students receive about providers' offerings, which enables them to make genuine choices about where to study on the basis of fitness for purpose and perceived quality. Institutions respond to students' choices and raise the quality of their provision accordingly.

Second, quality is best protected by institutions' own quality arrangements, which reflect and reinforce the values and professionalism of staff. The crucial information about quality is that provided to the institution by its internal processes, which usually include an element of externality. Quality is improved through the professional motivation to do better.

The main driver of the first view is efficiency in the use of resources; the main driver of the second is the need to match provision to requirements. As we saw in Chapter 2, this dichotomy between efficiency and effectiveness became clear as soon as the two quality processes introduced in 1992 began to take shape. It remains to this day.

Forms

The earlier emphasis on efficiency and competition through attracting students meant inevitably that external assurance through assessment had to focus on teaching and learning at subject/programme levels, had to involve explicit consequences for those concerned as a result of the evaluation, and had to involve graded (rather than threshold) judgements. As the White Paper said, 'Arrangements are needed to assess the quality of what is actually provided and these assessments should . . . inform the funding decisions of the Funding Council' (DES, 1991: 28–29).

As we saw in Chapters 4 to 6, this last phrase was to prove a major stumbling block in the successive attempts to agree a regime even though, ironically, the financial consequences were insignificant. By contrast, effectiveness could be tackled at any level within an institution (and indeed the overseas audits did work at sub-institutional levels), did not necessarily have any consequences for those being evaluated (since the report was made to the institution and not to an external agency), and did not in the early days involve even a threshold judgement.

Coverage

The 1991 White Paper proposed what was in effect a two-fold distinction in the coverage of the new external processes. While assessment looked directly at the quality of institutional provision for teaching and learning, audit looked at it indirectly through the scrutiny of institutions' quality assurance arrangements. While assessment looked at teaching – the process by which students are brought to a certain level of achievement – audit looked at institutions' arrangements for, among other things, maintaining academic standards. Accordingly the matters covered by the two processes differed. Over time some limited convergence took place. But of far greater significance was the sector's acceptance of the Dearing recommendation that the external quality regime should focus quite explicitly on academic standards, and that it should do so within collectively endorsed frameworks policed by a body external to the sector.

Fitness for purpose versus fitness of purpose

The Dearing report actually represented a significant shift in two senses: by extending external scrutiny to academic standards (with a recommended scaling-down of assessment of programme quality), and by moving quality assurance away from a 'fitness for purpose' approach towards a 'fitness of purpose' one.

At least in theory, both assessment and audit were quite explicitly against comparisons between institutions. The Dearing recommendations, and QAA's espousal of them by its initial chief executive, meant moving in the opposite direction. In future institutions' standards were to be judged against both their own criteria and those of the sector, mediated and orchestrated by the Agency. Of course there were limits to this approach, and certainly under the current management of QAA there has been some rowing back. But vestiges remain. For example, under the *Code of Practice*, external examiners are recommended to confirm whether the standards set by each institution 'Are appropriate for the awards, or award elements, by reference to published national subject benchmarks, the National Qualifications Framework and institutional programme specifications' (QAA, 2000: 15). In the wrong hands this could still turn into a backdoor route to a national curriculum, with external examiners becoming in effect Agency inspectors, although at present this seems unlikely.

The arrangements approved in March 2002 represented a compromise rather than a victory for one approach over the other. The outcomes of the new process are addressed both to the external agency (acting, inter alia, on behalf of the Funding Council) and to the institution being evaluated. But while there will no longer be either comprehensiveness of scrutiny at subject level or graded judgements on subject-level provision, there is a much stronger emphasis on the collection and publication of information about quality and standards. This goes not only beyond what has been required previously, but also beyond what the evidence on the demand for information suggests is actually necessary to inform students. Moreover the new framework continues to embrace academic standards, though there has been some retreat over the extent to which institutions will be expected (by the Agency) to comply literally with the quality infrastructure. Finally, there will continue to be consequences, including possibly financial consequences, for institutions that fall seriously foul of the auditors.[1]

Ownership

The arrangements for the ownership of quality assurance have also, since 1997, represented a compromise. Whether this aspect will be as unstable as the others remains to be seen.

As we saw in Chapter 2, the duality in the purpose of the quality processes introduced in 1992 was paralleled by a duality in ownership. Assessment was to be carried out on behalf of the Funding Council which also, with Departmental guidance, after consultation with the sector, and with the advice of a committee with institutional representatives, determined its key features. Audit was to be carried out on behalf of the academic community collectively, through the institutions and their representative bodies, by a body both legally owned and actually controlled by the institutions, through a board of which the overwhelming majority were heads of institutions appointed by the representative bodies (mostly vice-chancellors nominated by CVCP, now Universities UK). The Board of QAA, on the other hand, has 14 members (apart from its CEO), of whom four are appointed by the representative bodies, four are appointed by the funding councils, and six are independents. In effect, the duality has gone underground (David Parry, personal communication to the author, May 2003).

The rationale for the post-1992 division of ownership was that while quality was of interest to students and other stakeholders, academic standards were, and could only be, a matter for institutions and the academic community collectively. Legally this is still the case. But there was also a political reason. The vice-chancellors had only recently established the Academic Audit Unit. The Department was uncertain how they would react not only to the introduction of assessment, which was at that stage a fairly radical notion for institutions that had otherwise been largely free of external regulation, but also to the abolition of the binary line, of which the new quality arrangements were a necessary and unavoidable consequence. Just to be sure, however, the Department announced in the White Paper, and incorporated into the subsequent legislation, the reserve power for the Secretary of State to transfer to the funding councils collectively, or to someone acting on their behalf, the function of assessing the arrangements made by institutions for maintaining their academic standards. From the start, therefore, this was to be self-regulation within a statutory 'envelope'.

It was consistent with this pragmatic approach on the Government's part that it was not the Department but the institutions, through CVCP and its leadership, that sought to change things on the basis that a single agency, administering a single process, would reduce the regulatory demands upon them. Initially the Department was cool but eventually the lobbying paid off and a review was ordered. But even when, in the summer of 1995, agreement was reached on the bare bones of a new process, the Government made it clear that the new agency could never be, as HEQC had been, answerable chiefly to the institutions. The then CVCP Chair accepted this on the grounds that there was no way of keeping the Government out of quality.

Accordingly, while QAA's legal owners were, as with HEQC, the representative bodies, the majority of the new agency's board was to comprise independent members and Funding Council nominees. To add insult to injury, the request of the two representative bodies to be allowed to send observers to board meetings (as they had with HEQC) was humiliatingly refused, while similar requests from the Department and the NUS were accepted.

As we saw in Chapter 5, the vice-chancellors had by this time conceded that the new quality process would embrace standards. Historically they had made

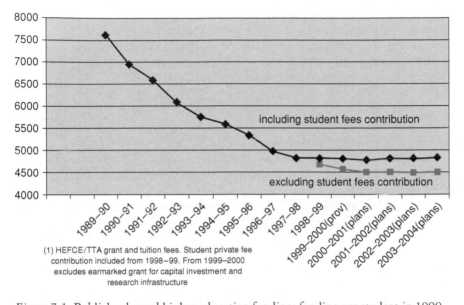

(1) HEFCE/TTA grant and tuition fees. Student private fee contribution included from 1998–99. From 1999–2000 excludes earmarked grant for capital investment and research infrastructure

Figure 7.1 Publicly planned higher education funding: funding per student in 1999–
2000 prices, England, 1989/90 to 2003/4
Source: Universities UK, DFEE

strenuous and mostly successful efforts to resist any external scrutiny of their courses or teaching; now they were accepting that an agency over which they had only limited control would not only scrutinize the standards of student achievement associated with their awards, but would do so in quite a thorough and comprehensive way. This was a considerable concession.

There are many ironies here. One of the biggest is that in return for accepting this greater degree of external regulation, and for giving up their own, increasingly respected and authoritative, self-regulatory body, the vice-chancellors did not receive, either then nor subsequently, any reward either in terms of reducing the famous burden (which was supposed to have happened as a result of the JPG report and the establishment of the new agency) or (as Figure 7.1 shows) in terms of securing any improvement in the funding of teaching (which was the quid pro quo, if there was one, for accepting the Dearing quality recommendations). Even by the universities' own standards, this represents a pretty poor outcome from nearly ten years' lobbying.[2]

The issue of ownership inevitably raises the question of the accountability of QAA. To whom is it accountable? Legally, the answer is that the Agency is accountable to the funding councils, and to the institutions, through separate service-level agreements. Practically, it is accountable to everyone (which includes of course the Minister for Higher Education and the Department) and to no one: there is no single person or body to whom the agency is answerable (except where it acts on behalf of the Department in giving advice on degree-awarding powers and university title). The irony — that this is an organization set up at the altar of accountability to enforce or ensure accountability on the part of others — is palpable.

So who was responsible for this sorry saga?

Responsibility

In his latest book, Ronald Barnett (2003) has described 'quality' as an 'ideology' which is contributing to the undermining of the liberal notion of the university as a site of rational discourse (cf Morley, 2003). He also notes that an agreed definition of ideology is hard to find. Using the word in the conventional sense, however, one can see that a preconceived view of what needed to be done to protect quality, on the part of the Government and HEFCE, was the root cause of the subsequent problems. The assumption that the way to improve quality was to get departments and universities to compete with one another, with the corollary that any external process had therefore to be capable of picking winners (and so had to scruitinize every provider in sufficient depth), together with the tenacity with which the Funding Council clung to this view right up to March 2001, limited the assessment regime's capacity to act as a vehicle for educational development, prevented the integration with audit into an appropriately comprehensive but selective assurance process, and doomed QAA's attempts to combine the JPG and Dearing recommendations.

It is not only with the benefit of hindsight that we can say that the post-binary quality regime should have started with an initial survey of the quality of institutions' teaching, should have identified the main strengths and weaknesses in the ways in which that quality was protected, and should have instituted a rigorous but selective regime aimed in the first instance at enabling institutions to identify and remedy their quality control weaknesses. This has never been done.

But if the Government and HEFCE bear the main responsibility for the nearly farcical, and certainly serious, waste of effort that so much of post-1992 quality assurance has represented, the institutions, and especially their representative bodies, cannot avoid some of the blame.

To begin with, the existing universities were slow to respond to the questions that Ministers and other were raising about their internal quality processes from the early 1980s onwards (the validity of which the early audit reports confirmed). They failed collectively to defend their own self-regulatory body (it often seemed that CVCP saw HEQC as more of a threat than the Funding Council), and it is impossible to imagine them taking the sort of action that Geoffrey Alderman has described the Southern Association of Colleges and Schools as taking, namely expelling an institution that was very clearly letting the side down (Alderman, 2003). They confused a valid concern (value for money) with an invalid one (the overall cost of the arrangements and the demands on them) in such a way as to play into the hands, time and again, of the Government and the Funding Council. It was always obvious that they would not get any substantial 'relief' (as they saw it) in return for giving up their own agency and accepting that external scrutiny should extend to academic standards, nor did they deserve it. It served them right when the agency appointed an avowed regulator as its chief executive and declined to give them observer status on the board.

This is a substantial catalogue, but actually the strongest criticism of the institutions is their failure to mount a reasoned critique of the Government's approach or to explore or present alternatives based on research and analysis. So far as the author is aware, no serious effort was made to compute the costs and distortions associated with assessment (other than the two attempts already detailed in Chapter 4). No survey of relevant international practice was ever commissioned. No reference was even made to past UK experience in the public sector of higher education with CNAA and HMI. No serious support was given to alternative QA approaches, either within UK higher education itself or outside it.[3] Most importantly of all, little or no reference was made to those in the sector in Britain (or abroad) with any knowledge or understanding of quality assurance. The literature on regulation summarized in Chapter 1 might as well never have existed for all the notice the vice-chancellors took of it.

Chapter 4 showed how those actually running the external processes were kept well away from the JPG. Allergy to experts seems to be a particularly British malady (Brown, 2001d). One might be prepared to forgive the civil servants, but given that higher education is supposedly all about basing one's arguments and propositions on a critical review of information and evidence garnered through research and scholarship, it is hard to forgive the vice-chancellors for such a serious failure (Brown, 2001f; cf Brown, 1997d).

Why, given its importance, did Universities UK not at any stage (at least to the author's knowledge) bring together at least some of those with relevant knowledge, experience and expertise to assist in developing its position, conducting relevant surveys and research in a suitably professional manner? There is an obvious contrast with their approach to policies on the funding of higher education. Was it simply that it would have shown up the ignorance of most vice-chancellors on these topics of crucial importance to their institutions, and their failure, frequently and painfully witnessed by the author, to discuss it in terms much more sophisticated than the 'four legs good, two legs bad' variety? Or was it that they actually *preferred* to have an external agency controlling these matters? This option left them free to criticize it while avoiding having to take the responsibility for doing the sometimes difficult things that are necessary if quality is to be maintained in the increasingly difficult environment in which their institutions have to operate; but it is for this that they are paid substantial salaries and accorded considerable honours. What price self-regulation in these hands?[4]

The future

The new quality framework

Against this somewhat discouraging background, how might the present quality framework be expected to evolve? A preliminary point is that the framework is still quite new. The first few new style audits have been completed (apparently without mishap), so it will be some while before any judgements can be made. The quality infrastructure is still being filled out. The information elements are also still being put into place, although they have already led to some controversy (Baty, 2003).

A further preliminary point is that since the framework was agreed, the Government and HEFCE have together published potentially far-reaching proposals for changing UK higher education (DfES, 2003a; HEFCE, 2003a). There is not space here for a detailed appreciation (but see Brown, 2003). For the purposes of this discussion, the key point is that there will be – or at least there is intended to be – a much sharper differentiation between institutions and what they provide. The main vehicle for this will be the introduction, from 2006, of the freedom for institutions to levy a tuition contribution (a top-up fee) of up to £3,000 (compared with the present £1,100) if certain conditions are satisfied. There has yet to be any proper discussion of the potential implications of this brave new world for quality assurance. But the HEFCE Chief Executive, Professor Sir Howard Newby, has already hinted that institutions that do not levy a top-up fee can expect closer external scrutiny (Goddard, 2003). This is bound to increase the pressure on the new framework.

As should by now be clear, the latest quality framework conciliates rather than resolves the conflicts about the purposes and forms of quality assurance that have been the subject of this book. So it is not possible to be over-sanguine about its chances of success. On the one hand, the institutions could yet again rebel at the demands, particularly the informational demands, being made on them (even though they have lost the main irritant from before, universal subject review). On the other hand, there could be further external pressures on the framework if Ministers, students and others feel that it is still not providing them with the information and assurance they see as necessary in a world in which, through the introduction of top-up fees, they regard themselves as sovereign paying customers. It should be obvious by now that the author does not think that any external regime can provide that information and reassurance; only effective self-regulation can do so.

In these circumstances the framework could evolve in one of two ways. If institutional pressures prevail, new-style audit could come over time to resemble institutional accreditation as it was practised under the CNAA. This could happen quite easily if the Agency were to abandon the gothic structures set out in the *Handbook* and rely instead on the technically superior criteria for taught degree-awarding powers. This would mean dumping the disciplinary audit trails and giving the reviewers a much freer hand (as in Scotland and Wales). If, however, external factors prevail, we could see a return to some form of subject review or even inspection by OFSTED.

This could happen anyway if the intended sharpening of the already severe differences in levels of institutional resourcing leads to real or perceived differences of quality.[5] Alternatively, there could be a sensible and final acceptance of the fact that institutional offerings are not realistically comparable, and therefore a swing back to the fitness-for-purpose approach which was articulated in the immediate aftermath of the abolition of the binary line.

All this is of course speculative. The past is not always a guide to the future, though Santayana's famous dictum – that a nation ignorant of its past is condemned to relive it – does come effortlessly to mind when one reflects on our quality assurance travails.[6] What is perhaps less speculative is that the new framework could have major problems of quality control.

Quite apart from the inherent tensions that have been described, there is the fact that the new framework is much larger, much more comprehensive (it covers far many more matters and involves both past and prospective judgements), and much more complex (in the way in which the various elements are to be brought together) than either audit or assessment. In itself the far larger number and types of auditors are bound to make the consistent application of the Agency's criteria much more difficult. Moreover it has simply been introduced; there has been no piloting. There are, to put it bluntly, just too many things that can go wrong, and institutions are of course much more attuned to these things – and with differential fees the stakes will be even higher – than previously. There is also the point that QAA has committed itself to certain quality standards in its work (see Chapter 6). This should help to improve the quality of the process, but it could also give institutions additional avenues of complaint.

So even if there is not a further radical change of the kind that we have seen several times since 1992, there is bound to be some simplification and refinement, overt or more likely covert, in the way the new process is operated. If there is one clear lesson from the last decade it is the mutability of external quality assurance processes. This in itself shows how they can never be fully consistent between institutions, or wholly immune from charges of unfairness. But it also reinforces the case for not placing excessive reliance on them, other than where an institution is in serious difficulty, as was the case with Thames Valley, or where the institution or sector is rapidly developing (as was the case with the former polytechnics in the early days of CNAA, and as is currently the case, in HE terms at least, with some of the further education colleges).

All this assumes, of course, that there will continue to be a single quality framework administered by a single quality agency. As some of us predicted when the heads of new universities chose to enter CVCP rather than keep their own representative body, Universities UK in its present form is capable of representing institutions' interests only to a limited degree.[7] Differential fees, if they come, will make UUK's task even harder. At what point will the heads of institutions accept that a single framework is simply not capable of doing justice to these differences, and that, for example, each group of institutions should have its own set of external examiners trained by a group agency?[8]

This in turn assumes, of course, that there has not been a further restructuring through the creation of a single agency devoted to quality improvement by combining the QAA and the new Academy for the Advancement of Learning and Teaching. It is time to return to the relationship between accountability and enhancement.

Accountability and enhancement

It would be comforting to think that some recognition on the part of the authorities – the Department for Education and Skills and the Higher Education Funding Council for England – of the limitations of an accountability-driven model of quality assurance was behind the recent increase in interest in quality enhancement and the proposal to establish the new academy. The actual reasons, however, were the government's desire, expressed in the White Paper, to raise the profile of teaching relative to research – something which as we saw in Chapter 3 goes back a very long way – and the widespread perception – confirmed by the TQEC report – that the existing organization of enhancement effort, through ILT, LTSN, HESDA and a number of voluntary groups like the Staff and Educational Development Association (SEDA) and the Society for Research in Higher Education (SRHE), as well as QAA, was sub-optimal. There were also questions about the longer-term viability of the ILT, or at least the funding model on which it was based.

In effect the new Academy takes us back to the Dearing Committee's original model for the ILT. In an article in the *Times Higher Education Supplement* on 9 August 2002 (Brown, 2002a), the author explained why the Dearing model had not been realized, a major factor being HEFCE's determination under its then chief executive to extend its control into all aspects of teaching and learning. As a result the balance of quality assurance effort had shifted to accountability, while the forces devoted to improvement, including the promotion of innovation, were fragmented. There needed to be a single agency that combined the enhancement of teaching with the strengthening of leadership and management, possibly on the lines of the NHS Modernisation Agency (cf Brown, 1998c).[9]

What challenges face the new academy? How should it relate to QAA? Is there indeed a case for a single agency covering both accountability and enhancement?

The new agency's immediate challenges will be to find a way of integrating the functions currently discharged by the various existing agencies, and to prepare itself to play a key part in implementing the Government's proposals for raising the profile and professionalism (as it sees it) of lecturers. These include additional funding for pay modernization, rewarding good teaching, more National Teaching Fellowships, 70 centres of excellence to reward good teaching and promote best practice, and 'new national professional standards for teaching' (DfES, 2003a: 46). But the Agency's most fundamental challenge will be to reconcile government and institutional perspectives about what needs to be done with the views of rank and file lecturers. The issues were well articulated in the response of the Centre for Learning and Teaching – Sociology, Anthropology and Politics to the TQEC report.

While welcoming the new Academy, and expressing the hope that the key features of the existing LTSN subject centres would be continued, this expressed concern about the underlying model:

> The TQEC report adopts a deficit model of staff, assuming that the problem is the recalcitrance of staff and a dose of strong leadership is needed to get them to improve their ways. . . . Just as enthusing students is crucial to improving their learning, so enhancement of the quality of teaching is about enthusing staff and engaging them in an intellectually rewarding process which maintains their commitment to continually improving their teaching.
>
> (C-SAP, 2003: para 1.7)

The response quotes the evaluation of the LTSN to the effect that enhancing teaching and learning 'is not a matter of straight adoption of practices, methods or resources. It is much more about the development of thinking, of reflection and discussion, of working together to find solutions and to become aware of how other people handle similar problems' (C-SAP, 2003: para 4.2). The issue then is how, and indeed whether, such a perspective can be reconciled with the pressures for accountability that have been depicted in this book.

In Chapter 1 we noted the views of Kells and Jackson about the difficulties of combining in a single quality regime the different purposes of accountability and improvement. This is something that has also been considered by Middlehurst and Woodhouse. Their conclusion is that: 'While it is possible to specialise a system towards *improvement* (original authors' emphasis), it is not possible to have a separate system solely for accountability, as it will inevitably overlap into improvement' (Middlehurst and Woodhouse, 1995: 266).

If there is not to be a single agency with improvement as its chief objective, there must in the authors' view be clear differences between the agencies, but with information being shared subject only to confidentiality. This of course is what the HEQC tried to do with the HEFCE Assessment Unit (see Chapter 3). In any event:

> Both accountability and improvement need to operate within a framework which sets out and builds upon guiding principles which are continually developed out of existing and emerging good practice. A balance of power and trust needs to be established between key stakeholders, supported by open communication and negotiating machinery. Quality involves judgements of value and these differ both at the level of accountability and improvement. To achieve a robust, cost-effective and fair system, different (but equally legitimate) purposes and interests must be accommodated at all levels of the system. Serious imbalances of power are likely to damage both quality and the integrity of the higher education enterprise.
>
> (Middlehurst and Woodhouse, 1995: 267)

However, a single agency for both functions is preferable. In the final section of this book I should like to state what, in the light of UK experience since 1992, I believe to be the requirements for a successful quality regime. I shall also outline how these might be met.

Key requirements for an effective quality assurance regime

The key requirements for an effective quality assurance regime are:

- The underlying purpose must be improvement, not accountability.
- The regime must focus on what is necessary for quality improvement.
- The regime must bolster, not undermine, self-regulation.
- The arrangements must be meaningful to, and engage, all those involved.
- The arrangements must promote diversity and innovation.
- There must be adequate quality control (of the regime).
- There must be clear accountability (of the agency).
- There must be proper coordination with other regulators or would be regulators.

The purpose of quality assurance

It has long been my view that accountability is a dead end and that it should be replaced, as the main purpose of quality assurance, by quality improvement. This is for two main reasons. First, UK universities and colleges already provide programmes which are nearly everywhere of an acceptable standard, at least according to the criteria currently employed: there have as we have seen been only a tiny number of below-threshold assessment judgments.[10] To have yet another quality process that is primarily focused on accountability is not therefore a particularly good use of resources if one is trying to raise quality. The issue is really how we can make better use of these resources. Second, the way to raise quality is to make accountability – in the sense of compliance with standards and rules – only a small part of quality assurance, and to appeal instead to the professional motivation of staff to do better by engaging in a constructive, professional dialogue of the kind envisaged in the CHES evaluation of assessment in England, and actually practised in the best HEQC audits.

Focusing on what matters for quality improvement

I have written previously of the irony that in spite of the enormous effort that has been cumulatively invested in them, the post-1992 quality arrangements actually tell us very little about quality in UK higher education:

> we have major developments in our midst which at the very least pose challenges for quality: the expansion in student numbers; the worsening of staff–student ratios; the fall in the real unit of resource; serious and continuing under-investment in the learning infrastructure and in staff development; the increasing use of communications and information technologies; the increasing resort to untrained, unqualified and poorly motivated 'teaching' staff; the increasing separation of 'teaching' and 'research'; increased student employment during the academic year etc. Yet hardly any of these has been seriously studied or evaluated for its impact on quality, any more indeed than the accountability regimes themselves have been.
>
> (Brown, 2000b: 10)[11]

This is because they have been focused on the wrong targets (comparative judgements of performance) when they should have been looking at what it is that assists quality improvement: as at Singapore, the guns were pointing out to sea. As Middlehurst and Gordon have pointed out, this means looking at the leadership and management of resources, especially staff, within a suitable framework of governance.

Strengthening self-regulation

It is not proposed here to repeat the argument in favour of self-regulation as the primary mode of regulation in higher education. However there is a clear danger that institutions will come to see periodic external regulation as all the regulation that is needed, and/or that their internal procedures will simply mimic those of the external agency.[12] What is important is that institutions have systems and procedures that are fit for their own purposes, but which are also capable of yielding the information and evidence that external regulators require without much additional effort or expense. This is a lot easier to describe than to achieve.

Making quality assurance more meaningful to those involved

One of the points that Jethro Newton made in his study of an institution in Scotland (see Chapter 4) is the distancing of quality assurance from the ordinary practices and values of academic staff. This is not confined to that institution but is a fairly common experience. One answer to this is to map quality assurance onto the activities that academic staff carry out and the structures through which they conduct them. A particular problem here is the distinction between 'teaching' and 'research':

> One of the greatest problems with the present accountability regime is the almost entirely artificial separation between activities which go under such titles as 'teaching', 'research' and (sometimes) 'other revenue generating activities'. In reality, teaching and research (each of which in turn covers a multitude of activities) are merely aspects or dimensions of the work of an academic entity – an institution, a research group or a department – which embraces a much wider range of things than can ever be captured in such simple terms. Such a separation is not only misleading but actually dangerous because it is the connections between these activities, and the ways in which they are capable of reinforcing one another, that distinguishes higher education from other forms of education. As John Brennan has said, if there is one single thing which could make external evaluation 'real' to those being evaluated, it is treating the activities of academic entities as a whole. The alternative is continued dysfunctional reductionism.
>
> (Brown, 2000b: 10)

Related to this is the need to map quality processes onto existing academic structures rather than invent new ones: 'subject provider', 'unit of assessment' and so on.

Diversity and innovation

Two of the greatest requirements of a successful mass higher education system are institutional diversity and innovation, and indeed the two are interrelated (Brown, 1999b, 1999c, 2000a). How far have the post-1992 arrangements served either requirement? In Chapter 4 we saw how, in spite of the avowed intentions of the Funding Council, assessment outcomes overwhelmingly favoured the established and better-resourced universities. Audit outcomes were more balanced. In so far as assessment reinforced the existing 'hierarchy of esteem', it served to undermine real diversity at institutional level, since one of the preconditions for that is that there should not be too great a disparity of esteem. In contemplating still greater resource differentials, the recent White Paper will make this even worse (Brown, 2003). There is also an argument that the post-Dearing quality infrastructure is anti-diversity. This is certainly an inherent danger, but since the infrastructure is still being implemented, we can only reserve judgement at this stage. What is most striking is its sheer conservatism, or rather the conservatism that it reflects.

As regards the impact of the post-1992 arrangements on innovation, we lack an authoritative, up to date, study of the kind that Hannan and Silver made in 2000 (incidentally confirming the view of the anonymous auditor who contributed to the AAU's first annual report about the negative impact of the RAE on innovation in teaching; see Chapter 3). The general argument is that the post-1992 arrangements discouraged innovation in two ways: by rewarding institutions and departments that were good at delivering a tried and tested product at the expense of those that were innovating to develop a better one, and by diverting to quality assurance resources that might have been used for curriculum innovation. There is also the point that the current obsession with audit (Chapter 1) discourages enterprise at all levels in the institution. Certainly as the head of an institution I find that there is an inherent conflict between the desire one has to encourage colleagues to show enterprise and take risks, on the one hand, and the need to respect the audit requirements of external regulators, on the other. However we currently lack detailed studies and evidence that might enable us to test this hypothesis, the unhelpful but unavoidable corollary of which is that quality assurance can actually be detrimental to quality![13]

Quality control

Chapter 1 concluded by referring to the quality control of external quality assurance. This is a striking, and ironic, lacuna in the literature on quality assurance in higher education. Yet as argued in 1999 (Brown, 1999a), one of the basic tests of any quality assurance regime must surely be whether it can be delivered to an adequate standard of quality: that is, to an acceptable degree of validity, reliability (including consistency) and transparency. And one test of that is whether the operating agency has explicit standards for these variables, *and* the means of monitoring performance against them (and adjusting process and/or standards as a result).

This was less of a problem with audit than with assessment, where every head of institution had a tale to tell of what happened when the assessors came to call, some merely risible, others positively Ortonian. QAA has added an annex to the *Handbook for Institutional Audit* that deals with this, and there are now service standards for audits. It has also committed itself as an agency to the principles of integrity, professionalism, accountability and transparency (QAA, 2002d: 36). Blackmur has written, 'External quality assurance of higher education should involve a process of audit against appropriate standards by an organisation whose own performance quality is periodically assessed' (Blackmur, 2002: 21; cf Alderman, 1998). It is not clear when, how or by whom QAA's performance has been or will be assessed, although an evaluation of the new framework is envisaged for 2005.

Accountability

The absence of an explicit focus on quality control on the part of those designing and operating quality assurance is not the least of the many ironies of the past decade. But perhaps the greatest irony of all concerns accountability: after all, we must never forget that all of this has been done in the cause and name of accountability!

Commenting on the proposal in the January 2003 White Paper for an 'access regulator' to regulate institutions' admissions policies and procedures, and writing in a personal capacity, Christopher Hood, Professor of Government at the University of Oxford, said:

> If an access regime is to be stable, transparent and independent, the standards should be enshrined in statute, not regulation; regulators should be subject to a strict open-government regime; and the standards should be monitored and applied by a commission whose members are appointed for staggered terms, not by a single individual. (Naturally, the commissioners should be chosen in a way that is consistent with the principles they themselves apply.) Regulation by a tsar with uncertain powers is not the answer.
>
> (Hood, 2003)

Quis custodiet?

Coordination

It was of course the duplication between audit and assessment that was used to justify CVCP's push for a single system, although no evidence of such duplication was ever adduced, as the author pointed out publicly as long ago as February 1997 (Brown, 1997a). Audit and assessment were different processes aiming at different purposes and with different outcomes.

Needless to say, none of this prevented the point being made, any more than the information collected for the CVCP Committee showing that assessment and audit together absorbed only a tiny fraction of institutions' overall resources for teaching prevented the vice-chancellors from continuing to complain about the regulatory burden. Nor, ironically, did QAA make any serious effort to integrate the two processes until it was forced to abandon assessment. Had even a tiny fraction of the political and administrative effort that went into the single system negotiations and the creation of a single agency been put into making the two existing agencies collaborate more effectively, we should all have been a lot better off! Had HEFCE dropped its obsession with comparability, and had CVCP expressed real confidence in HEQC – or even any understanding of its rationale and purpose – the two agencies could have worked together, since their roles were generally complementary, and relationships at the professional level were good.

There is clearly an argument for better coordination between the various bodies concerned with the regulation of higher education: not only QAA and the funding council but other agencies such as the Teacher Training Agency and the NHS. As we saw in Chapter 6 this argument was accepted by the Better Regulation Task Force, although their conclusion was disappointingly lame: to establish a task force under the Department when it is the government that is the cause of the problem! What is really needed is a separate, independent organization with clear lines of accountability.

A higher education audit commission

In October 2000 the author put forward proposals for a single body, answerable to Parliament, that would regulate all aspects of institutions' academic activities (Brown, 2000b, 2001a). It would administer a single process with the following main elements:

- a single evaluation regime covering all aspects of an institution's academic activities: teaching, research, scholarship, knowledge transfer and so on, *seen in the context of an institution's mission*;
- a regime focusing on the achievement of objectives at institutional and local, usually departmental, levels;
- a regime using an audit methodology;
- a regime looking at all the academic activities of an institution or department;
- a regime aiming primarily at quality improvement.

The overall purpose would be to help improve the quality of the work of institutions by evaluating and reporting on their effectiveness in achieving their objectives, and by supporting them in their efforts to do so. To achieve this the commission would:

- Appoint, train, set standards for, and regulate auditors.
- Conduct, or accredit others to conduct, audits of institutions and, on a sample basis, academic units, and publish the outcomes. There would be a single threshold judgement accompanied by a profile of strengths and

areas for strengthening. The agency would also conduct 'thematic reviews' of specific topics across the sector, as was done by both CNAA and HEQC and is now intended in Scotland.

- Carry out value for money studies, facilitate benchmarking, conduct applied research and disseminate best practice.
- Give advice to Parliament, the Government, the Funding Council and other bodies about management, quality and standards in higher education.

The agency would make an annual report to Parliament about the quality of institutions' academic activities, the main challenges to this, and how (and how successfully) these challenges were being addressed. It could also:

- scrutinize the claims made by the institutions about the quality and standards of their provision (if not done as part of a routine audit); and
- investigate complaints from students and others about services offered by an institution that had not been successfully resolved through internal institutional procedures; and/or
- support institutions in their efforts to develop appropriate professional standards for their staff.

The commission would itself be subject to periodic (say five-yearly) review to ensure that it was fulfilling its objectives. The advantages of such a regime were summarized in the following terms:

- it would aim at quality improvement, which at the end of the day is the only real basis and justification for an external evaluation regime;
- it would concentrate on the key factor – leadership and management of staff and other resources – determining the quality and effectiveness of the 'services' provided by universities and colleges;
- it would make quality assurance, in the broadest sense, more meaningful because it would avoid or reduce the amount of games playing and compliance, audit being a very much harder methodology to traduce than assessment;
- it would cover all institutional activities, without the artificial and often meaningless distinction between research, teaching, scholarship etc;
- it would map onto existing institutional structures and means of delivery;
- by bringing the existing accountability regimes under a single roof, it would both save costs by reducing duplication and raise quality by giving a higher priority and profile to quality improvement;
- by making it directly accountable to Parliament, it would reduce the susceptibility of the present agencies to influences, formal or informal, from government, if not from politics, whilst enabling a properly independent and credible view to be taken of quality across the sector,

something which the existing representative bodies are unable to achieve however hard they try.

(Brown, 2001a: 17–18)[14]

Such a mission-focused scheme would also fit in well with the renewed emphasis in the White Paper and the HEFCE Strategic Plan on institutions 'playing to their strengths' and developing more distinctive missions. It should be noted that the agency would have both on accountability and an improvement role. While the difficulty of combining these functions is not to be underestimated, there need be no ultimate incompatibility between the two functions, provided everyone is clear that the ultimate purpose and justification of regulation is not to 'pick winners' but to raise quality across the sector, and that the best way to do this is to work with the institutions and others in identifying and removing the barriers to improvement, including poor or inappropriate leadership.[15]

Envoi

My final plea is that we devote some resources to the study of regulatory regimes and their impact on higher education. Whilst the existence of evidence is in itself no guarantee that anyone will pay it any attention (Brown, 2001c), the sad story of waste and confusion told in this book surely demonstrates the potential benefits to be gained from the careful collection of evidence in relation to particular propositions or hypothesis. It can only be hoped that those responsible for developing quality assurance regimes not only in Britain but elsewhere will heed this lesson. If this book assists in this, this in itself will be sufficient justification for having written it.

Notes

1 The second Aim of the HEFCE draft Strategic Plan published in March 2003 is 'Enhancing excellence in teaching and learning'. Successful implementation of the new quality framework is placed first. One of the key performance targets is to the effect that at least 95 per cent of QAA audits identify satisfactory provision throughout the Plan period (2003–8). Indeed paragraph 14 states, 'all institutions receiving our grant will be expected to achieve satisfactory audits by the QAA'. The new framework does not of course have a category of 'satisfactory' (HEFCE, 2003a: 19).
2 Over the past year or so QAA has made a considerable effort to portray itself as the sector's own body, culminating in an article in the *Times Higher* by Peter Williams about the values inherent in higher education (Williams, 2003). This is all very well, but we need to be mindful both of what happened to the last such agency to attempt to articulate the values of higher education, and of the fact that, unlike HEQC, the majority of board members are nominated by the funding councils or are independent. QAA is not, and never can be, the sector's own body.

3   Some were described in an HEQC publication *Managing Quality and Standards in UK Higher Education* (HEQC, 1997d). These included methods of departmental review developed by Goldsmiths University of London and the Engineering Professors Conference (see also Tannock and Jackson quoted in Jackson and Lund, 2000) and a profiling model devised by Gethin Williams at University of Wales College Newport (Williams, 1994). There is also the Association of Commonwealth Universities University Management Benchmarking Programme which has operated since 1996. Most recently, the HEFCE has funded a number of programmes exploring a more holistic approach to quality management and improvement, some using the European Foundation for Quality Management (EFQM) Excellence Model as a basis. (Consortium for Excellence in Higher Education, 2003; Improving Higher Education, 2003; Raban and Turner, 2003).

4   See also Wolf, 2003. There was also a failure to consult in-house experts within institutions. As Chief Executive of HEQC I regularly attended meetings of the Chudley Group of pro-vice-chancellors, mainly in the new universities, to talk about quality issues. I lost count of the number of times I was 'assailed' by them and similar groups for the policy pronouncements that had come from the vice-chancellors' own body.

5   It is not generally appreciated just how big a discrepancy there already is in the funding that institutions receive. In 2001/2 the most prosperous mainstream university (Imperial College) received over nine times the income – in terms of gross income per full-time equivalent student – of the poorest (Anglia Polytechnic University). This gap will be bound to increase if the stronger institutions charge the full £3,000 fee, as the government clearly envisages. This point has already been picked up by the Standard & Poor's credit rating agency (MacLeod, 2003).

6   Others may prefer Sir Arthur Streeb-Greebling's comment, after wasting most of his life attempting to teach ravens to fly under water: 'I've learnt from my mistakes and I'm sure I can repeat them' (Cook, P, 2003).

7   In 1992, as Chief Executive of the Committee of Directors of Polytechnics, the author proposed that both CVCP and CDP should dissolve themselves and be replaced by an entirely new, federal, body which would comprise separate 'colleges' representing heads of institutions, chairs of university councils, registrars, finance officers and so on. These groups would come together to form an overall body which would lobby on matters of common interest; other matters would be dealt with by the sectional groups. This effectively is how the American Council on Education operates, and the then CVCP Secretary visited Washington in 1992 to get further details. The passage of time has only strengthened the author's conviction that the only effective representative body for British higher education is one that recognizes and celebrates the plurality of institutions and interests, something Universities UK in its present form clearly cannot.

8   It is rumoured that several years ago the Russell Group explored having its own external examining system. There might still be a role for QAA as an accrediting body for the individual agencies, while it continues to discharge functions such as advice on degree-awarding powers and university title.

9   The NHS Modernisation Agency was established in April 2001 to help NHS staff and their partner organizations improve services for patients. The agency works in close partnership with strategic health authorities to align its work to local priorities, and commits funding, resources and expertise to local modernization objectives (NHS Modernisation Agency, 2003).

10 The PA Consulting report *Better Accountability for Higher Education* (2000), commissioned by HEFCE, stated:

The extent and detail of these requirements, and the uniform level of rigour applied across all institutions, would appear to reflect stakeholder perceptions that HEIs represent high levels of risk to the taxpayer. Yet no stakeholder we interviewed expressed this view. Indeed, and despite signal exceptions, most remarked on the infrequency of control and/or performance lapses in the higher education sector, and on the minor nature of those problems which have occurred.

(P A Consulting, 2000: 17)

This was confirmed by the Better Regulation Task Force: 'there is no evidence that the sector as a whole is particularly prone to financial and/or management failures or failures to deliver on academic performance. The National Audit Office considers the HE sector to be a low risk sector in terms of fraud or malpractice' (Better Regulation Task Force, 2002: 10).

11 Martin Trow has commented that 'the only aspect of university life that seems to be immune to "assessment" is the quality and wisdom of central government toward higher education' (Trow, 1994: 13).

12 An example comes from the continuation audit report on the University of Sheffield, where it is clear that the university's scheme of independent teaching assessments was established primarily to give the university a means of preparing for periodic external assessments (QAA, 1997b: para 3.5.1).

13 There is an increasing consensus that the most effective form of student learning involves cognitive or intellectual change and transformation of the person. Transformation is about students as participants in their learning, where they are both enhanced through the knowledge, skills and abilities they acquire and also empowered. Abilities that enable someone to think critically and reflect, to cope with change and to question and challenge all contribute to such empowerment. For such change to occur, a learning environment conducive to 'deep' learning is needed. This involves relating ideas to knowledge and experience, looking for patterns and meanings, considering evidence and conclusions, and in the process critically considering arguments. As three authors on the subject say, 'Clearly, if improvement of transformative learning processes is to be facilitated, then an institution has to empower staff, especially teaching staff, to provide the freedom necessary to question the status quo and to seek alternative and innovative ways of providing such learning' (Corder, Horsburgh and Melrose, 1999; cf Harvey and Knight, 1996; Hodson and Thomas, 1999, 2003). I am aware of no authoritative study that finds any correlation between the effectiveness of quality assurance arrangements – external or internal – and actual quality, howsoever defined.

14 It is interesting that under recently published government proposals the new access regulator will report to Parliament (DfES, 2003b: 22).

15 It is ironic that the White Paper announces the creation of a new and separate Leadership Foundation for Higher Education (DfES, 2003a: 76): yet further fragmentation of effort as yet another agency is formed!

Appendix 1   Definitions used in the book

Quality assurance has been defined as:

> All those planned and systematic activities to provide adequate confidence that a product or service will satisfy given requirements for quality.
>
> (HEQC, 1994c: 61)

Throughout this book, the term 'quality assurance' is used to denote quality assurance conducted by, or under the aegis of, an agency external to the institution concerned. Strictly speaking, this is incorrect. Only those who design and deliver programmes of study, and assess and accredit the resulting learning, can actually 'assure' the quality of those processes. Moreover, using the term in this way equates quality assurance with external quality regulation. This is both misleading and dangerous. It is misleading because external quality assurance can only ever be a fraction of the total quality assurance taking place in relation to a particular programme or qualification. It is dangerous because it implies that the necessary reassurance can only come from external regulation. Yet it is only in the exceptional circumstances, when a system is in rapid development or where there is a serious crisis in quality at a particular institution, that external regulation really comes into play, and both of these are pretty rare in mature systems. For these reasons, external quality 'evaluation' is the correct term. Nevertheless 'quality assurance' is the term used in the book.

For simplification, the various processes aimed at evaluating the quality of teaching and learning at subject/discipline level – Teaching Quality Assessment, Subject Review, Academic Review – are all referred to here generically as 'assessment'. (Where we are talking about the assessment of students this is made clear in the text.) Similarly, the various processes aimed at evaluating the effectiveness of institutions' quality assurance arrangements (academic quality audit, continuation audit, institutional review) are here known collectively as 'audit'. Finally, 'accreditation' is used in two main senses: to denote approval of a particular programme for purposes of professional recognition (by a professional or statutory body) and/or to indicate a process whereby an institution's total provision receives approval or authorization by an external regulatory body.

Appendix 2 Chronology of attempts to achieve an external quality assurance regime

- **September 1993:** the CVCP Annual Conference resolved to reduce the perceived duplication and overlap between the two processes by seeking a single quality regime under a single quality agency.
- **December 1994:** following sustained lobbying by the CVCP Chair, the Secretary of State for Education and Employment invited the HEFCE Chief Executive, Professor (now Sir) Graeme Davies, to begin a review to see if there was a way of combining the processes.
- **June 1995:** Professor Davies proposed that assessment should be the core method, with audit only taking place where assessments disclosed issues requiring a wider look at the institution concerned. Although the proposal obtained the support of the CVCP Chair, Dr Kenneth Edwards, it was thrown out by the CVCP Main Committee.
- **July 1995:** HEQC proposed a method by which the effectiveness of internal reviews of groups of programmes would be tested by periodic institutional audits. This was immediately disowned by both CVCP and HEFCE. Later that month, after much toing and froing, agreement was reached between CVCP and HEFCE on the principles of a new framework that would incorporate both assessment and audit.
- **September 1995:** the Secretary of State approved these proposals while emphasizing that assessment could not be conducted 'on a self-regulatory basis'. A Higher Education Forum was jointly established by CVCP and HEFCE to conduct preliminary fact-finding meetings with HEQC and the assessment staff of the Funding Council.
- **December 1995:** HEQC published an interim report on how institutions defined and protected their academic standards, the Graduate Standards Programme. The report suggested a number of ways in which institutions might make these more explicit and transparent.
- **December 1995:** CVCP and HEFCE announced the establishment of a Joint Planning Group (JPG) consisting of senior representatives of the funding councils and the representative bodies. The group was to be chaired by Sir William Kerr Fraser, lately Principal of Glasgow University.

- **December 1996:** the JPG recommended that a new framework bringing together assessment and audit should be administered by a new agency. This would carry out the assessment functions of the funding councils, and the audit and other functions of HEQC. In the same month HEQC published the final report of the Graduate Standards Programme.
- **March 1997:** the new agency (the Quality Assurance Agency for Higher Education or QAA) was incorporated as a company limited by guarantee, with the bodies representing the institutions as its legal owners, but with directors nominated by the funding councils and a number of independent directors together having an overall majority on its board. In the following month, and after a selection process, John Randall, Head of Professional Development at the Law Society, was appointed as its Chief Executive: the Chair was (and is) Christopher Kenyon.
- **July 1997:** the report of the National Committee of Inquiry into Higher Education chaired by Lord Dearing made a number of wide-ranging recommendations about ways in which the external scrutiny of academic standards should be subsumed within the new framework. The report suggested moving to a 'light touch' method of assessment. The report also proposed the establishment of a new body, the Institute for Learning and Teaching (ILT), to accredit lecturers and promote and disseminate good practice in learning and teaching. In general these recommendations, which built on HEQC's work on standards and quality enhancement, were accepted by both the government and the representative bodies.
- **August 1997:** QAA took over the quality functions of HEQC and HEFCE. The HEQC Chief Executive became redundant and a number of other staff left.
- **October 1998:** the new agency consulted the sector and other stakeholders about a new quality framework which would flesh out the principles in the JPG Report and incorporate the relevant Dearing recommendations.
- **November 1999:** following further consultation, QAA published the details of the new framework. This was to comprise three elements: programme outcome standards, the quality of learning opportunities, and institutional management of quality and standards. This was to be achieved through a combination of subject reviews and institutional reviews. Economy was to be secured by the close alignment of external and internal review events. In addition there was to be 'variation in intensity': departments that had previously received good assessments would in future receive less intense scrutiny and vice versa.
- **January 2000:** after further negotiations with the funding councils and the representative bodies, QAA announced how the outcomes of subject review (now incorporated in a process to be known as 'academic review') would in future be reported. This was endorsed by the representative

bodies. In April 2000 QAA published a detailed handbook describing how the new method would operate, and (from October) it began to apply it in Scotland.

- **August 2000:** HEFCE published a consultants' report estimating the annual measured costs of external quality assurance as being likely to exceed £45–50 million.
- **March 2001:** the Secretary of State announced new 'lighter touch' arrangements for the new method. University departments that had achieved good scores in the current round of assessment would be exempt in the next one, apart from a small proportion to be sampled 'by agreement'. Taken together with the planned further reduction in the average length of reviews, the aim was to secure a reduction of 40 per cent or more in the volume of review activity.
- **July 2001:** HEFCE, the representative bodies and the QAA together published a consultative document on yet another new quality process. QAA's institutional audits would incorporate subject reviews on a selective basis, the aim being to test how well the institution's internal processes were working, the reliability of the information being provided, and the outcomes being delivered. These new-style audits would begin in October 2002, although the new method would not come fully into force until 2005. In the meantime a task force under Sir Ron Cooke, Vice-Chancellor of the University of York, would determine the minimum information about academic effectiveness that each institution should publish.
- **August 2001:** the QAA Chief Executive resigned.
- **November 2001:** QAA announced that there was a broad measure of support for the new process.
- **March 2002:** the Minister for Higher Education gave her approval to the new process. The Cooke Committee published its recommendations about the information on quality and standards to be published by institutions.
- **July 2002:** QAA published the *Handbook* setting out the details of the new process.
- **August 2002:** another committee chaired by Sir Ron Cooke (the Teaching Quality Enhancement Committee or TQEC) published an interim report about national arrangements for quality enhancement.
- **January 2003:** TQEC proposed a new single quality enhancement agency. This was endorsed in the White Paper *The Future of Higher Education* published in the same month.
- **May 2003:** Professor Leslie Wagner was appointed to lead the development of the new enhancement agency.

Appendix 3   Information requirements

Information which should be available in all HEIs

Information on the institutional context

- Relevant sections of the HEI's corporate plan.
- Statement of the HEI's quality assurance policies and processes.
- The HEI's learning and teaching strategy and periodic reviews of progress.

Information on student admission, progression and completion

- Student qualifications on entry.
- The range of student entrants classified by age, gender, ethnicity, socio-economic background, disability and geographical origin as returned to the Higher Education Statistics Agency (HESA).
- Student progression and retention data for each year of each course/programme, differentiating between failure and withdrawal.
- Data on student completion.
- Data on qualifications awarded to students.
- Data on the employment/training outcomes for graduates from the First Destination Survey (FDS).

Information on the HEI's internal procedures for assuring academic quality and standards

- Information on programme approval, monitoring and review:
    - programme specifications;
    - a statement of the respective roles, responsibilities and authority of different bodies within the HEI involved in programme approval and review;
    - key outcomes of programme approval, and annual monitoring and review processes;
    - periodic internal reports of major programme reviews;

- reports of periodic internal reviews by the institution of departments or faculties;
- accreditation and monitoring reports by professional, statutory or regulatory bodies.

• Information on assessment procedures and outcomes:

- assessment strategies, processes and procedures;
- the range and nature of student work;
- external examiners' reports, analysis of their findings, and the actions taken in response;
- reports of periodic reviews of the appropriateness of assessment methods used.

• Information on student satisfaction with their HE experience, covering the views of students on:

- arrangements for academic and tutorial guidance, support and supervision;
- library services and IT support;
- suitability of accommodation, equipment and facilities for teaching and learning;
- perceptions of the quality of teaching and the range of teaching and learning methods;
- assessment arrangements;
- quality of pastoral support.

• Information and evidence available to teams undertaking HEIs' own internal reviews of quality and standards in relation to:

- the effectiveness of teaching and learning, in relation to programme aims and curriculum content as they evolve over time;
- the range of teaching methods used;
- the availability and use of specialist equipment and other resources and materials to support teaching and learning;
- staff access to professional development to improve teaching performance, including peer observation and mentoring programmes;
- the use of external benchmarking and other comparators both at home and overseas;
- the involvement of external peers in the review method, their observations, and the action taken in response.

Information for publication

Quantitative data

• HESA data on student entry qualifications (including A levels, access courses, vocational qualifications, and Scottish Highers).

- Performance indicators and benchmarks published by the higher education funding bodies on progression and successful completion for full-time first degree students (separately for progression after the first year, and for all years of the programme).
- HESA data on class of first degree, by subject area.
- Performance indicators and benchmarks published by the higher education funding bodies on first destinations/employment outcomes for full-time first degree students.

Qualitative data

- Summaries of external examiners' reports on each programme.
- A voluntary commentary by the HEI at whole-institution level on the findings of external examiners' reports.
- Feedback from recent graduates, disaggregated by institution, collected through a national survey.
- Feedback from current students collected through HEIs' own surveys, undertaken on a more consistent basis than now.
- A summary statement of the institution's learning and teaching strategy as presented to the HEFCE under the Teaching Quality Enhancement Fund programme.
- Summary statements of the results of, and the actions taken in response to, periodic programme and departmental reviews, to be undertaken at intervals of not more than six years.
- Summaries of the HEI's links with relevant employers, how the institution identifies employer needs and opinions, and how those are used to develop the relevance and richness of learning programmes. These should be included as part of learning and teaching strategies (see above) and in individual programme specifications.

Source: HEFCE (2002).

Appendix 4 Benchmark statements

Phase 1 (22 statements)

Accounting
Archaeology
Architecture, architectural technology and landscape
General business management
Chemistry
Classics and ancient history
Computing
Earth science, environmental sciences and environmental studies
Economics
Education studies
Engineering
English
Geography
History
Hospitality, leisure, sport and tourism
Law
Librarianship and information management
Philosophy
Politics and international relations
Social policy and administration and social work
Sociology
Theology and religious studies

Phase 2 (25 statements)

Agriculture, forestry, agricultural sciences, food sciences and
   consumer sciences
Anthropology
Area studies
Art and design
Biomedical science

Biosciences
Building and surveying
Communication, media, film and cultural studies
Dance, drama and performance
Dentistry
Health studies
History of art, architecture and design
Languages and related studies
Linguistics
Materials
Mathematics, statistics and operational research
Medicine
Music
Optometry
Pharmacy
Physics, astronomy and astrophysics
Psychology
Town and country planning
Veterinary science
Welsh/Cymraeg

References

Aitkenhead, D (1998) On examination, Chris Woodhead's Ofsted is a very expensive flop, *Guardian*, 11 Jun

Albjerg Graham, P, Lyman, R and Trow, M (1995) *Accountability of Colleges and Universities: An essay*, Trustees of Columbia University in the City of New York

Alderman, G (1995) *Audit, Assessment and Academic Autonomy*, inaugural lecture, 27 Nov

Alderman, G (1996) *Quality Assessment in England: A worm in the bud?* Paper presented at the Eighth International Conference on Assessing Quality in Higher Education, Australia, 14–16 Jul

Alderman, G (1998) Who inspects the inspectors? *Independent*, 27 Sep

Alderman, G (2003) Regain the right to self-regulate, *Times Higher Education Supplement*, 3 Jan

Allen, M (1993) Reasons to resign from a teaching quality assessment exercise, *Times Higher Education Supplement*, 6 Aug

Amann, R (1995) *A Sovietological View of Modern Britain*, professorial lecture, Edinburgh University, 1 Dec

Ayres, I and Braithwaite, J (1992) *Responsive Regulation: Transcending the deregulation debate*, Oxford University Press, Oxford

Baker, K (1989) *Higher Education 25 Years On*, speech at University of Lancaster; Department for Education and Science press notice, London

Barnard, N (1998) '£1bn' inspection regime fails to raise standards, *Times Educational Supplement*, 16 Jan

Barnett, R (2003) *Beyond All Reason: Living with ideology in the university*, Society for Research into Higher Education (SRHE)/Open University Press, Buckingham and Philadelphia

Barron, D (1999) Quality controls, *Times Higher Education Supplement*, 3 Sep

Baty, P (1999) TVU report was 'flawed', *Times Higher Education Supplement*, 5 Nov

Baty, P (2001) Randall's exit imperils light touch regime, *Times Higher Education Supplement*, 24 Aug

Baty, P (2003) Student survey plans fall apart, *Times Higher Education Supplement*, 21 Mar

Bauer, M and Henkel, M (1997) Evaluation systems in the UK and Sweden: successes and difficulties, *European Journal of Education*, **32** (2), pp 129–43

BBC Radio 4 [accessed 12 April 2002] *Reith Lectures 2002: A Question of Trust*, Radio 4 [Online] http://www.bbc.co.uk/radio4/reith2002

Beckett, F (2001) Brideshead inspected? No, sir! *New Statesman*, 7 May

Better Regulation Task Force (2002) *Higher Education: Easing the burden*, Cabinet Office, London

Biggs, J (2001) The reflective institution: assuring and enhancing the quality of teaching and learning, *Higher Education*, 41, pp 221–38

Birnbaum, R (2000) The life cycle of academic management fads, *Journal of Higher Education*, 71 (1), pp 1–16

Blackmur, D (2002) *Issues in Higher Education Quality Assurance*, 16th Australian International Education Conference, Hobart, Oct

Bleiklie, I (1998) Justifying the evaluative state: new public management ideals in higher education, *European Journal of Education*, 33 (3), pp 299–316

Brennan, J (1999) Coming to terms with mass higher education, *The New UK Quality Assurance System, Higher Education Digest*, special supplement, 33, QSC/CHERI, Open University, Milton Keynes

Brennan, J (2001) Quality management, power and values in European higher education, in *Higher Education Handbook of Theory and Research*, ed J Smart, vol 16, Agathon Press, New York

Brennan, J (2002) [accessed 27 May 2002] A combined approach, *Guardian Unlimited*, 28 Jan [Online] http://education.guardian.co.uk/universityteachinginspection/story/0,7348,640828,00.html

Brennan, J, Goedegebuure, L, Shah, T, Westerheijden, D and Weusthof, P (1991) Comparing quality in Europe, in *Higher Education in Europe*, CEPES/UNESCO, Bucharest

Brennan, J, Frederiks, M and Shah, T (1997), *Improving the Quality of Education: The impact of quality assessment on institutions*, HEFCE, Jul

Brennan, J and Shah, T (1997) Quality assessment, decision-making and institutional change, *Tertiary Education and Management*, 3 (2), pp 157–64

Brennan, J and Shah, T (2000a) *Managing Quality in Higher Education: An international perspective on institutional assessment and change*, OECD/SRHE/Open University Press, Buckingham

Brennan, J and Shah, T (2000b) Quality assurance and institutional change: experiences from 14 countries, *Higher Education*, 40 (3), pp 330–49

Brennan, J and Shah, T (2000c) Territorial disputes: the impact of quality assurance on relationships between academic and institutional values, in *Higher Education and its Communities*, ed I McNay, SRHE/Open University Press, Milton Keynes

Brighouse, T (1998) In search of infallibility, *Times Educational Supplement*, 27 Nov

British Educational Research Association (2003) The White Paper: The Future of Higher Education: Comments on Research in Relation to Teaching, Research Intelligence (in italics), No 83

Brown, R (1997a) *If at First You Don't Succeed . . . Creating a single system of external quality assurance in UK higher education*, inaugural lecture, Institute of Education

Brown, R (1997b) The new quality assurance arrangements in England and Wales, *Higher Education Quarterly*, 51 (4), pp 270–85

Brown, R (1997c) Developing effective overseas partnerships: lessons from Britain, *Journal of International Education*, 8 (1), Spring, pp 15–21

Brown, R (1997d) Future analysis or rhetoric? More research into education, *Times Higher Education Supplement*, 1 Aug

Brown, R (1998a) Co-operation or compliance? The National Committee of Inquiry proposals on quality and standards, *Quality in Higher Education*, 2 (1), pp 85–96

Brown, R (1998b) Institutional responsibility: Reality or myth? *Higher Education Review*, 30 (3), pp 7–22

Brown, R (1998c) The post-Dearing agenda for quality and standards in higher education, *Perspectives on Education Policy*, Institute of Education, University of London

Brown, R (1999a) *Measuring Quality in Higher Education*, lecture for the British Council International Seminar, Quality Assurance and Standards in Higher Education, 7–12 Mar, Oxford

Brown, R (1999b) *Diversity in Higher Education: Has it been and gone?*, professorial lecture, Goldsmiths, University of London, 11 Mar

Brown, R (1999c) Criteria for the external quality assurance of teaching and learning, *Journal of the International Network for Quality Assurance Agencies in Higher Education*, 18, pp 12–14, Jul

Brown, R (1999d) The new quality framework, *perspectives*, 3 (2), Summer, pp 1–5

Brown, R (2000a) Diversity in higher education: do we really want it? *perspectives*, 4 (1), Jan, pp 2–6

Brown, R (2000b) *Accountability in Higher Education: have we reached the end of the road? The case for a higher education audit commission*, professorial lecture, University of Surrey Roehampton, 24 Oct

Brown, R (2000c) The new UK quality framework, *Higher Education Quarterly*, 54 (4), pp 323–42

Brown, R (2001a) Accountability in higher education: the case for a higher education audit commission, *Higher Education Review*, 33 (2), Spring, pp 5–20

Brown, R (2001b) *Comments on HEFCE 01/45 Quality Assurance in Higher Education*, comments on the proposals in a note to SCOP, Jul

Brown, R (2001c) *Quality Assurance in Higher Education: Proposals for consultation*, notes on the consultation, circulated to members of the SCOP Quality Group, 31 Jul

Brown, R (2001d) *Evidence Based Policy Making or Policy-Based Evidence? The case of quality assurance in higher education*, inaugural lecture, City University London, 11 Dec

Brown, R (2001e) *Scholarship*, Southampton Institute, Southampton

Brown, R (2001f) *What Should Be the Role of Research in Higher Education?*, Sir James Matthews Lecture, University of Southampton, 15 Nov

Brown, R (2002) A case of quantity over quality, *Times Higher Education Supplement*, 9 Aug

Brown, R (2003) What future for higher education? *Higher Education Review*, 35 (3), pp 3–22

Budge, D (1998) Inspection 'push standards down', *Times Educational Supplement*, 23 Oct

Cabinet Office (2000) [accessed 9 June 2003] *Strengthening Leadership in the Public Sector: A research study by the PIU*, Performance and Innovation Unit, London [Online] http://www.strategy.gov.uk/2000/leadership/leadershipreport/piu-leadership.pdf

Calman, K, Hunter, D and May, A (2002) *Make or Break Time? A commentary on Labour's health policy two years into the NHS plan*, School for Health, University of Durham

Cave, M, Dodsworth, R and Thompson, D (1995) Regulatory reform in higher education in the UK: incentives for efficiency and product quality, in *The Regulatory Challenge*, ed M Bishop, J Kay and Mayer, pp 85–118, Oxford University Press, Oxford

Centre for Higher Education Studies (CHES) (1994) *Assessment of the Quality of Higher Education: A review and an evaluation*, Report for the Higher Education Funding Councils for England and Wales, Institute of Education, University of London, Jan

Centre for Learning & Teaching – Sociology, Anthropology and Politics (C-SAP) (2003) *C-SAP's Response to TQEC Report*, Mar

CHES *see* Centre for Higher Education Studies

Clark, P (1994) *Quality Assessment: Present position, future directions*, address to University of Newcastle upon Tyne

Clark, P (1996) *Quality Assessment in English Higher Education: Achievements and prospects*, Eighth International Conference on Assessing Quality in Higher Education, Broadbeach, Australia, 14–16 Jul

Committee of Vice-Chancellors and Principals (CVCP) (1985) *Report of the Steering Committee for Efficiency Studies in Universities* (Jarratt Report), CVCP, London

CVCP (1986) *Academic Standards in Universities* (Reynolds Report), CVCP, London

CVCP (1992) *Annual Report of the Director 1990/91*, Academic Audit Unit, CVCP, London

CVCP (1993) *Accountability for Teaching: Background paper*, paper for main committee meeting 21–23 Sep, CVCP

CVCP/Committee of Directors of Polytechnics (CDP)/Standing Conference of Principals (SCOP) (1991) Quality assurance arrangements for higher education, letter to Kenneth Clark MP, 10 Oct

CVCP/Higher Education Funding Council for England (2000) *The Business of Borderless Education: UK perspectives – analysis and recommendations*, Jul, CVCP, London (see especially ch 11 on quality)

Consortium for Excellence in Higher Education (2003) [accessed 30 May 2003] *About the EFQM Excellence Model*, Consortium for Excellence in Higher Education [Online] http://excellence.shu.ac.uk /model/

Cook, P (2003) *Tragically I Was An Only Twin: The complete Peter Cook*, ed W Cook, Century, London

Cook, R (2001) Have things got this much better? An analysis of Subject Review scores 1998–2000, *Higher Education Review*, 33 (3), pp 3–11

Cook, R (2003) Was that it? An analysis of the Subject Review system from October 2000 to June 2002, *Higher Education Review*, 35 (3), pp 92–106

Cook, R and Underwood, S (2002) Making the translation from subject to academic review: does 6*4 = 4*C (or c + 3e)?, *Higher Education Review*, 34 (2), pp 3–14

Cooke, R (2003) External examiners: report from the Teaching Quality Enhancement Committee, letter from Sir Ron Cooke, Chair of TQEC to Sir Howard Newby, Chief Executive, HEFCE, 22 Jan

Cope, S and Goodship, J (1999) *Comparing Regulatory Regimes in the New Governance*, paper for Political Studies Association Annual Conference, University of Nottingham, Mar

Corder, M, Horsburgh, M and Melrose, M (1999) Quality monitoring, innovation and transformative learning, *Journal of Further and Higher Education*, 23 (1), pp 101–8

C-SAP *see* Centre for Learning & Teaching – Sociology, Anthropology and Politics

CVCP *see* Committee of Vice-Chancellors and Principals

de Vries, P (1996) Could 'criteria' used in quality assessment be classified as academic standards? *Higher Education Quarterly*, 50 (3), pp 193–206

Department of Education and Science (DES) (1985) *The Development of Higher Education into the 1990s*, Cmnd 9524, HMSO, London

DES (1987) *Higher Education Meeting the Challenge*, Cmnd 114, HMSO, London

DES (1991) *Higher Education: A new framework*, Cmnd 1541, HMSO, London

DES (1992) *Letter of Guidance to the new Funding Council*, Jun, DES, London

Department for Education and Skills (DfES) (2003a) *The Future of Higher Education*, Cmnd 5735, The Stationery Office, London

DfES (2003b) *Widening Participation in Higher Education*, Apr, The Stationery Office, London

Dill, D (1998) Evaluating the 'evaluative state': implications for research in higher education, *European Journal of Education*, 33 (3), pp 361–77

Dill, D (1999a) *Quality Assurance and Standards in the UK: A US perspective on the QAA consultation paper*, QSC Digest Briefing, Open University, Milton Keynes

Dill, D (1999b) 'Who will rid me of this meddlesome priest?', *The New UK Quality Assurance System, Higher Education Digest*, special supplement, 33, QSC/CHERI, Open University, Milton Keynes

Doe, B (1998) Tory competition fails to raise standards, *Times Educational Supplement*, 9 Jan

Drennan, L (1999) [accessed 30 May 2003] Influences on teaching quality assessment scores on the Scottish universities, *Education-line* [Online] http://www.leeds.ac.uk/educol

Drennan, L (2001) Quality assessment and the tension between teaching and research, *Quality in Higher Education*, 7 (3), pp 167–78

Edwards, K (1994) Quality and standards of teaching and learning in universities, letter from Dr Kenneth Edwards to Rt Hon John Patten MP, 30 Jun

Edwards, K and Roberts, G (1995) Developing quality assurance in partnership with the institutions of higher education, letter from Dr K Edwards and Professor G Roberts to Rt Hon Gillian Shephard MP, 19 Jul

El-Khawas, E and Shah, T (1998) Internal review to assure quality: comparative perspectives on evolving practice, *Tertiary Education and Management*, 4 (2), pp 95–101

Elton, L (1986) Quality in higher education: nature and purpose, *Studies in Higher Education*, 11 (1), pp 83–84

Elton, L (1996) Partnership, quality and standards in higher education, *Quality in Higher Education*, 2 (2), pp 95–104

Elton, L (2002) *Quality Assurance through Quality Enhancement*, unpublished paper, personal communication to the author

Foreman-Peck, L (2001) Regulating teachers, *Journal of Educational Enquiry*, 2 (1), pp 23–32

Fry, H (1995) Quality issues in higher education, *Viewpoint*, 1, Institute of Education, University of London, Jun

Gaither, G (1998) *Quality Assurance in Higher Education: An international perspective*, Jossey-Bass, San Francisco

Gaster, L and Squire, A (2003) *Providing Quality in the Public Sector: A practical approach to improving public services*, Open University Press, Maidenhead and Philadelphia

Goddard, A (2003) Low fees may win extra HEFCE cash, *Times Higher Education Supplement*, 14 Mar

Gordon, G (2002) Learning from quality assessment, in *The Effective Academic: A handbook for enhanced academic practice*, ed S Ketteridge, S Marshall and H Fry, pp 201–17, Kogan Page, London

Gordon, G and Middlehurst, R (1995) Leadership, quality and institutional effectiveness, *Higher Education Quarterly*, 49 (3), pp 267–85

Gosling, D and D'Andrea, V (2001) Quality development: a new concept for higher education, *Quality in Higher Education*, 7 (1), pp 7–17

Government Statistical Service (1993) *Education Statistics for the United Kingdom: 1992 edition*, HMSO, London

Graham, J and Barnett, R (1996) Models of quality in teacher education, *Oxford Review of Education*, 22 (2), pp 161–78

Hannan, A and Silver, H (2000) *Innovating in Higher Education Teaching, Learning and Institutional Cultures*, SRHE and Open University Press, Buckingham

Harris, R (1990) The CNAA, accreditation and quality assurance, *Higher Education Review*, 22 (3), pp 34–54

Harrison, M, Lockwood, B, Miller, M, Oswald, A, Stewart, M and Walker, I (2001) Higher education: trial by ordeal, *Guardian*, 30 Jan

Harvey, L and Knight, P (1996) *Transforming Higher Education*, SRHE/Open University Press, Buckingham

HEFCE *see* Higher Education Funding Council for England

HEFCW *see* Higher Education Funding Council for Wales

Henkel, M (1991) The new 'evaluative state', *Public Administration*, 69, pp 121–36

Henkel, M (2000) *Academic Identities and Policy Change in Higher Education*, Jessica Kingsley, London

HEQC *see* Higher Education Quality Council

Her Majesty's Government *see* HM Government

Higher Education Funding Council for England (HEFCE) (1993) *Assessment of the Quality of Education*, Circular 3/93, Feb, HEFCE, Bristol

HEFCE (1994) *The Quality Assessment Method from April 1995*, Circular 39/94, Dec, HEFCE, Bristol

HEFCE (1995) *Report on Quality Assessment 1992–1995*, Nov, HEFCE, Bristol

HEFCE (2001) *Quality Assurance in Higher Education: Proposals for consultation*, HEFCE 01/45 consultation, Jul, HEFCE, Bristol

HEFCE (2002) *Information on Quality and Standards in Higher Education: Final report of the Task Group*, HEFCE 02/15 report, Mar, HEFCE, Bristol

HEFCE (2003a) *HEFCE Strategic Plan 2003–08*, HEFCE 2003/12 consultation, Mar, HEFCE, Bristol

HEFCE (2003b) [accessed 27 May 2003] Professor Wagner leads the development of new enhancement academy, *HEFCE News and Events*, 16 May [Online] http://www.hefce.ac.uk/News/hefce/2003/wagner.htm

HEFCE/Higher Education Quality Council (1994) *Joint Statement on Quality Assurance*, M 1/94, Jan, HEFCE, Bristol

HEFCE/Scottish Higher Education Funding Council/Higher Education Funding Council for Wales/Department for Employment and Learning (2003) [accessed 30 May 2003] *Joint Consultation on the Review of Research Assessment: Consultation by the UK funding bodies on the review by Sir Gareth Roberts*, HEFCE 2003/22 consultation, May, HEFCE, Bristol [Online] http://www.hefce.ac.uk/pubs/hefce/2003/03_22.htm

HEFCE/Universities UK (UUK)/Standing Conference of Principals (SCOP) (2002) [accessed 30 May 2003] *Teaching Quality Enhancement Committee Interim Report*, Aug [Online] http://www.hefce.ac.uk/learning/tqec/tqec_report.pdf

HEFCE/UUK/SCOP (2003) [accessed 30 May 2003] *Final Report of the Teaching Quality Enhancement Committee on the Future Needs and Support for Quality Enhancement of Learning and Teaching in Higher Education*, Jan [Online] http://www.hefce.ac.uk/learning/tqec/final.htm

Higher Education Funding Council for Wales (HEFCW) (1994) *The Assessment of Quality in the Higher Education Sector in Wales: Future directions*, HEFCW, W94/36HE, 31 May

Higher Education Quality Council (HEQC) (1994a) *Choosing to Change: The report of the HEQC CAT development project*, HEQC, London

HEQC (1994b) *Choosing to Change: The report of the HEQC CAT development project, executive statement and summary*, HEQC, London

HEQC (1994c) *Guidelines on Quality Assurance 1994*, HEQC, London

HEQC (1994d) *Learning from Audit*, HEQC, London

HEQC (1995a) *Choosing to Change: The report of the HEQC CAT development project, outcomes of the consultation*, HEQC, London

HEQC (1995b) *Code of Practice for Overseas Collaborative Provision in Higher Education*, HEQC, London

HEQC (1995c) *Guidelines on the Quality Assurance of Credit-Based Learning*, HEQC, London

HEQC (1995d) *Learning from Collaborative Audit: An interim report*, HEQC, London

HEQC (1995e) *Notes of Guidance for the Audit of Collaborative Provision*, HEQC, Birmingham

HEQC (1995f) *Some Questions and Answers for Participants in HEQC Collaborative Audit Visits*, HEQC, London

HEQC (1995g) *Notes for the Guidance of Auditors*, Quality Assurance Group, Birmingham, Mar

HEQC (1996a) *Improving Institutional Capacity for Self-Regulation*, HEQC, London, Dec

HEQC (1996b) *Improving the Effectiveness of Quality Assurance Systems in Non-Medical Health Care, Education and Training*, National Health Service Executive/HEQC, London, Sep

HEQC (1996c) *Learning from Audit 2*, HEQC, London

HEQC (1996d) *Quality Enhancement within HEQC 1995–96*, HEQC, London

HEQC (1996e) *Strengthening External Examining*, HEQC, London

HEQC (1997a) *Assessment in Higher Education and the Role of 'Graduateness'*, HEQC, London

HEQC (1997b) *Graduate Standards Programme Final Report, vol 1*, HEQC, London

HEQC (1997c) *Graduate Standards Programme Final Report, vol 2, Supplementary material*, HEQC, London

HEQC (1997d) *Managing Quality and Standards in UK Higher Education: Approaches to self-evaluation and self-regulation*, HEQC, London

HM Government (1988) [accessed 30 May 2003] Education Reform Act 1988 (c.40), The Stationery Office, London [Online] http://www.hmso.gov.uk/acts/acts1988/Ukpga_19880040_en_1.htm#tcon

HM Government (1992) [accessed 28 May 2003] Further and Higher Education Act 1992 (c.13), The Stationery Office, London [Online] http://www.hmso.gov.uk/acts/acts1992/Ukpga_19920013_en_5.htm#mdiv70

HM Government (2001) *Report of the Public Inquiry into Children's Heart Surgery at the Bristol Royal Infirmary 1984–1995: Learning from Bristol*, CM 5207(I), July 2001

Hood, C (2003) Tsar-tsar galore . . . , *Times Higher Education Supplement*, 31 Jan

Hodson, P and Thomas, H (1999) Towards an enterprise culture: will the Quality Assurance Agency help or hinder? *Higher Education Review*, 32 (1), pp 24–33

Hodson, P and Thomas, H (2003) Quality assurance in higher education: fit for the new millennium or simply year 2000 compliant? *Higher Education*, 45 (3), pp 375–87 [Online] http://www.tandf.co.uk/journals

Hughes, G, Mears, R and Winch, C (1997) An inspector calls: regulation and accountability in three public services, *Policy and Politics*, 25 (3), pp 299–313

Hunter, D (2002) Will the medics strike back?, *The Stakeholder*, pp 11–12

Hunter, P (1998) Just take confidence, *Times Educational Supplement*, 16 Jan

Improving Higher Education (2003) [accessed 30 May 2003] *Information,* Improving Higher Education [Online] http://www.improvinghe.livjm.ac.uk/Default.asp

Jackson, N (1997a) Academic regulation in UK higher education, part I: the concept of collaborative regulation, *Quality Assurance in Education*, 5 (3), pp 120–35

Jackson, N (1997b) Academic regulation in UK higher education, part II: typologies and frameworks for discourse and strategic change, *Quality Assurance in Education*, 5 (3), pp 165–79

Jackson, N (1997c) *The Role of Evaluation in Self-Regulating Higher Education Institutions in HEQC, Managing Quality and Standards in UK Higher Education – Approaches to self-regulation*, HEQC, London

Jackson, N (1998) Academic regulation in UK higher education, part III: the idea of 'partnership in trust', *Quality Assurance in Education*, 6 (1), pp 5–18

Jackson, N and Lund, H (2000) *Benchmarking for Higher Education*, Society for Research into Higher Education, Buckingham and Philadelphia

James, E and Neuberger, E (1981) The university department as a non-profit labour co-operative, *Public Choice*, 36, pp 585–612

Jenkins, A (1997) Quality matters, so let's get serious about it, *Times Higher Education Supplement*, 18 Apr, p 14

Johnston, R (1996) Quality in research, quality in teaching and quality in debate: a response to Graham Gibbs, *Quality in Higher Education*, 2 (2), pp 165–70

Joint Planning Group for Quality Assurance in Higher Education (JPG) (1996a) *Minutes of the Meeting of the Joint Planning Group*, 11 Jan, JPG, London

JPG (1996b) *First Report*, CVCP, Apr

JPG (1996c) *Final Report*, CVCP, 17 Dec

Kells, R (1992) *Self-Regulation in Higher Education: A multi-national perspective on collaborative systems of quality assurance and control*, Higher Education Policy Series 15, Jessica Kingsley, London and Philadelphia

Kettl, D (1997) The global revolution in public management: driving themes, missing links, *Journal of Public Policy Analysis and Management*, 16, pp 446–62

Kogan, M and Hanney, S (1999) *Reforming Higher Education*, Jessica Kingsley, London

Larrington, C and Lindsay, R (2002) [accessed 27 May 2003] Equal among firsts: reviewing quality in psychology, *Psychology Learning and Teaching*, 2 (1) [Online] http://www.psychology.ltsn.ac.uk/21larrington.pdf

Lindop, N (1985) *Academic Validation in Public Sector Higher Education: Report of the Committee of Inquiry*, HMSO, London

Lukes, S (1974) *Power: A radical view*, Macmillan, London

MacLeod, D (2003) Rich to get richer, *Guardian Education*, 25 Mar

Mansell, W (2001) Tomlinson expected to ease inspection burden, *Times Educational Supplement*, 4 May

Marston, S (2002) Training and development for external examiners, letter to Professor Sir Ron Cooke, Chair of TQEC from Stephen Marston, Director for Institutions, HEFCE, 16 May

McBarnet, D and Whelan, C (1991) The elusive spirit of the law: formalism and the struggle for legal control, *Modern Law Review*, 54, pp 847–73

McDowell, L (1998) *Assessment As An Episode of Learning: Reflections on the experience of subject specialist assessors*, Paper for one-day national conference, The Impact of Quality Assurance on UK Higher Education, 15 May

Middlehurst, R (1997a) Enhancing quality, in *Repositioning Higher Education*, ed F Coffield and B Williamson, SRHE/Open University Press, Buckingham

Middlehurst, R (1997b) Reinventing higher education: the leadership challenge, *Quality in Higher Education*, 3 (2), pp 183–98

Middlehurst, R and Woodhouse, D (1995), Coherent systems for external quality assurance, *Quality in Higher Education*, 1 (3), pp 257–68

Milton, P (1996) *Quality Assurance in English Higher Education: An attempt to rationalise disparate systems*, HEFCE, Bristol

Moran, M (2002) Review article: understanding the regulatory state, *British Journal of Political Studies*, 32, pp 391–413

Morley, L (2003) Quality and Power in Higher Education, SRHE and Open University Press, Berkshire and Philadelphia

National Committee of Inquiry into Higher Education (NCIHE) (1997) *Higher Education in the Learning Society*, HMSO, London

Neave, G (1988) On the cultivation of quality, efficiency and enterprise: an overview of recent trends in higher education in Western Europe, 1986–1988, *European Journal of Education*, 23 (1, 2), pp 7–23

Neave, G (1998) The evaluative state reconsidered, *European Journal of Education*, 33 (3) pp 265–83

Newby, H (2003) Teaching Quality Enhancement Committee (TQEC): External examiners, letter to Baroness Warwick, Chief Executive, Universities UK from Sir Howard Newby, Chief Executive, HEFCE, 27 Jan

Newton, J (1997) Opportunities for partnership in quality improvement: responding to the challenge of teaching quality assessment in Wales, *Quality in Higher Education*, 3 (1), pp 37–50

Newton, J (1999) An evaluation of the impact of external quality monitoring of a higher education college (1993–98), *Assessment and Evaluation in Higher Education*, 24 (2), pp 215–35

Newton, J (2000) Feeding the beast or improving quality?: academics' perceptions of quality assurance and quality monitoring, *Quality in Higher Education*, 6 (2), pp 153–63

Newton, J (2001) *Views from Below: Academics coping with quality*, keynote presentation at Sixth QHE seminar in association with EAIR and SRHE, Birmingham, 26 May

NHS Modernisation Agency [accessed 30 May 2003] *About the Agency*, NHS Modernisation Agency [Online] http://www.modernnhs.nhs.uk/scripts/default.asp?site_id=43&id=11935

O'Leary, J (2001) Why we need league tables, *The Times*, 29 Mar

O'Neill, O (2002a) [accessed 12 April 2002] *Lecture Two: Trust and terror*, BBC Radio 4 [Online] http://www.bbc.co.uk/radio4/reith2002/lecture2_text.shtml

O'Neill, O (2002b) [accessed 20 April 2002] *Lecture Three: Called to account*, BBC Radio 4 [Online] http://www.bbc.co.uk/radio4/reith2002/lecture3_text.shtml

Osborne, D and Gabler, T (1992) *Reinventing Government: How the entrepreneurial spirit is transforming the public sector*, Addison-Wesley, Reading, MA

P A Consulting Group (2000) *Better Accountability for Higher Education: Summary of a review for the HEFCE by PA Consulting*, Report August 00/36

Parry, D (2002) Quality assurance in higher education, *Perspectives*, 6 (1), pp 3–7

Perellon, J-F (2001) *The Development of Quality Assurance Policy in Higher Education: A comparative analysis of England, the Netherlands, Spain and Switzerland*, University of London, Institute of Education unpublished PhD thesis, Aug

Pollitt, C (1987) The politics of performance assessment: lessons for higher education? *Studies in Higher Education*, 12 (1), pp 87–98

Pollitt, C (1993) *Managerialism and the Public Services: Cuts or cultural change*, 2nd edn, Blackwell, Oxford

Power, M (1994) *The Audit Explosion*, Demos, White Dove Press, London

Power, M (1997) *The Audit Society: Rituals of verification*, Oxford University Press, Oxford

Pyke, N (1998) Chief inspector's role 'out of control', *Times Educational Supplement*, 27 Mar

Quality Assurance Agency for Higher Education (QAA) (1997a) Work of the agency, *Higher Quality*, 1, Jun

QAA (1997b) *University of Sheffield Quality Audit Report*, QAA, Gloucester, Oct

QAA (1997c) Progress on the Dearing quality agenda, *Higher Quality*, 2, Nov

QAA (1997d) *Subject Review Handbook October 1998 to September 1997*, QAA, Gloucester, Dec

QAA (1998a) An agenda for quality, *Higher Quality*, 3, Mar

QAA (1998b) The way ahead, *Higher Quality*, 4, Oct

QAA (1999a) Assuring quality and standards, *Higher Quality*, 6, Nov

QAA (2000) *Handbook for Academic Review*, QAA, Gloucester

QAA (2001a) World class standards, *Higher Quality*, 8, Jan

QAA (2001b) Reaping the benefits, *Higher Quality*, 9, Nov

QAA (2001c) *Annual Report and Financial Summary 2000/2001*, QAA, Gloucester

QAA (2001d) [accessed 20 April 2003] Chief Executive of higher education quality agency to resign, QAA Press release, 21 August [Online] http://www.qaa.ac.uk/aboutqaa/news/pressreleases/21_Aug_2001.htm

QAA (2002a) *QAA External Review Process for Higher Education in England: Operational description*, QAA 019, QAA, Gloucester, Mar

QAA (2002b) Continuous improvement, *Higher Quality*, 10, Jul

QAA (2002c) *Handbook for Institutional Audit: England*, QAA, Gloucester, Aug

QAA (2002d) Anyone for enhancement?, *Higher Quality*, 11, Nov

QAA (2002e) [accessed 30 May 2003] *QAA Evaluation Report: Department of Health prototype reviews of health profession programmes*, QAA, Gloucester, Nov [Online] http://www.qaa.ac.uk/public/depthealth/Evaluation_report_short.pdf

QAA (2002f) [Accessed 20 May 2003] *Service Standards*, QAA, Gloucester [Online] http://www.qaa.ac.uk/public/inst_audit_hbook/service_standards.htm

QAA (2003) *Handbook for Enhancement-Led Institutional Review: Scotland*, QAA, Gloucester, Apr

Raban, C and Turner, E (2003) [accessed 10 June 2003] *Academic Risk: Quality risk management in higher education*, HEFCE Good Management Practice Project, Interim Report, Jan [Online] http://www.bathspa.ac.uk/quality-and-standards/risk-management/qrm-interim-report.pdf

Randall, J (1997) Taking the last and only chance, *HEFCE Gazette*, Summer

Randall, J (1998) Flexible friends, *Times Higher Education Supplement*, 16 Oct

Randall, J (2000) A profession for the new millennium? in *Higher Education Re-formed*, ed P Scott, Falmer Press, London and New York

Randall, J (2001) A question of quality, *Guardian Education*, 28 Aug

Roberts, R (1997) [accessed 11 April 2003] Our graduate factories, *The Tablet*, 11 Oct [Online] http://www.thetablet.co.uk/cgi-bin/archive_db.cgi?tablet-00120

Russell, C (2001) *Academic Freedom*, Routledge, London

Salter, B (2000) *Trust Me, I'm A Doctor*, Working Paper 3, Nursing and Midwifery Research Unit, University of East Anglia, Oct

Salter, B (2002) Medical regulation: new politics and old power structures, *Politics*, 22 (2), pp 59–67

Salter, B and Tapper, T (2000) The politics of governance in higher education: the case of quality assurance, *Political Studies*, 48 (1), pp 66–87

Scott, P (2000) *Higher Education Re-Formed*, Falmer Press, London and New York

Segal Quince Wicksteed (1999) *Providing Public Information on the Quality and Standards of Higher Education Courses*, Segal Quince Wicksteed, Cambridge

Sharp, S (1995) The quality of teaching and learning in higher education: evaluating the evidence, *Higher Education Quarterly*, 49 (4), pp 301–15

Shephard, G (1994) Speech by the Secretary of State Rt Hon Gillian Shephard MP to the Committee of Vice-Chancellors and Principals, 2 Dec

Shephard, G (1995) Developing quality assurance in partnership with the institutions of higher education, letter to Professor Gareth Roberts, Chair of CVCP from Rt Hon Gillian Shephard MP, 21 Sep

Shore, C and Selwyn, T (1998) The marketisation of higher education: management discourse and the politics of performance, in *The New Higher Education: Issues and directions for the post-Dearing university*, ed D Jary and M Parker, pp 3–27, Staffordshire University Press, Stoke-on-Trent

Shore, C and Wright, S (1999) Audit culture and anthropology: neo-liberalism in British higher education, *Journal of the Royal Anthropological Institute*, 5 (4), Dec, pp 557–79

Sikka, P (2002) We are a nation of accountants, *Guardian*, 20 Feb

Silver, H (1990) *A Higher Education: The Council for National Academic Awards and British Higher Education 1964–1989*, Falmer Press, London

Silver, H (1993) *External Examiners: Changing Roles? A study of examination boards, external examiners, and views of the future*, Council for National Academic Awards, London, Feb

Silver, H, Stennett, A and Williams, R (1995) *The External Examiner System: Possible futures*, Report of a project commissioned by the Higher Education Quality Council, Open University, Milton Keynes

Southampton Institute (2000) *The Relationship between Research and Teaching in Higher Education: Present realities, future possibilities*, Conference at Chilworth, 19–20 Jan

Swain, H, Tysome, T and Baty, P (1999) Leak reveals quality 'A' team, *Times Higher Education Supplement*, 30 Apr

Times Higher Education Supplement (THES) (1992) Quality assurance arrangements are going wrong, *THES*, 11 Dec

THES (2000) Over 80% vetoed blueprint, *THES*, 28 Jan

THES (1993) V-Cs reject quality red tape, *THES*, 22 Jan

Trow, M (1994) Managerialism and the academic profession: quality and control, *Higher Education Report*, 2, Quality Support Centre, May

Trow, M (1996) *On the Accountability of Higher Education in the United States*, paper for the Princeton Conference on Higher Education, 21–23 Mar, University of California, Berkley

Tysome, T (1999) Setback for quality watchdog power bid, *Times Higher Education Supplement*, 10 Sep

Underwood, S (1998) Quality assessment: some observations, *Perspectives*, 2 (2), pp 50–55

Underwood, S (2000) Assessing the quality of quality assessment: the inspection of teaching and learning in British universities, *Journal of Education for Teaching*, 26 (1), pp 73–91

Vroeijenstijn, A (1995) Government and university: opponents or allies in quality assurance? *Higher Education Review*, 3, pp 18–36

Wagner, L (1993) The teaching quality debate, *Higher Education Quarterly*, 47 (3), Summer, pp 274–85

Warren-Piper, D (1994) *Are Professors Professional? The organisation of university examinations*, Jessica Kingsley, London

Warren-Piper, D (1995) *Assuring the Quality of Awards*, paper for Conference on Academic Standards Higher Education Quality Council, 30 Mar, Coventry

Warwick, D (2003) TQEC: external examiners, letter to Sir Howard Newby, Chief Executive, HEFCE from Diana Warwick, Chief Executive, Universities UK, 13 Feb

Watson, D (1995) Quality assessment and 'self-regulation': the English experience, 1992–94, *Higher Education Quarterly*, 49 (4), pp 326–40

Watson, D and Bowden, R (1999), *Unto Him That Hath: Prosperity and university league tables*, UK HE Prosperity Index, University of Brighton, Oct

Watson, D and Bowden, R (2001) *Can We Be Equal and Excellent Too? The New Labour stewardship of UK higher education, 1997–2001*, Education Research Centre, University of Brighton, Occasional Paper, Jun

Williams, G (1994) *Achieving Quality in Higher Education: A student centred approach to self-evaluation, proposals for student progression profiling model*, Gwent College of Higher Education

Williams, P (1996) From audit to institutional review: a brief survey of the evolution of academic quality audit, communication to the author

Williams, P (2002) [accessed 9 December 2002] Largest ever review of UK higher education completed, Press release, QAA, 29 Jul [Online] http://www.qaa.ac.uk/aboutqaa/news/pressreleases/pr29_Jul-2002.htm

Williams, P (2003) Rest assured – we will defend the core values, *Times Higher Education Supplement*, 14 Mar

Wolf, A (1998) Two sides of A4 will not do the trick, *Times Higher Education Supplement*, 22 May

Wolf, A (2003) The history of the QAA shows how supine our dignitaries have become . . . Dr Johnson would not see V-Cs as fit champions for a great sector in crisis, *Times Higher Education Supplement*, 30 May

Woodhead, C (2000) Outsiders looking in, *Times Higher Education Supplement*, 10 Mar

Wragg, T (2000) Woodhead was my sick joke, *Times Educational Supplement*, 17 Nov

Wright, P (1989) Access or exclusion? Some comments on the history and future prospects of continuing education in England, *Studies in Higher Education*, 14 (1), pp 23–40

Wright, P (1996) Mass higher education and the search for standards: reflections on some issues emerging from the 'Graduate Standards Programme', *Higher Education Quarterly*, 50 (1), pp 71–85

Index

Academic Audit Unit (AAU) 45, 50–62
academic autonomy 10, 85–8
academic guild 23–4
academic review 7, 126–7, 132–3, 134, 139, 145–6
academic standards 69
Academy for the Advancement of Learning and Teaching in Higher Education 138, 160–1
access courses 70
accountability 21–2, 100, 155–6, **160–2, 166**
accreditation 70, 71, 129, 173–4
Alderman, Geoffrey, Professor 85–6, 96–7, 100, 156
Amman, Ron 4, 17–18
argument of the book 3–4
Ashworth, John, Professor 103
assessment 39, 73–100; academic autonomy 85–8; arguments against 80–1; arguments for 79–80, 84; benefits to teaching and learning 81–4; Britain's reputation 90; compliance culture 85–8; definitions 173; establishment of 46; evaluation 77–8; institutional bias 94–7; institutions, demands on 84–5; managerialism 88–90; Scotland 98–9; Wales 98–9
method 74–84; of performance 23, 25–6; politics 25–6; quality of process 91–4; of students 56; value for money 97–8
audit society 15–19
audit(s); Academic Audit Unit 50–62; commission for higher education 167–9; continuation 61–2;

evaluation 55–6; institutional 133, 145–6; learning from 56, 60–1; overseas 58–60, 145; QAA 145–6; for validation 57–8

Baker, Kenneth 9
Barnett, Ronald 18–19, 156
benchmarking 69, 140–1, 142, 143, 144, **181–2**
Better Accountability for Higher Education (PA Consulting) 170
Better Regulation Review Group 100, 136–7, 171
bias 94–7
Blackmur, D. 166
Bleiklie, I. 13–14
Blunkert, David 131
Booth, Sir Clive 41, 90
Brennan, John 7, 82, 143
Brown, R. 32, 130, 134, 163, 164, 167
Bush, Peter, Professor 114

Calman, K. 22–3
Campbell, Carolyn 70–1
categorization of provision 74
Cave, M. 24
CDP *see* Committee of Directors of Polytechnics (CDP)
centralization 100
Centre for Higher Education Studies (CHES) 77–8
choices 105
Choosing to Change (HEQC) 70
chronology 175–7
Chudley Group 170
Circular 3/93 74–7
Circular 39/94 77, 88
Clark, Paul, Dr. 46, 47, 79, 89, 91, 112

clinical governance 20–3
CNAA (Council for National Academic
   Awards) 30, 36, 37, 45, 102
*Code of Practice for the Assurance of
   Academic Quality and Standards in
   Higher Education* 141
codes of practice 141, 142
collaborative provision 57–60, 122
Committee of Directors of Polytechnics
   (CDP) 11, 45; on quality
   assurance 45–6; on the White
   Paper (1991) 41, 42
Committee on Standards in Public Life
   (Nolan) 118
Committee of Vice Chancellors and
   Principals (CVCP) 11, 157, 170;
   on audit 51, 52, 53, 54; on
   HEQC 45–6, 167; on quality
   assurance 45–6; Residential
   Conference 103–4; single system
   1, 103, 106–7, 108–9, 118;
   White Paper (1991) 41; working
   party (Sir Frederick Crawford)
   104
communication 19, 20
comparative ratings 28
compliance culture 81, 82, 85–8, 100
consistency 93, 100
consultation 124–31
continuation audit(s) 61–2
control 16–17
Cook, Roger 76, 91, 95, 96, 97
Cooke committee 84, 137
Cooke, Sir Ron, Professor 84, 133,
   137, 138
Coopers and Lybrand 55
coordination 166–7
costs 85, 102–3, 115
Council for National Academic Awards
   (CNAA) 30, 36, 37, 45, 102
Crawford, Sir Frederick 103, 104
credit accumulation and transfer 70
Crispin, Alan 70
CVCP *see* Committee of Vice
   Chancellors and Principals
   (CVCP)

Davies, Sir Graeme, Professor 1–2, 46,
   104, 105, 150
Dearing Committee *see* National
   Committee for Inquiry into
   Higher Education
Dearing, Lord Ron 46, 69, *see also*
   Dearing Report

Dearing report 2, 82, 117–18, 124,
   125, 152–3
definitions 173–4
degree-awarding powers 144–5
Dill, David 23, 142, 143, 147
disagreements 3, 151
diversity 164–5
Dodsworth, R. 24
dual system 1
Dublin descriptors 149
duplication 122, 125, 129, 138

economic ideology 11–12, 86, 87
ECTS (European Credit Transfer
   System) 71
Education Guardian 131
Education Reform Act 10
Edwards, Dr. Kenneth 67, 103–4,
   106–7, 109, 118
effectiveness 151–2
efficiency 13, 18, 25–6, 151–2
Enhancement Group 123
Enterprise in Higher Education 71
European Credit Transfer System
   (ECTS) 71
evaluative state 12–14
excellence 94–5
external examining 53, 56, 60, 61,
   64–7, 125, 138–9, 147
external regulation 24, 30–1, 31
external reviews 7, 126–7, 132–3, 134,
   139, 145–6

feedback 53, 54
fitness of purpose 87–8, 152–3
fitness for purpose 87–8, 152–3
Floud, Roderick, Professor 48
*Framework for Higher Education
   Qualifications (FHEQ)* 140
franchising 57
Frazer, Malcolm, Dr. 44
funding 42, 74, 155, 170
funding councils 10–11, 39, 45, 111,
   113, 116, 127; Higher Education
   Funding Council for England
   (HEFCE) 46–8, 106
Further Education colleges 97
Further and Higher Education Bill 43
The Future of Higher Education (White
   Paper 2003a) 2, 48

General Certificate of Secondary
   Education (GCSE) 9
Giddens, Anthony, Professor 131

good practice guidelines 63
Gordon, G. 30
government policy 10–11
grading 31, 78, 99, 130; Academic
    Review method 96; institutional
    76; quality 7; subject 76, 92–3,
    98
Graduate Standards Programme (GSP)
    50, 67–9, 108, 149
Graham, J. 18–19
Green Paper on higher education
    (1985) 10
GSP (Graduate Standards Programme)
    50, 67–9, 108, 149
Guidelines on Quality Assurance 1994
    (HEQC) 63

Handbook for Academic Review (QAA)
    129
Handbook for Institutional Audit 135,
    148–9
Harris, Sir Martin, Professor 116
HEFC *see* Higher Education Funding
    Council for England (HEFC)
Henkel, M. 33
HEQC *see* Higher Education Quality
    Council (HEQC)
Her Majesty's Inspectorate (HMI) 37,
    45, 46
Hibbert, Alan, Professor 46
Higher Education: Easing the Burden
    (Better Regulation Task Force)
    136
Higher Education: Meeting the Challenge
    (White paper 1987) 10
Higher Education: a New Framework
    (White Paper 1991) 1, 35;
    analysis 39–41; progress review
    37; quality assurance 38; reactions
    41–3
higher educationaudit commission
    167–9; government policy 10–11;
    new framework 37–8; regulation
    23–5
Higher Education Funding Council for
    England (HEFCE) 48; relationship
    with HEQC assessment unit
    46–8
Higher Education in the Learning Society
    (NCIHE) 117, 118
Higher Education Quality Council
    (HEQC); 1992–97 49–71;
    constitution, organization and
    resourcing 43–4; and CVCP
    45–6, 167; incorporation 1;
    international impact 149;
    relationship with HEFCE
    assessment unit 46–8;
    representative role 11–12; single
    system 102, 106, **107–10**, 110,
    115, 118, 122
Higher Education Quarterly 79
Higher Quality 121, 122, 123, 126,
    144
Hilbourne, John, Professor 64
HMI (Her Majesty's Inspectorate) 37,
    45, 46
honours degrees 68–9
Hood, Christopher, Professor 166
Howarth, Alan 43
Hunter, D. 21, 22–3, 190

*Improving the Effectiveness of Quality
    Assurance Systems in Non-Medical
    Health Care, Education and
    Training* (HEQC) 64
In Focus 63
incorporation 10, 44
incrementalism 29
information 23–4, **83–4**, 129, **137**,
    178–80
Initial Teacher Training 37
innovation 164–5
Institute for Learning and Teaching in
    Higher Education 117
institutional bias 94–7
institutional prosperity 96–7
institutional review 126, 132
internal examiners 65
internal processes 128, 132
internal regulation 30–1
international links 70–1

Jackson, N. 26–8, 31
James, E. 24
Jarratt Committee 11
Jarrold, Ken 64
Joint Planning Group (JPG) 110–16,
    143
Jones, Philip 70
Journal of International Education 59
JPG (Joint Planning Group) 110–16,
    143

Kells, R. 26–8
Kenyon, Christopher 116, 119
Kerr-Fraser, Sir William 101, 110,
    119

leadership 7, 30, 151
league tables 83, 97
Learning from Collaborative Audit: An Interim Report 57–8
learning opportunities 127
Learning and Teaching Support Network (LTSN) 132, 148
Lindop Committee 64
Loughborough University 100
LTSN (Learning and Teaching Support Network) 132, 148
Lucas, Colin, Professor 131

McDowell, Liz 82
managerialism 14, 88–90
Managing Quality and Standards in UK Higher Education (HEQC) 169
Marston, Stephen 138
Matterson, Claire 56
May, A. 22–3
medical profession 20–3
methodology 4–5
Middlehurst Robin 48, 67, 123, 161–2
Middlehurst, Robin 29, 30
Middleton, Graham 44
Milton, Peter 147
Mitchell, Harry 44, 48, 70
modular courses 61, 65
Moran, M. 14–15
motivation 29

National Committee for Inquiry into Higher Education (Dearing) 2, 82, **116–18**, 124, 125, 152–3
National Health Service (NHS) 20–3, 47, 140, 160
National Union of Students (NUS) 84, 149
Neave, G. 12–13
neo-liberalism 16
Neuberger, E. 24
Newby, Sir Howard 139, 158
Newton, Dr. Jethro 90, 164
NHS (National Health Service) 20–3, 47, 140, 160
Northern Ireland 73, 110
NUS (National Union of Students) 84, 149

OD (Operational Description) 134–5
O'Neill, O. 17
Open University 66, 81
Operational Description (OD) 134–5
'Options Paper' 105–6

overseas audits 58–60, 145
ownership 153–6

PA Consulting 85, 100, 170
partnerships *see* collaborative provision
Patten, John, M. P. 49, 50
PCFC (Polytechnics and Colleges Funding Council) 10–11, 45
peer review 91, 92, 93
performance assessment 23, 25–6
plan of the book 5–7
policy panic 21
Pollitt, C. 25–6
polytechnics 45, 86
Polytechnics and Colleges Funding Council (PCFC) 10–11, 45
postgraduate students 61
power 19, 20
Power, M. 15
professional regulation 19–23
professional training 37, 52–3, 54, 143–4
profiles 78, 99, 128–9
programme review 126–7
public sector 10, 36–7

QAA (Quality Assurance Agency) 121–50
QEG (Quality Enhancement Group) 56, 62–3, 67
Qualifications Framework 122
quality 18–19, 87, 89; damage to Britain's international reputation 90; developmental stages 28–9; ideology 156
quality agencies 63–4
quality assurance; accountability 160–2; CDP views 45–6; coordination 166–7; coverage (past) 152; CVCP views 45–6; definitions 173; effectiveness, key requirements 162; enhancement 160–2; fitness for purpose vs fitness of purpose 152–3; forms (past) 152; future 158–60; making it more meaningful 164; new arrangements 38, 158–60; ownership (past) 153–6; past 151–8; pre-1992 arrangements 35–7; purpose(s) 151–2, 162–3; responsibility (past) 156–8
Quality Assurance Agency (QAA) 121–50; 1997 to 2001 146–7; better regulation task force

136–7; chief executive 123–4; consultation 124–31; degree-awarding powers 144–5; enhancement 137–8; external examining 138–9; incorporation 101; information 137; inheritance 118; institutional audit 145–6; January 2001 to August 2002 131–5; March 1998 to December 2000 124–31; professional training 143–4; quality infrastructure 140–3; quality process 124–35, 139–40; Scotland 135–6; subject review 145–6; Thames Valley Affair 146; university title 144–5; Wales 135–6

Quality Assurance and Enhancement Network 63, 123

quality control 165–6

quality enhancement 28–30; and accountability 160–2; Higher Education Quality Council (HEQC) 62–9; Quality Assurance Agency (QAA) 137–8

Quality Enhancement Group (QEG) 56, 62–3, 67

quality evaluation 19, 54

quality improvement 90, 99, 163

quality infrastructure 140–3

RAE (Research Assessment Exercise) 91, 96, 165

Randall, John 78, 116, 121, 122, 123, 133, 144, 146, 147

ratings 79

Registered External Examiners (REEs) 124–5, 125

regulation; external 30–1, 31; higher education 23–5; internal 30–1; professions 19–23; quality of 32–3; by the state 14–15; teaching and learning 30–2, *see also* self-regulation

Reith lectures 17

Report on Assessment 1992–1995 (HEFCE) 94, 95

research 53, 54, 60–1, **63**, 84, **95–6**, 164

Research Assessment Exercise (RAE) 91, 96, 165

resources 95–6, 97–8

responsibility 156–8

Reynolds, Philip 36

Roberts, Sir Gareth, Professor 58, 109, 113, 119

Robertson, David, Professor 70

Rogers, Lady Bridget 63

Russell Group 131, 140, 148

Salter, B. 11, 21, 22

SCOP (Standing Conference of Principals) 11, 144

Scotland 70, 98–9, 110, 122, 135–6

Scott, Peter 123

self-assessment 75

self-regulation 3–4, 15, 26–8, 110, 123, **163–4**

Sharp, Norman 70

Sharp, S. 91

Shephard, Gillian 71, 104, 105, 109, 110, 116

Shore, C. 16–17

Silver, Harold 65

single system 47, 101–18; Dearing committee 116–18; December 1994 to September 1995 104–7; HEQC's position 107–10; QAA's inheritance 118; September 1993 to December 1994 102; September 1995 to October 1997 110–16

Soviet Union 17, 18

A Sovietological View of Modern Britain 4

staff development 52–3, 84

standards 67, 117, 127

Standing Conference of Principals (SCOP) 11, 144

Stewart, Professor (Lord Sutherland) 36, 48

Stoddart, John 5, 44, 45, 50, 67, 106, 110, 112, 114

Strengthening External Examining 66

student assessment 56

subject reviews 132–3, 134, 139, 145–6

subject specialists 132

Tapper, T. 11

teacher education 18–19, 19–20, 37

Teacher Training Agency 19–20, 144

teaching 3, 7, 53, 81, 164

teaching and learning; assessment 81–4; innovation 52, 54; regulation 30–2

Teaching Quality Assessment (TQA) 40, 82–3

Teaching Quality Enhancement
    Committee (TQEC) 2, 161
Thames Valley Affair 146
Thomas, Alun 46
Thompson, D. 24
threshold standards 67
Times Higher Education Supplement 99,
    101, 143, 169
top-up fees 158
Total Quality Management (TQM) 103
TQA (Teaching Quality Assessment)
    40, 82–3
TQEC (Teaching Quality Enhancement
    Committee) 2, 161
TQM (Total Quality Management) 103
training *see* professional training
transformative learning 171
Trow, Martin 88–9, 151
Tuning Project 149

UFC (Universities Funding Council)
    10, 11
Underwood, Simeon 75, 83, 91, 93,
    98, 100
unit size 96
universities 35–6, 45
Universities Funding Council (UFC)
    10, 11
Universities UK 154, 157, 160, 170

University of Sheffield 171
university title 144–5
University of Warwick 131

validation audits 57
value for money 97–8
VandeLinde, David, Professor 137
de Vries, Peter 75, 86–7

Wagner, Leslie 77, 102–3, 138
Wales 70, 98–9, 110, 135–6
Warren-Piper, David, Professor 64–5
Warwick, Baroness of Undercliffe 71,
    114, 118, 119, 139
Watson, David, Professor 41, 46, 47,
    79, 80, 87, 89, 90, 112, 113
White Paper (1987) 10–11
White Paper (1991) *see Higher
    Education: a New Framework*
    (White Paper 1991)
White Paper (2003a) 2, 48
Williams, Peter 44, 50, 52, 112, 139,
    141, 169
Wolf, Alison, Professor 143, 150
Woodhouse, D. 161–2
Wright, Peter 141, 147, 150
Wright, S. 16–17

Yorke, Mantz, Professor 44, 48, 63